Dedi

To my w
the best gamble

Other Books By Keith Sobey

How to Win at Horsracing Betting
will be published in October.
It does what it says on the tin.

The Phoenix Rises
will be published in Spring 2018.
It is a sequel to Stick or Twist

Keith's sensational debut novel **Migrants**
can be purchased from Amazon and is on bookshelves now.
www.migrantsthenovel.com

A sequel **Nomads** will be published before Christmas

PART 1
LIFE BEFORE CENTAUR

6. The Beginning
7. The Early Years
20. The Entrepreneurial Flame Begins To Burn
28. Sex, Love, Marriage and Death
48. Life Goes On
62. Friendship
100. Climbing the Greasy Pole
127. Life in the Audit Commission
144. Life At The Top

PART 2
THE RISE AND FALL OF
THE CENTAUR EMPIRE

170. The Early Days of Centaur
189. Rebranding
215. Centaur Moves Into The Investor Market
222. Living My Dreams
229. Centaur Bloosdstock Stars
263. Centaur Bloodstock Trainers
291. Centaur Jockeys
299. Centaur Greyhounds
327. Trouble and Strife
340. The Big Idea
351. Centaur Move To The City
367. 2011 An Annus Horribilis
376. Betfair To The Rescue?
381. The End
384. The Phoenix Rises

PART 1

LIFE BEFORE CENTAUR

THE BEGINNING

The Epsom Derby, run on 5TH June 1948, took place in front of a crowd of 1million people on Epsom Downs. Hard to believe but this was in the days before every household had the ability to watch the race on television.

The race was won by the French challenger My Love who came from last to first to win at the odds of 11to1.

The result was a good one for bookmakers in the United Kingdom. However, another event that took place on that Derby Day was to herald massive future losses for the bookmaking industry in the future.

On that day, in The Green Hospital, Wallsend-On – Tyne a son, named Keith, was born to Thomas Henry and Winnifred Alice Sobey, weighing in at 8lb and 4 ounces.

THE EARLY YEARS

Sport, Sport and More Sport

My father was a policeman and the policy in the Northumberland County Police Force at that time was to move personnel around. By the time I was 11 years of age I had lived in Wallsend, Newbiggin –by-the Sea, Amble, Ashington, Whitley Bay and finally Wallsend again where my dad was promoted to Sergeant.

My father was a keen sportsman. He was on Everton's books before the war and played alongside Billie Wright in midfield for the Army in Africa where he was stationed. When he returned home in 1946 he played football and cricket for Northumberland County Police.

My earliest memories were of being taken to watch my father play and running around playing with his fellow policemen on the sidelines. However there was one other aspect of my father's life that made a bigger impression on me and that was his love of horse racing and gambling.

I used to pester him to be taken to the races whenever he got to attend on overtime on his days off. By the time I was seven I was a regular member of the party whenever my dad and his mates went racing. This was not done for any philanthropic reasons on their part. I was their computer database! Dad discovered I had a photographic memory one day when I was able to narrate all the runners at Newcastle without looking at the newspaper and I also recalled all results from previous meeting –I was a walking talking version of today's Racing Post!

In those days I used to drive my mum up the wall. I would make makeshift racetracks out of Meccano and other items in the living room and used my marbles to hold imaginary races, keeping a record of the results in a notebook. It was not unusual for family members to go careering into the furniture if I had failed to clear up all of my "horses".

My photographic memory was also developing and it almost led to my life taking a completely different path. My father was a keen musician and song writer, he was quite successful and used to put on a few shows at the theatre in Whitley Bay and we frequently had well known performers calling round in the evening for dinner or tea. Visitors included Frankie Vaughan, of "Green Door" fame. Frankie was a very handsome guy and there was a lot of curtains fliuttering in the neighborhood when he came round not to mention my sisters hearts!

On occasions I used to watch my dad play on the piano and then one day when he and my mum were in the dining room having their lunch, they heard the piano playing one of my dad's songs. Taken aback they went into the sitting room and there I was sitting on the piano stool playing his song. I had never had a lesson and was only four years old!

Unsurprisingly this caused quite a stir and it was not long before an article appeared in the Newcastle Journal, the main newspaper for the region. My parents were delighted and sent me for lessons, something they could hardly afford. However my talent was a gift and did not respond too well to the discipline of formal learning. That, combined with my dad being put on permanent nightshift, meant I could not play during the day, led to the decline and eventual termination of my piano- playing career. This is something that I regret today as I have always had a love of music and would have loved to be able to play an instrument well.

My organisational skills continued to develop. A few years later I organised a Subbuteo league among my primary schoolfriends using the set I had been bought for Christmas. My friends, most of who had the game too, and I would collect teams with different strips and ancillary items such as corner flags and referees and we would have our own world cup after school. Things got quite competitive and if you know subbuteo, you would know that there is considerable scope for pushing rather than flicking the players to hit the ball. In the end we always had to have a third party to referee!

Subbuteo helped to get me interested in football and obviously the family genes had an influence too. I started playing for school teams in the second year of senior school and eventually became a useful left side midfield player. I helped the teams I played in to win a few trophies. The most prestigious was the Northumberland and Durham under 18 trophy. I played for Wallsend -On -Tyne Grammar School, a brilliant side that contained several players who went on to play league football.

I could have gone for trials with a number of clubs at the time for football or cricket for that matter, I used to open the bowling for the District Schools cricket team but cricket and football came second by a long way to my love of tennis.

I started playing tennis for the first time at the age of nine. At the time my dad was stationed at Whitley Bay police station and my mum used to do the cooking and organise the domestic services for a young policeman's hostel. The hostel was two adjacent Victorian 6 bedroom dwellings, which had a massive concrete area at the back of the house and around one side.

Wimbledon fever was starting to sweep the nation in the summer and it was impossible to get on the public courts. I had watched the mighty Lew Hoad slaughter Ashley Cooper in the 1957 final and I was infested with the tennis bug. I persuaded my mum to buy me a cheap tennis racket and some tennis balls and I was in play. I did not need any of my friends to play, I marked out half a tennis court with coloured chalk up the side of the court and the wall was my opponent!

I used to play for hours every day against the wall and I replayed the whole of the Wimbledon draw once I had developed the ability to keep the ball coming back time after time. This went on for the following two years and although some of my friends came round to play against the wall I never played on a proper tennis court. In reflection, I must have developed a good level of ability as there were two windows on the side of the house and they were never broken in two summers of playing an average three hours a day.

In my twelfth year I plucked up courage to ask my dad if he would take me to the public courts for a game. He was a useful player who represented the Northumberland Police team. My dad was very competitive and he explained before we started that, after he had shown me how to serve and how to play a forehand and backhand, he did not believe in mollycoddling and would play properly against me as I would learn faster that way. I did not say anything and I could see the look of surprise on his face when I served the ball in and hit it over the net hard on both the forehand and backhand sides in the warm up. He had an even bigger surprise when he lost the first two games!

Eventually my dad proved too strong for me that day but in the months that followed we played at least once a week and by the time I was thirteen I was winning our weekly matches. By that time my dad had been transferred to Ashington, some twenty miles north of Newcastle and I started attending Ashington Grammar School. My best friend at school Malcolm Taylor could also play tennis and he lived at Newbiggin -by -The Sea some 6 miles from Ashington.

Newbiggin had some excellent red shale tennis courts, quite a change from the tarmacadam I had been used to and the faster surface encouraged me to serve and hit the ball harder. Malcolm and I played every day, weather- permitting, that summer in 1961 and we came to the attention of some of the adults who played in the tennis club there. They did not have a coach but I picked up a couple of tips with regard to the correct grip to use for the backhand which was enough for me to win the mens singles in the club championship.

Malcolm and I had started our daily routine in the summer of 2002 when one of the club members came and had a chat with me. He said that he thought I was very good and I should enter the Northumberland Junior Championships. I said that these took place at Jesmond in Newcastle and that it was not practical for me to get the bus every day. However my objections were removed when he offered to take me by car every day if my parents agreed.

A couple of months later I was stepping on court at Jesmond in my new tennis outfit with a Maxply racquet that my parents had bought me for my birthday and Christmas present. I had entered the under 15 and under 18 championships as my mentor said why not as I was used to playing against older opponents. I did not know what to expect in my first match which was in the under 15's but as things turned out I won easily. At that time I had not been coached and used to play an all out attacking game hitting my second service just as hard as my first, both flat without any overspin. I used to accept the inevitable occasional double faults as worth being always on the front foot.

My second match turned out to create quite a stir. I was drawn to play the number two seed in the under 18 singles. He was 17 and was also number one for the county junior side. The number one seed for the tournament was the 12- year old David Lloyd who was number one in England at the time for the age group under 13 and had travelled up from Essex to play. We were placed on an outside shale court as no one had heard of the boy from Newbiggin.

We started off and I had never faced a service anything like it before .The first service whistled past me and when it didn't the second service had a vicious kick on it that I had never played against before. I was doing okay on my own service but hardly won a point on my opponents' service and lost the first set 6 games to At the end of the first set Bob, who had driven me from Newbiggin, came to the chair and suggested I stand back from the base line a couple of yards and that I might be able to return the service. I was not used to this but thought I had nothing to lose so started to step back. It made a difference and gradually I began to get into my opponents service games and then to put pressure on him. It took him a while to adjust to the fact that he was in a match and before he did I had won the second set six games to four.

By now the bush telegraph was working and a crowd was building up around the outside court. By the time we were halfway through the final set, it was standing room only and there was a fantastic atmosphere. I was not used to this, I had never played in front of a crowd before and this probably cost me the match as although I broke service to lead 4 games to three I could not close it out and eventually lost 7-5.

After the match many of the crowd stayed to congratulate me although I did not know what for – this was the first tennis match I had lost in two years! Among them was an elderly gentleman called Sid Evans. Sid was the coaching professional at Jesmond and he said that he had watched the game and was prepared to give me free coaching if I could come every Saturday morning winter and summer. I explained about the transport issue and he said that the county would also pay petrol expenses if I could get a driver. Bob said he would do what he could as my dad could not make every week due to the shift system.

I sped through the under 15 tournament to the semi finals without dropping a set and then had my first experience of playing on grass courts. The semi finals and final were played in front of the grandstand on superb lawn courts, which were like bowling greens. In the semi –final I played against another newcomer to county tennis , John Reilly who came from Blyth. Although just fourteen John was already over six feet tall and had a massive service. We ended up playing three very long sets and there was only one service break in each set and I was fortunate in that John could not take any of the three match points he had in the final set.

John and I became firm friends after this epic match and as Blyth was much closer to Newbiggin we began to play each other every weekend. Meanwhile I had a final to play against top seed David Lloyd. David was the latest product in the Lloyd family tennis assembly line. Although only 12 years and smaller than me, in betting parlance he was probably 20 to 1 on having already won the under 18 final easily.

Playing against David was an education for me. He never made a mistake and no matter how hard I tried to hit the ball it came back forcing me continually backward. Still, encouraged by a partisan crowd, I managed to win six games losing 6-2 6-4 two games more than David's opponent won in the under 18 final.

I lived for tennis in the next 5 years. Syd Evans stripped back my home taught approach and equipped me with an all round game and a more controlled service action which virtually eliminated double faults. This took a lot of perseverance on my part and at first my match results suffered quite badly as the new grip and footwork I was using took a while to take hold and for those who know me, patience has never been one of my strong suits.

I had four great summers playing county and tournament tennis with my expenses paid for and won a number of junior titles over this period but I have to say they were all for boys doubles and mixed doubles. To my and my dad's disappointment I lost 4 Northumberland Closed and Northumberland and Durham open singles finals. For some reason the fact that I was favourite in these matches weighed heavily on me and I could never finish off my opponent, in colloquial terms I developed "the elbow". In the 1965 final I even lost to my doubles partner Geoff Lowe who I had played against over 100 times and never lost!

Tennis and football gradually disappeared from my life when I got married and started to study for professional qualifications but one pursuit that did not was chess.

I learnt to play chess at the lunchtime chess club at Ashington Grammar School when I was 12. However although I had a natural ability, it did not take hold till we moved back to Wallsend when I was 14. Wallsend Grammar School had a great reputation for sport and for chess and when I found out that members of the school chess team regularly got afternoons off school to travel to play other schools in Northumberland and Durham my ability improved rapidly.

The break through in chess came when Mr Brown the deputy Headmaster who managed the chess team explained to me the need to read chess books and to learn openings defences and end game theory. In stepped my photographic memory which seemed to still work when I was interested in subjects and by the time I was 17 I was not only playing top board for the school but also for the Northumberland County Team. The highlight of my school chess career came when our school team defeated the mighty Royal Grammar School team for the first time ever to win the Northumberland Schools Trophy.

Chess remained a driving interest for me until I moved to London at the end of the 1980's and I wished I had got started ten years earlier as I missed out on the years when my mind would have been capable of assimilating the data that would have taken me to the highest level of the game rather than being a strong county player. This was brought home to me when in 1976 I played in a big chess tournament at the Norbreck Castle Hotel at Blackpool and saw Nigel Short in action at first hand.

Nigel at thirteen years of age was already Britain's greatest ever chess player. He was taking part in the International Masters Tournament being held at the Norbreck, while I and over a thousand other chess players took part in parallel tournaments that weekend . These were sorted into tournaments based upon player's ratings.

Some 30 players from all over the world were taking part in the International Masters tournament and they could be seen hunched over the board for the four- hour duration of their matches That was all the players bar one, Nigel was outside with his brother and friends playing football on the beach for most of the day. He would then return to the board some one and a half hours behind on the clock and proceed to demolish his opponent using the latter's time taken to make his moves in extremely complex positions in order to develop his own winning strategies. I eventually finished runner up in the third of 6 levels winning £125 for the weekend but was blown away by watching true greatness in action. Nigel went on to challenge for the world championship but was beaten in the final by Kasparov in 1993.

With all this sport going on in my life it was not surprising that my academic achievements were somewhat less than outstanding. My annual reports were pretty consistent " Keith is capable of making the top set but seems to just do enough each year to achieve comfortable mediocrity. He must work a lot harder if he is to get top grades."

To me however if I could get the eight O level and three A level passes that were necessary to get into University without spending hours studying each weekend, that was good enough for me. As it turned out I missed out on the three A levels getting an A in History and C in Geography but failing English Literature which prevented my getting a scholarship for Cambridge in History unless I re-sat and got a B.

My supreme academic achievement came in the O level Latin translation paper. I completed the one and a half hour exam in 15 minutes having memorised the relevant parts of Homer's Iliad.

So came to an end the school years of my life, now for the real world.

THE ENTREPRENEURIAL FLAME BEGINS TO BURN

From Little Acorns……………………

As an only son with three sisters, there is no doubt that I led a pretty spoiled existence growing up, particularly due to my sporting prowess. However as I grew older I realised that if I wanted to be able to behave as equals with the public school boys and girls who mainly made up the county tennis team, I needed more disposable income than it was fair to ask my parents for.

I had a paper round from when I was 13 but it was when I got a part time job as a collector with Tenovus Cancer pools in 1963 that I started to nurture my entrepreneurial talents. The pools were similar to Littlewoods Pools, with profits, after prize money and administration expenses, going towards Cancer research. The Newcastle –Upon-Tyne office was based in Heaton, a suburb to the east of the City Centre.

I applied for and got a collection round in Walker, a run down area of the city. My collection used to take me two hours on a Thursday and Friday evening and I received commission on the money I collected plus a small bonus if any of my customers won. I retained this round for about a year and built it up quite a bit so that I was earning around £6 per week, which at that time was good for part time work.

However I soon came up with an idea that massively increased my income. There were a number of high rise blocks in Walker and the adjacent Byker suburb, I asked who collected in those areas and was told they were too rough an area for people to collect in and the lifts and lights were usually out of order in the high rise blocks. I asked and was given permission to collect there and put my plans into action.

I went to each of the blocks and hung around for a couple of summer evenings. I approached some of the local teenagers and asked if they would be interested in a well -paid part time job collecting in their own block. I would be their agent and would collect from them each Friday evening. There was obviously a risk in this operation that they would not pay over all of the money they collected, however I used my intuitive skills in recruiting those teenagers who seemed to be into sport and worked hard at school. I also let all my sub contractors know that they were running a massive risk of a severe beating if they did not pay over money collected from some of their customers who were well known villains.

The network of sub collectors that I created meant that I was earning on average around £30 per week .Put in context, this was over 50% more than my first full time employment salary at Refuge Insurance and then Northumberland County Council when I started work two years later. I had had my first experience of creative thinking paying off handsomely.

The income I was earning went to furnish my wardrobe and I told my parents that I did not need them to buy my clothing any more, which certainly benefitted my sisters. It also went to fund my gambling, I would like to say that I could prove I was a winning gambler all my life but I am sure that was not the case in my earlier years when I lacked discipline and failed to keep records. I can certainly recall one or two occasions when I had to walk the 8 miles home from Newcastle races having lost my bank and my bus fare home.

As it happened it did not really matter if I won or lost backing my own fancies as I had come across a sure fire way to make money from gambling thanks to a friend of mine. George Dalgliesh. George lived on a big council estate at the north of Wallsend close to the main road that links Newcastle to Whitley Bay and Tynemouth on the east coast.

George was a close friend who played football for the school football team at right back but was even more effective in the school cricket team as an opening bowler. We used to open the bowling together for the school team and the District team and while I got quite a few wickets the lion share went to George who was devilishly quick and got a lot of lift from his deliveries. Had George come from a well to do family I am sure he would have been a regular in a major county team, as it was he went on to open the bowling for Northumberland County in the Minors.

We used to go to each other's houses quite a lot when we were in the lower sixth form as we had a lot of free periods. This time was supposed to be spent studying but in most cases we used to gravitate to the local betting shop to have a bet. Betting shops became legal in the UK in May 1961 but the shops that existed in the 1960's were a million miles from the technological marvels that exist today beaming in live sport from all over the world.

In Wallsend town centre in 1964 there were two betting shops, which had a blower that received live commentaries from one or more racecourses. The remaining results used to be rung in from on course bookmakers. The shops were owned by a prominent North East bookie called Joe Simpson. The local gossip held that Joe had made his start up capital by milking the back street bookies bag system that existed before betting was legalised.

Joe had recently opened a smaller betting office on Georges' estate. This shop did not have a blower and all results were rung in to the clerk by the staff in the main shop in Wallsend. George and I were regulars in the main shop, even though we were below the legal age of 18, and we noticed that on many occasions there was a bit of a delay before the staff rang in the result to the satellite office. An idea germinated in our minds- was it possible to contact George outside the satellite office when a horse was clearly winning in time for him to get a bet on it?

Our research established that there was a telephone kiosk less than 100 yards away from the satellite office (There were no mobile phones in those days!). The next step was for us to pluck up the courage to put our plan into action. We decided that George would put the bet on after he picked up my telephone message, as he was better known in the betting shop. I waited until there was a National Hunt meeting taking place and listened to the commentaries until in one race a horse was well clear jumping the last hurdle. I sprinted out to the nearby telephone box and rang George who picked up the message and ran in to the betting shop to put a bet on with the "winner". To our delight the horse won and George got paid out.

For another 12 months we had a licence to print money. We refined our system to put the "winner " into doubles and trebles with other horses still to run but including a non-runner so that we had a guaranteed return. George needed to spend time in the betting shop and have other bets to avoid suspicion and there were other drawbacks such as one or other of the telephone boxes being occupied or an occasional defeat for the horse we had selected. However, in the year before the satellite office installed its own blower system, we won around £400.

Perhaps my greatest entrepreneurial achievement prior to creating Centaur was the Wallsend Grammar School Word League, which I created and operated during 1965 and 1966 when I was in the lower and upper sixth forms. I have already mentioned that I had plenty of spare time in the lower sixth form and you know what they say idle hands make!

History was my favourite subject at school. I was really interested in it and unlike some other students I needed no encouragement to research lessons and do my homework. I was always top in the annual exams and got an A grade in my O level exam. I was being encouraged by the school to sit the Cambridge entrance exam.

Much of the credit for this was due to my History Teacher, Mr Rodgers. He was a dimunitive man who exuded passion, not only about history which to me he made come alive in his lessons but in local politics where he frequently made the headlines for being ejected from Gateshead Borough Council meetings!

In most of Mr Rogers lessons he would get carried away about some aspect of history that he was outlining and use a wide range of descriptive words by far his most well used was "fantastic" but "truly,"amazing" and "outrageous" were also widely used. At first I started monitoring the use of the favourite words, then the idea came to me to create a word "league" which grew from involving a few classmates to having most of the school involved.

The Word League started in late 1965, there were 16 word teams, which played fixtures against each other in history lessons and a league table was compiled based upon the results. From this small beginning came a social phenomenon, which took over the whole school. By early 2006 there was a fanzine for each team and a weekly magazine covering matches played that week. I was never slow on the uptake and soon word teams could be sponsored for a small fee and there was a flourishing transfer and betting market.

Once again I had created another income source, my earnings from Tenovus covered me against a run of bad results and in no time I was turning over £20 per week in Word League bets. Customers could bet at fixed odds on individual matches and also for the league championship. You might ask how we could guarantee the integrity of the published results- simple I appointed two referees for each match who both kept a tally –if there was any disagreement we halved the difference.

Word League amazingly lasted over 6 months before we were betrayed. It all ended suddenly, The Deputy Headmaster Mr Brown burst in to a history lesson and grabbed every notebook in sight. The game was up and I confessed that it was all my idea. In today's education environment I would have got away with the apology I freely gave to Mr Rogers however in the 1960's no opportunity for corporal punishment was ever spurned. Mr Brown told me I could shout out any word I liked while he was doing the administering!

This wonderful example of entrepreneurial spirit and commercial organisation brought to an end my early academic career as for reasons you will read about later I did not go on to college or university. I did take Mr Rogers out for a coffee in the last week of term and said I hope that there were no hard feelings. He laughed and said of course not, he said he had never lectured a class for so long who hung on every word he spoke!

SEX, LOVE, MARRIAGE AND DEATH

A Voyage Through The Sea of Emotions

I am going to interrupt the chronological nature of this book here to talk about love and friendship and how both of these essential elements of life impacted upon me.

From the age of 16 I had lived in a terraced house that my parents had bought in Wallsend when they received an assurance from the Chief Constable that my father would not be transferred again in his last 10 years of service. There were six of us in the three bedroomed house at first, I had three sisters, Valerie who was the eldest child, 5 years older than me, Enid Jill who was two years younger than me and my baby sister Caroline who was 13 years younger than me. Valerie moved out to her own flat in 1966.

The Word League increased my profile hugely among my female schoolmates and playing for the school football team did no harm either. My years in the sixth form seemed to consist of sport, sport and more sport during the week and a constant stream of parties on Friday and Saturday nights.

These exposed me to a wide range of temptation. I was never one for taking drugs and to be fair there was not that much about in the 1960's however I soon developed quite a taste for " Rocket Fuel " as

Newcastle Brown Ale was termed. This lifestyle was bad enough in its own right but did nothing for my appetite for revision for my A levels and led to a considerable decline in my commitment to my tennis career.

Sex started to rear its ugly head at these weekend soirees and I have to admit that my sexual prowess for some time was way below my abilities on the sports field. Not for my generation the benefits of sex education or Internet porn on demand –we had to find our own way or be guided by a more experienced partner. It was hardly surprising that there were many many unwanted pregnancies and even a few shotgun weddings amongst my year group.

My recall is that I lost my virginity to Anna, a friend of one of my sixth form classmates, who went to La Sagesse private school in Newcastle. Her father was a judge and I hate to think of the sentence he would have passed on me if he knew what we got up to during the summer holidays. We went our separate ways when I got a job as a temporary postman while waiting for my A level results and kept falling asleep in the afternoons and failing to turn up for our dates.

I had left school now and was experiencing the transition in life that most of you over the age of 18 will recognise. No longer was sport laid on a plate, you had to go out and join a team or club and social life was far less structured. I soon found out that I was no longer a big fish in a small pool and my life began to go through some major changes.

I started to go to discotheques and clubs in the evening, I had plenty of money thanks to my entrepreneurial success and was quite a fashion icon for a while,. My pride and joy was a full- length suede coat which I wore in true "mod" style over a polo shirt, three quarter length jeans and boots. I wore this during the winter and in summer replaced it with my rainbow cotton madras jacket.

My favourite haunt was the Club Agogo in Newcastle, which was famous for being a haunt of The Animals and Alan Price but regularly had top line R and B artists on stage like Long John Baldry, Julie Driscoll and a very early Rod Stewart. I was more into soul music but that was catered for too with gigs by such big names as Wilson Pickett and Sam and Dave.

1966 was the year that England won the World Cup and Newcastle was buzzing. I can remember going to a world cup dance at the Mayfair, which was a major dance hall in the city centre. However I cannot remember too much more about that evening as I woke up the following morning in hospital.

My friend Les Perceval visited me later that day and filled me in on the blanks. Apparently we had had a couple more bottles of Newcastle Brown than usual. That had not prevented us from scoring with a couple of attractive girls. Neither Les nor I could drive so the options for finishing the night off were limited. We eventually decided to go to one of the winding alleyways opposite Newcastle Railway station for a snog.

Things were going pretty well when a young man walked past and looked into the doorway where I was romantically entwined. Unsurprisingly I did not take kindly to this and told him to sling his hook but in more explicit terms. He walked away and I did not think anything more of it. Les told me that five minutes later he returned with six mates. Les shouted for me to run and he got away, however I did not. Apparently the gang of yobs kicked the you- know-what out of me and then started hitting me with bottles. That was the story according to two railway policemen who had stood and watched it all from the safety of Newcastle Central Station!

The catalogue of injuries I sustained included a broken nose, shattered front teeth, broken ribs and a minor fracture in my skull. I was definitely not a pretty site. My mum was really upset when she came to see me and my dad went and had a few strong words with the two railway policemen about their manhood.

It was some time before I was able to go out again and still had one or two tasty scars. I had lost my job on the post and my Tenovus job in the interim and needed to make a big decision. Did I re-sit my English Literature exam as scheduled and go to University or should I get a job. I was still making my mind up in early 1967 when an event happened that shaped the rest of my life. I met my first wife Pat.

I had stopped going to Newcastle for nights out following the beating I took and had started going to Whitley Bay and Tynemouth. On Friday nights I used to go to the Rex ballroom, which used to attract several hundred under twenty fives for their weekly dances. These usually featured live bands (I once saw Bryan Ferry play there with his first group The Gas Board).

On this particular night I was feeling pretty good as I had just had a good win on the horses and had treated myself to a new bottle green suit and a new pair of shoes. I was standing near the exit to the toilets which featured a massive gold full length mirror, checking that I was ready to make some girl's night when all of a sudden all hell broke loose. Apparently a Mods V Rockers fight had broken out in the middle of the dance floor and soon some 50 people were involved with glass flying everywhere and screams galore.

There was no way I was going to get involved following my recent experience in Newcastle and was preparing to exit via the staircase when all of a sudden a young woman cannoned into me as she was running away from the dance floor. She fell over as she had high heels on and I bent down to pick her up, it was then that I looked into her face and I was a goner. Patricia Ann Taylor was only sixteen years of age but I am sure that, had we been in today's reality show era, she would have been snapped up for Britain's Top Model. She had the most beautiful natural blonde hair which she wore straight down to the middle of her back she had a real peaches and cream complexion which was exaggerated at the time by her blushing furiously as I picked her up. When she stood erect I could not help but notice as she wore a cherry mini dress that she had the most incredible long legs which her mum would often say went all the way to her bum!

People often debate whether there is such a thing as love at first sight. The only thing I would contribute to that debate is that even though I am a pretty analytical sort of person and have dated many many women in my life, with Pat and then later with my second wife Hazel I knew from the very first hours I spent with them that I wanted to be with them constantly.

I scored big brownie points with Pat immediately as she had sustained a nasty cut on her arm caused by flying glass and I insisted on bandaging it up with a handkerchief and taking her to the nearby Tynemouth infirmary. I waited for her to receive treatment and got a taxi to take her home. Maybe it was out of gratitude that she agreed to go out with me the following week, particularly as my brand new green suit was mixed with a lot of red before the end of the evening. However, I think we both knew after our first few dates that we wanted to be together.

For the next 2 years we saw each other nearly every day even though we still lived at home. After our first holiday together in August 1967 in Torquay, the first time we had been able to sleep together, we got engaged and saved hard until we eventually got married at Percy Main Methodist Church in October 1969.

All plans of going to university went out of the window after I had met Pat and I started my working career in Spring 2007 as a claims assistant with Refuge Assurance in Newcastle City Centre. I never really settled in this job and eventually moved at the end of that year to get a job as a trainee accountant with Northumberland County Council. The early part of my working life is described in more detail later in the book.

I should state at this point that although Pat and I were engaged and spent nearly every day together, we entered into married life with very little idea of what living together was like. Both of our parents did not believe in sex before marriage and my father and Pat's dad who was a six foot two trawlerman were not people you took risks with. We did however take as many holidays and mini breaks as we could afford!

There is one event I should share with the reader under the headline of " How to Make an Impression On Your Future In-Laws". Pat had been coming to my house for several weeks for her tea after work. She worked at the Ministry of Social Security at

Longbenton as a data input operator, which was a bus ride away. However she was extremely nervous about inviting me to her house because her father's behaviour could be pretty unpredictable. Eventually though I was invited for Sunday Lunch.

I was told to arrive at midday and I thought that this was pretty normal as we always had our Sunday dinner early at home. However, after introductions were made to Pats mum Eva, her dad George and her brother Norman I was told that the men were off to the Social Club and that we would have dinner on our return at 2.30pm. Pat whispered to me "Be careful" in my ear as we went out the front door but I thought to myself what could go wrong?

Two hours and 12 pints of exhibition later I had to be supported by my future in- laws up the street and up to the house. I had failed my initiation test. Pat was in tears and her mum was not best- pleased and scolded George and Norman while we ate lunch, or everyone else did. My head kept lurching towards my plate of roast beef and two veg only to be saved at the last minute by George's powerful arm. The final humiliation came when I announced I was going to the toilet and after climbing the stairs then proceeded to collapse on the toilet with my trousers around my ankles. I was eventually rescued and put to bed. Amazingly our relationship survived after this although I ate very few meals at Pat's house over the next two years.

Our wedding went very well and the following morning after a night in a local hotel we set off for our new life in Manchester. We should have started with something better in terms of a honeymoon however I was in a down cycle on my betting in the 3 months before the wedding. Pat forgave me for losing our honeymoon fund as I had paid for two or three holidays with my winnings over the previous two years and to her credit, she never brought it up over the next fourteen years we were together. However this was an important lesson learnt for me, never count on winning in betting and spend your winnings in advance.

We lived in Greater Manchester for 3 years, initially in a furnished flat and then in a nice two bedroom unfurnished flat in Heaton Moor, which was a nice area. We made some great friends during this period and I describe these friendships in the next paragraph. Financially I gave Pat full control over our joint bank account. I got a part time job on Saturdays in a local bookmakers and I was allowed to gamble my wages. We made good headway on the savings front over the next two years, as we were both working and earning reasonable salaries. Then in 1970 tragedy struck.

My dad was due to retire from the police force in 1972 and he and my mum were planning on getting a static caravan in Devon with his lump sum and spending a few years in the warm south west climate. Then one day on a day off, after he left the bookies and started the short walk home he collapsed on Station Road in Wallsend. He had suffered an aneurism and never recovered consciousness. Pat and I travelled straight up by train and were able to see him in hospital before he died . However I never got the chance to tell him I loved him and to recall all of those great days we shared at the races, playing tennis and in the all night domino marathons we played every weekend when Hazel and I travelled up from Manchester.

My dad's death left my mum to look after my two sisters, although Jill was courting and looked like getting married soon. Pat and I took two weeks leave and at the end of this we sat down and talked through things with my mum. We agreed that we would move back to the North East if District Audit would allow me to transfer. My mum said she would give us a loan to top up our savings so that we could buy our own house.

This became reality in early 1971 and we moved into a new two bedroom flat in Cramlington- New-Town. We needed two bedrooms because Pat was pregnant with our first child. Christopher, Thomas (after my dad) Sobey was born on the 20th October 1971, weighing in at a healthy 8lb and 4 oz. I was gutted that I was not present at the birth as I was decorating at the flat when the call came through from the hospital and by the time I got to Newcastle the birth was complete.

We lived in Cramlington for 2 years and moved up to a new three bedroom semi-detached house in 1972, when I passed the first stage of my accountancy exams. Things were pretty tough financially then as we did not have Pat's income coming in and, for the only time in my life, gambling let me down. All in all I have gambled on horse racing for over 50 years and although I did not keep formal records until the mid 1990's I am pretty sure that I have only had two losing years during that period, 1973 and 2007.

I was pretty much at full stretch in 1973 with a young baby and studying long hours for my accountancy exams. I don't know if that had anything to do with my having a disastrous losing run on the horses but the fact is that I had one. Worse, I concealed it from Pat, getting a personal loan for £2,000 to cover the mortgage arrears that had developed. In those days it was unusual for women with young children to go back to work and although Pat tried to, she found she missed being with Christopher too much and in the spring of 1973 she fell pregnant with our second child.

I passed the second of my three stage CIPFA exams in 1973, which led to a small salary increase but things were still tough financially. In November 2003 I saw a job advertised in the local government press for Chief Internal Auditor at Eden District Council, based at Penrith in Cumbria. This job offered a fully qualified salary but the Council stated in the advert that they would interview candidates who were sitting their final CIPFA exam and they also offered housing assistance. I discussed the advert with Pat and my mum and although both had reservations, the fact that Penrith was only 70 miles from Newcastle and was in the Lake District, which would be a great place to bring up our kids, won the day for me.

The fact that I had 5 years experience with District Audit meant that I breezed through the job interview. Eden District did not exist when I took up the post; it was a new District Council. It combined the former rural district councils of Penrith, Appleby, and Kirkby Stephen, none of which had previously had an internal audit function. This was certainly a huge challenge as I had to create the function from scratch and what it meant in practice was that I could not be spared for full time or day release study leave.

It took me until 1983 to pass my final CIPFA examination after several intermissions. I was only given a dispensation to have one final attempt upon the intervention of our Chief Executive who explained to the exam board that I had been unable to study effectively due to the demands placed upon me by the Council who had recently promoted me to Assistant Director of Finance.

Pat and I had 10 happy years in Penrith and made some really close friends (more details later). It took us a few years to reconcile ourselves to the lack of privacy living in a small town where the population at the time was only 14,000. Perhaps the best illustration of small town life I can think of was when our second son Darren was born on the 10th of January 1974. Once again I was unable to be present at the birth, as Pat had gone into labour in the middle of the night. I had dropped her off at the hospital in Penrith late the previous evening but had to return home to look after Christopher. As soon as it was daylight I knocked a neighbour up and asked if they would mind looking after Christopher till I got back from hospital.

We lived less than a mile from the hospital and I decided to run in. To my utter disbelief, as it was only 6.30 in the morning, three people stopped me on my way in and congratulated me on the birth of a baby boy! Clearly Africa is not the only place where the jungle drums beat!

Once I had organised things at work so that the Internal Audit function was performing well and winning awards, I took up sport again. In the mid 1970's I represented Cumbria at both tennis and squash and became a lifetime vice president of the tennis and squash club when I obtained a grant from the Sports Council to build four new tennis courts and a new squash complex.

I also created Penrith Chess Club, which within three years won the Cumbrian Championship and I organised an annual international Chess Congress in the town, which brought in a lot of money for the local economy.

My gambling returned to profitability and in 1976 I had a really big yankeee come up, the fourth winner being a first time out hurdling debutante of Stan Mellor's named Willy What who won at 33/1. We put down a deposit on a new 4 bedroom detached house and furnished it with the winnings and still had enough left over to have a holiday abroad in Tunisia.

Pat liked living in Penrith and soon developed her own circle of friends based around the children. She took up squash, even though she had never played sport before. She worked really hard at it and progressed to play for the women's first team in the Cumbria League. In 1983 we took a major decision. We bought a sub post office in Castletown, a major suburb of Penrith, which meant we were intent on staying in Penrith for good. So much for life's great plans, a year later Pat was dead and I was being threatened with eviction from our home!

Pat had always suffered a lot from migraine and I put down the fact that they seemed to be increasing to her having to do the complex paperwork associated with being sub-postmistress. Then I came home one Friday evening in February to find out that Pat had had to call in emergency assistance from the Main Post Office and was ill in bed with violent headaches and sickness.

Then followed the weekend from hell .The pain increased significantly and the local GP, who was also a friend, told me that he was worried by Pat's symptoms. Eventually on the Sunday evening Pat was taken by ambulance to Cumberland Infirmary in Carlisle. I was about to set off from work the following morning to see Pat when I received a phone call from the Infirmary saying that they were transferring Pat to the Neurology Centre at Newcastle RVI hospital immediately and I should go there as soon as possible.

I had to make some domestic arrangements to make sure the children would be cared for after school then set off on the one and a half hour drive to Newcastle, a drive that I would come to know well over the next few weeks. I went straight to the ward number I had been given on arriving at the RVI but on arrival was told by the sister on duty that the consultant wanted to see me before I went in to see my wife.

Then followed the worst half hour of my life. The consultant asked me to sit down and, after I had refused his offer of a cup of tea, proceeded to tell me that the results of the brain scan undertaken at Cumberland Infirmary was that he was pretty certain that Pat had an inoperable brain tumour and had only a few weeks to live.

I am someone not known for showing their emotions publicly and have an extremely high pain threshold but that afternoon, as I was sitting listening, my tear ducts opened and I blubbered like a new born. The consultant told me that the probable prognosis was that they could keep Pat pain free and through medication give her at least four more weeks of a reasonable quality of life. At some stage though she was likely to sustain a massive and fatal heart attack due to the infection spreading throughout her brain. He told me that I had three important decisions to take, first did I tell Pat, second did I tell anyone else i.e. family or friends and third would I consent to an exploratory operation in the unlikely event that they may be able to identify a way of delaying the inevitable.

Afterwards I went in to see Pat. Although slightly confused she looked as beautiful as ever and was in no pain. I sat and talked to her for two to three hours but was in a mental fugue trying to rationalise the information I had obtained. When I eventually left, I rang my friends John and Joan who were looking after Christopher and Darren and asked if they could look after them overnight and I would pick them up from school the following day.

The next twelve hours seemed like twelve days, I drove down to St Mary's Island on the coast and sat looking out to sea thinking until around 7am in the morning. I pretty much killed the raging emotions within me during that time and came to a decision that I would not tell Pat or anyone else that she was going to die. Also, in the hope that the operation might uncover a miracle cure I would allow them to go ahead.

The next four weeks were like living in suspended animation. On the one hand I was able to spend as much time as possible with Pat. My boss Peter Farmer, the Treasurer at Eden District council allowed me to work half days until Pat came out of hospital and John and Joan had the kids for a few days at a time. I went to the hospital every day, taking the children with me as often as possible. There were even some days when the hospital allowed me to take Pat out in the afternoon for a drive.

I leave it to you to imagine what it was like seeing Pat with the children, family and friends, putting on a cheerful face for the next five weeks, knowing the inevitable. It tore my insides to pieces and even today, over 25 years later if I am watching a film with highly emotional content in the house or at the cinema I can burst into tears without warning. Whatever I had to put up with was of course nothing whatsoever compared to what Pat had to go through, I will never forget the day of the exploratory operation when they had to shave off all of that beautiful golden hair.

As the weeks passed, self-doubt began to gnaw at me as to whether I was doing the right thing by not telling family and friends. I decided to ask the one person whose opinion I would trust the most, our friend John. John was a Cumbrian smallholder who also worked as a transport manager. His wife Joan was headmistress of a village school near Clifton where they lived in a converted farmhouse. We had known them for eight years and been close friends for six.

John was untypical as far as Cumbrian's go as he had an amazing sense of humour and was for ever playing practical jokes on his friends. Underneath this Jack the lad exterior however was the most dependable person I have ever met and no job or task was ever too much for him. I asked John if he could meet be for lunch on the 8th March before I travelled over to Newcastle. We met in a popular pub in Penrith and were surrounded by other diners. I told him that I needed to confide in him about something that was really important. To my amazement before I could tell him he burst into tears and walked quickly out of the pub. He returned five miniutes later and said to me he had seen what I had been going through over the last few weeks and thought he knew what I was going to say. So much for my trying to conceal things!

John was a tower of strength for me over the next year and he was the only person who had guessed the truth, On the 15th March 1984 it was all over. That day as soon as I went in to see Pat in hospital I could tell she had deteriorated. Her skin had turned into a greyish pallor and she seemed to be having difficulty in concentrating. I said I would leave her to rest for an hour and went to see the ward sister. She told me that they had seen that Pat was deteriorating and had sent for the consultant but unfortunately he and his senior registrar were both operating.

I did not see Pat alive again. She had a massive heart attack and although the consultant did come as soon as he could, she had gone into a coma and had to be kept alive by breathing apparatus. I stayed by her bedside till the following evening when, on the advice of the consultant, I gave permission for the apparatus to be switched off.

Other than telling Christopher and Darren, that was one of the hardest things I have ever had to do. The next month seemed to be a blur of emotional numbness. I constantly met people to tell them about Pat's death, arranged the funeral and then came back to live in a house where I could see Pat wherever I turned. This continued for several months. I had two car accidents during this period, as my mind was not fully concentrating .

Pats death had a profound effect on me. Not just the impact upon my emotions and trying to cope with the grief and to go on living a normal life at the Town Hall and trying to keep our shop going after the post office was closed and trying to bring up the children properly. There was no grief counselling in those times, however, the weeks I spent in hospital had made me acutely aware of the suffering that other families were going through. It made me realise that my thought process until then had been insular and I had pretty much ignored what was going on around me.

From that point on, I hope I became a better person in that I made it a priority to always consider other people's feelings when making decisions. I hope that this improvement extended to my managerial career as well as my personal life.

LIFE GOES ON

Lightning Strikes Again.

The next two years were spent trying to cope with being a single parent. I learnt just how much I had relied on Pat to provide a rock for our marriage. Coping with the domestic side was relatively straight-forward. In time I came to enjoy cooking and got the kids involved in my weekly Saturday cookathon.

Each week I prepared enough food for the following week and put it in marked containers in the freezer so the kids could heat up the containers for their tea if I was delayed by work or buying stock for the shop. There were one or two failures on the way such as the day I came up with the idea to make a giant pizza. Common sense is not one of my greatest assets and while the pizza contents looked great on the kitchen table it would have worked far better if I had rolled out the base first and then added them in!

At a personal level I found I could not sleep and decided to use this to get fit. I began running and exercising after I had put the kids to bed. After a year I had lost three stone in weight and was running half marathons and marathons. I also did a number of things that I had always wanted to do such as a parachute jump and a bobsleigh run.

The impact of their mum's death had a major impact, as you would expect upon Christopher and Darren.

Christopher was at the beginning of his teenage years and up until then had done well at school. He was closest to his mother and they used to regularly sit huddled up on the couch watching late night horror films on Friday and Saturday nights. He was away on a school trip in London when Pat died and missed seeing her body in hospital. This had a profound effect upon him and a year or two later he told my friend Barry's wife Maureen who he had always been close to that he still expected his mum to be there when he got home from school. I deliberately moved house after six months, even though this made running the shop more difficult, because I felt pretty much the same as Christopher.

What made matters a lot worse for Christopher was that Pat's mum Eva, who had been coming over to lend a hand for a week at a time, suffered a heart attack when she was alone in the house with Chris and died even though he had rung for the ambulance and applied CPR.

It is not surprising that Chris had a really bad adolescence after this and he virtually gave up at school. He also made life pretty difficult for Hazel and I when we started living together and his late teen years were pretty badly messed up with drink and drugs. In amongst this he displayed a lot of ability at football and rugby. I tried my best to use these to try to strengthen the father and son bond and took over the under-16 football team he played in at weekends at his request (as if I did not have enough to do in my life!).

Despite the hassle of dealing with the parents and getting the kit washed every week I really enjoyed this two years and was immensely proud when we won the County Under 16 Cup and Chris won the man of the match award after capping a brilliant display with a truly stunning goal from 35 yards.

He deserves the utmost credit for pulling his life round. He stayed in Penrith when Hazel and I moved to Carlisle and London for a few years and then eventually joined us in London. While he was there with us he worked his way up from kitchen porter to Head of Purchasing at the 5- star White House Hotel. Chris left this job to come and work for Centaur in 2001. He managed the Seahouses office for several years, being responsible for setting up most of our administrative systems. He was also our tennis correspondent and analyst and subsequently carved out a trading role. He also managed to fit in visits to the Australian and French opens as well as Wimbledon.

Darren was only 9 at the time of his mum's death and had a bad time at school for a while due to the cruelty of other children. However this toughened him and although Christopher tended to push himself away from the family, Darren and I became very close as he did with his Nanna who spent most of 2005 and 2006 helping me to bring up the kids and run the shop. I had got into distance running as I could not sleep and Darren ran the Great North Run with me when he was just 11 and he and I would regularly go running and walking in the beautiful Lakeland fells.

While Christopher was always tall and well built, he is six foot two, Darren was of a slim build and it is only in adult life that he has built up his weight through exercise. Darren has always been a model son and quite simply I have never known him do one wrong thing in his life, he has an extremely strong sense of right and wrong. However, this cannot be mistaken for being soft or being someone who can be pushed around as some people have found out to their cost.

I still remember the day when I was summoned from working at the Cumbria County Council audit by the Head Mistress at Darren's new school in Carlisle shortly after we had moved there. On the way in to her office I passed Darren and another boy sat outside the head's office, both had cuts on their faces and they looked pretty dishevelled. It transpired that Darren had been leaving the school to go home when he had been teased and tormented by four bullies who had taken his bag and emptied it.

They had picked on the wrong boy. Darren soon had had enough and launched himself at the ring-leader. Another boy who had been nearby and was a classmate of Darren's had seen what was going on had come to his assistance. The upshot was that two of the gang had had to be taken to hospital with facial and other injuries. The Head proceeded to give me a lecture on violence and how it would not be tolerated at her school. I told her that I hoped she was giving the parents of the assailants the same lecture. Strangely enough Darren was never ever tormented or bothered again after this episode and he and Richard became firm friends.

Another example of Darren's ability to look after himself came when he was playing for Saracen's colts at Rugby after we had moved down to London. Darren had become a promising rugby player at school where he played rugby union and at weekends where he played Rugby League, which he much preferred, for Whitehaven Under 18 team. When we moved to London in 2000, we lived less than a mile away from Saracen's ground, which was then in North London in north Southgate. Darren went to the ground to ask if he could train and was soon playing centre in the Colt's team. He did not enjoy this role and much preferred to play loose forward however the coaches told him he simply did not have sufficient body mass for that role.

Hazel and I went to watch Darren as often as we could and one Sunday they were playing against a touring Australian Under 18 team. The Aussies were considerably heavier than Saracens and were winning easily and dominating the scrums. They were also dishing out the stick and two of the Sarrries front- row forwards were taken off injured.

After the second injury the coach was just about to send on another lamb to the slaughter when Darren ran over to him and told him he was going in the front row and to send on a substitute back. All seemed pretty quiet until the next scrum, which is where the Australian's were dishing out the treatment. All of a sudden the scrum broke up and Darren was tussling with one of the big props. The next thing to happen was one of the best uppercuts I have ever seen and the prop was laid out flat on his back. Needless to say Darren was sent off however it was some time before the crowd stopped chanting his name!

Darren tried hard but was only an average student at school, coming out with four "o" levels. After a brief flirtation with office work, which he hated, and three years as a scaffolder, which he loved, he joined the Parachute Regiment in 1996. Since then he has worked his way up to be Staff Sergeant and has been decorated several times during his four stints in Afghanistan, two in Kosovo and two in Iraq. Running stayed with Darren and he ran in endurance races for the Parachute Regiment after he joined the Army at the age of twenty- one.

Darren settled in Plymouth with his fiancée Michelle and Harvey her son from a previous marriage some 10 years ago and they were married in March this year. I have not seen him much over the last 15 years compared to Christopher who lived near us in

Seahouses and worked for Centaur but he is always in my thoughts and I am extremely proud of him.

A typical day in my life between 1984 and 1986 was;

Get up 5.am

Open Shop and lay out newspapers and magazines.

Hand over to shop assistant at 7.30 am

Have a shower and get kids ready for school.

8.45 take Darren to school

9am Start work as Assistant Director of Finance at Eden District Council

12.30 Go back to shop for shift changeover and lunch

1.30 Back at work

5.30 Back to shop for evening hand over

5.45 Upstairs to cook kids tea

6.30 Play sport with kids/go for a run

8 Go to cash and carry for shop stock

9.30 Housework and TV

11-1 Running/exercise

1.30 - Bed

Weekends were spent taxiing the kids to matches or friends and cooking.

This hectic schedule was a blessing in some ways as it prevented me from succumbing to the overwhelming sense of loss that overcame me when I was alone. However it also prevented me from restarting my love life. This was something that I never thought I would do but eventually it began to fill my thoughts more and more as I realised there was a huge hole in my life after Pat. Eventually in early 1985 I asked my mum if she would look after the kids every other weekend and I began to go out pubbing and clubbing.

I have to say, both sexes have it easy today with the proliferation of dating sites and there is no excuse for loneliness. In 1985 there was nothing like this and I needed to develop a very thick skin in order to put up with the many knockbacks I received as I tried to chat up women who were inevitably socialising in groups. I did have a number of things in my favour however including being extremely fit, my all night running phase had resulted in my weight dropping from 14stone to 11 stone. I also owned a new BMW 315,which I bought with my winnings from the 1984 Cheltenham Festival.

Having got married at twenty- one to pretty much my first girlfriend, I had to learn how sexual politics had changed over the previous 15 years, but eventually I got my act together and started to go out with an ever increasing number of very attractive women. They tended to be five to ten years younger than me due to the fact that there were few places to meet women of my age. Most of these women were frightened off because of my lifestyle, which required a high degree of organisation and gave priority to my children but I did have two or three longer relationships, which lasted two to three months. In my mind however i was set on remaining single for at least five years in order to let the kids grow up significantly.

One girlfriend who made me a hero in my male friend's eyes in Penrith was Judith. Judith managed a small craft shop in Penrith and worked as a barmaid in the most popular pub in town, the Gloucester Arms. I used to go to the Gloucester for a drink with friends once a week and Judith regularly cropped up in the conversation as being the sexiest woman in Penrith. I tended to agree but was not keen on going out with local women because of the gossip factor.

Matters were taken out of my hands however when I took Darren on a bus trip to Blackpool organised by local residents of Castletown, which was where I lived. We sat down on the bus and who should come and sit down behind us but Judith and her son, We ended up spending the day together and taking the kids to the Pleasure Beach. On the way home Judith surprised me by asking me if I would like to go to her house the following week for a drink after she had finished working in the pub.

Judith and I were soon the subject of town and work gossip however I have to say that it was worthwhile from my point of view. She certainly matched the two John's fantasies. We split up eventually because she was essentially a free spirit who had never married and I was probably not mature enough to cope with that. I went back to spending weekends in Newcastle and London where a friend let me have the use of his house at weekends.

In August 1986 I booked to take the kids to the Commonwealth Games taking place in Edinburgh for a holiday. By that time I thought I had got my life in order at work, the shop was doing really well and my social life was anything but boring. I was going to travel back home direct but changed my mind and decided to spend the evening at my mum's house and go and see my sister Jill, then travel home in the morning. That turned out to be one of the best decisions I have made in my life.

It must have been about 7pm when I arrived at Jill's house and when I went through to the living room, an extremely attractive young woman was sitting there. We had a great evening full of laughter and I really hit it off with Jill's guest, who happened to be her best friend from work Hazel. I took the kids back to Penrith the next day but I had made my mind up that I would try to get Hazel's number and ask her out on a date. However I had reckoned without Jill, She told me in no uncertain terms that she did not want Hazel to become the latest notch on my bedpost and no matter how hard I tried she would not relent. Fortunately I recalled that Hazel had said that she worked at Brims Construction and I soon tracked her down and managed to eventually get a "yes"to meet me for a drink.

That was in July 1986. By October we were living together in Penrith and Hazel had given up her job. I was completely stricken and thankfully she was too. Even the weather seemed to be on my side as on our third date we went for a walk along the Northumbrian coast from Craster to Dunstanburgh Castle some two miles in distance terms. The plan was to have lunch afterward in Craster but on the walk back the heavens opened and we got absolutely soaked. We were forced to go back to my mum's house to change out of our wet clothes. Neither of us went back to work for two days!

I like to think I am quite romantic and I proposed to Hazel one weekend when we went for a walk in the lakes and climbed up the waterfall behind the Swiss Lodore Hotel near Keswick. We were sitting looking down on the truly beautiful view overlooking Derwentwater when I plucked up the courage and I like to think it was my words and not the climb that left her breathless.

Hazel and I got married on 20th November 1987 and we celebrated our twenty- fifth wedding anniversary in 2012 with a dinner for family and friends and a romantic weekend in Prague. Over the last twenty five years I can remember only one occasion when we went to bed not speaking to each other and after spending the first part of her life in one house with her parents in Wallsend, we have subsequently lived in Penrith, Carlisle, London twice, The Lake District, Seahouses in two homes, Ireland and Tenerife.

Hazel is a fantastic home- maker and as our wealth grew we both derived a lot of pleasure from refurbishing and furnishing our home in the Lake District and the converted farmhouse we lived in in Seahouses. She is very much an introvert, however when people get to know her they realise what a wonderful person she is.

She really came out of her shell when we lived in London when she developed a lot of friendships at work and our house became renowned both in District Audit and C and A for the many great parties and dinner parties that we threw. These included our annual fancy dress party at Christmas at which we would often have over 200 people crammed into our three- bedroomed terraced house in Southgate.

The most memorable event was in 1998 when Hazel threw a surprise 50th birthday party for me. When I returned home from work the whole street was decorated and there must have been half of LASER Audit Commission and C and A Marble Arch staff inside.

As you can imagine there was an incredible amount of noise throughout the evening but then, at about

8pm. there was a gasp from the 30 or so people in the kitchen. Hazel had just had a new range cooker installed and Jim Mcwhirr, LASER's Regional Director was holding court in the kitchen when all of a sudden came a shout from the doorway " Get your fat arse off my cooker!" Jim had been leaning back against the controls and had switched on one of the cooker rings, which was burning the protective cover. The thought that my career in District Audit had ended flashed through my mind but fortunately Jim made a joke out of it and it was funny to see the ripple of gossip and laughter run through the house in the next couple of minutes as the news spread as to what had happened.

One of the things that made our marriage so strong is a total trust in each other. We have had a joint bank account since we got married and I cannot remember ever having looked at it. Hazel controls all the money side of things however she never hesitates when I ask her for sums as much as £10,000 to have a bet.

Probably the most memorable time in our married life from my perspective was when I was rushed to hospital at Chase Farm in Enfield around our 5th wedding anniversary with a burst appendix. After a twenty-hour operation, due to complications, I spent the next two weeks in the Intensive Care unit drifting in and out of consciousness. Whenever I regained my faculties, day or night, Hazel was there, holding my hand. She did not go into work for three weeks until I was on the road to recovery and throughout our marriage I have been privileged to enjoy this level of love and devotion.

FRIENDSHIP

The Chosen Few

Before I revert to my professional and entrepreneurial careers I will devote this chapter to the friendships I have formed in my journey through life. I don't know if I am typical but sitting down here writing this autobiography it is surprising how few friends I can recall as having had a major impact upon my life. Yes I have had hundreds of friendly associations with colleagues both at work, in sport and socially but I have shared my innermost feelings with very few people as I progressed along the tapestry.

Maybe that says something about me. Most people would describe me as an outward going, genial character and I have heard words such as "natural leader" and "open and entertaining" used to describe me. I certainly do believe that smiling and respecting people's dignity costs nothing, disarms potential adversaries in situations of conflict and often affords you time to collect your thoughts and assess individuals. But, if I were to assess myself I would say that I am an analytical thinker who can be ruthlessly pragmatic on occasions.

In the years between leaving school in 1966 and getting married in 1969 I did not develop any real friendships and pretty much gave up sport as I spent all of my spare time with Pat. In fact it was a bit difficult coming up with a best man candidate, I eventually settled for Les Perceval who had been my best mate after school until I met Pat. He had remained footloose and fancy free and repeatedly tried to get me to stray but eventually realised he was fighting a lost cause.

We live in an age of mass social interaction with the delights of Twitter and Facebook with individuals sharing the most mundane aspects of their life with the world at large. The fact that the world had become a goldfish bowl was first drawn to my attention when my wife Hazel enrolled me in Friends United, a website designed to reignite school friendships. She told me that she had mentioned the fact to me that she was putting my profile on the site but I have to say that the possibilities did not register with me or I would not have agreed.

This happened at the height of Centaur at which time I used to deal with around 100 e-mails per day. All of a sudden I was starting to receive tens of e -mails from individuals, who said they were my best-friend 40 years ago, and copious invitations to attend school re-unions. I can honestly say that I did not recall any of the e mailers who wished to interact with me, even the female ones, which was a bit disturbing. I disappeared from the site pretty quickly and to this day remain un-reunited.

However, there were two notable occasions when my life re-connected with former school -mates. The first was in the 1980's when I met up with Bill Brown again. Bill had played inside right alongside my inside left for Wallsend Grammar School under 18 team. He was a really good footballer, a Jimmy Greaves type of player who could have made it professionally had he wished but went off to university instead.

I was attending a North West CIPFA regional meeting to give a speech on " Privatisation of Local Authority Stores" something I had pioneered at Eden District that was creating a lot of national interest. There were about a hundred practitioners present and I was having a coffee in the refreshment area prior to speaking when I felt a tap on my shoulder. It was Bill, I recognised him immediately despite the passage of time and we went for a drink at the end of the day to catch up.

Bill had done well, at the time he was Chief Internal Auditor for Lancashire County Council, but of much more interest was that like me he had become a keen horse- racing fan who went racing regularly. We ended up having a late one and kept in touch at future meetings until our paths separated again when he became a senior partner at one of the big six accountancy firms and I moved to the Audit Commission.

My other school friend re-union was much more remarkable. Pat and I had started to go abroad for our holidays with the children when they had both reached school age. We liked Tenerife and were having our third holiday there in 1981 at Bajamar, a small town in the north of the Island. Some friends at the hotel we were staying at had children of a similar age to Chris and Darren and offered to look after them one night if we wanted an evening out to ourselves.

We did not need to be asked twice and decided to go to a very remote fish restaurant that we had noticed when we were touring during daylight. It took some finding in the dark but we made it and settled down with a bottle of wine and ordered the local fish speciality. The restaurant was quite large but there was only one other group of four people at a table near the bar. We could tell that they were English from the snippets of conversation that drifted over but I thought nothing of it until one of the group a young man mid to late twenties walked up to our table.

Imagine my surprise when, in one of the remotest places I had been in and in a foreign country, he said " Excuse me but you are Keith Sobey aren't you?" The gentleman in question turned out to be Barry Mitchell who was a year behind me at Wallsend Grammar but had played in the football and chess teams. Not only that but I had gone to his house in Wallsend quite often to play chess with him and his younger brother. I probably hadn't recognised Barry straight away because his hair had changed considerably over the last 15 years.

We could not stop laughing at the remarkable coincidence that had led to us meeting up and we had a good evening with his wife and her parents reminiscing and catching up. Barry was travelling back to England the following day but we agreed to meet when we returned to England. Over the next three years we met up occasionally, Barry had done well and was a Senior Accountant for the Electricity Board, more remarkably he too had become a horse racing fan and our weekends when we met up were usually dominated by form study and betting. I lost touch with Barry after Pat's death. I found it extremely difficult to spend time with people who had known us as a couple.

That holiday also featured one of the most remarkable "friendships" I developed in my life. The hotel we were staying at had a tennis court and table tennis tables and held tournaments. As well as playing in these in which we pretty much swept the board, Pat and I used to play through the day quite a lot with the kids. One day we were playing when a gentleman came up to me and asked me in an eastern European accent if I would mind giving him a game of table tennis. I said I would be happy to but was slightly surprised when he asked if I would mind playing at his house, a fabulous villa, which overlooked the hotel.

Thus started an absolutely bizarre week. Ivan was Russian and one of the most competitive people I have met. We played against each other at table tennis, chess and with each other at doubles at tennis against another Russian couple. After the first day he insisted that Pat and I and the children move to the villa from the hotel and we enjoyed sensational hospitality including being taken to the two best Russian restaurants on the island.. The week flew by and Ivan drove us to the airport with his partner Vanya,whom Pat got on really well with, and Ivan said he would write to me.

Ivan wrote periodically over the next year and was particularly keen on keeping up to date with the prices of fashion goods and jewellery, I never found out what he did for a living other than it involved importing and exporting. Then the following summer we got an invitation to spend two weeks at his villa and he would also pay the flights. We were only too glad to accept. Over that fortnight the sport continued unabated and I began to get to get to know Ivan, I noticed that he was not as carefree as the previous year and he referred on several occasions to how difficult life was becoming in Russia.

The highlight of the holiday for me was representing Russia in a Russia v Germany chess match, which Ivan had organised with the owner of a German restaurant that we ate in regularly. This was organised like a world championship event and there were many spectators present. I played board four and after 4 hours the match was poised at two and a half points each with my game going into extra time. It seemed certain to be drawn as we were well into the end game and had equal material when my opponent made the fatal mistake of pressing too hard for a win and ended up losing a piece for a pawn. I converted this into a win and the whole place erupted.

I have never drunk so much in my life that day and had a ferocious hangover the following day, I also found out that Ivan had a $10,000 side bet with the restaurant owner. He had tried to give Pat $2000, as he knew I would not accept it but she would not take it. However Vanya bought her a diamond watch when they were out shopping. That broke her stiff upper lip, we all know about women and diamonds.

We invited Ivan and Vanya to visit us in the UK that Autumn. He promised they would but when we returned there were no more letters. I hope that Ivan survived what ever troubles he was going through but I am afraid that he probably did not as he never answered any of my letters including the one in which I wrote telling him of Pat's death. Ivan gave Pat a set of Russian dolls when we said goodbye at the airport and when we got home and separated them in one of the bodies we found $2000.

Most of my enduring friendships have come during my married life, first with Pat and then with Hazel. The first real friendships I developed were when we lived in Stockport between 1969 and 1971. As we were single and had no children we spent quite a few nights in our local pub, The George and Dragon. The pub was just starting up a Sunday morning football team and I got roped in to playing in the trials. I walked into the team, as I was one of only a handful of triallists who turned up sober!

The captain of the team was Barry D'arcy and as I played left half and he played left back we soon struck up an on- field relationship. That soon translated itself into an off- field friendship too. Barry and his wife Doreen were market traders and already had a wide circle of friends but took us under their wings. I can honestly say that the two years we spent in Stockport before moving back to the North East were one of the best periods in my life. Barry introduced us to Rodney Ernil a well known local chef and we became pretty much inseparable, playing golf and football and going out to country pubs until the early hours of the morning (I did not drive then).

Rod is one of the funniest people I have ever met. The first time we met, he and his then wife Cindy came to our flat for supper and a few drinks. He was lying on the floor opposite me and beside Barry who was seated but had taken his shoes off. Rod spent the whole evening stuffing Barry's shoes with grapes and Satsuma segments and Pat and I found it extremely difficult to keep a straight face especially when Barry stood up!

Another evergreen moment came one winter morning when we were playing golf. It was sheeting down with rain and visibility was not great. Barry played his second shot from the rough from a hilly lie and fell over as he struck the ball. No one had seen where it went so after looking for the ball he took his penalty and we finished the hole. The sun eventually came out a few holes later and we felt safe to take off our waterproofs. As we did so a ball dropped out of the hood in Barry's jacket. The ball he struck must have gone straight up in the air and landed in Barry's hood as he lay on his back after he had slipped. It took ten minutes before Rod and I stopped laughing and we could finish the game.

After I moved away from Manchester we all kept in touch and often spent weekends at each others'houses and there was always the annual Cheltenham saga. For almost 20 years Barry, Rodney, their friend Mike and I went to Cheltenham for festival week. We were joined by another close friend Barry, about whom you will read more later

The Cheltenham saga became an annual pilgrimage. I would travel down to Manchester on the Sunday and we would all meet for breakfast on the Monday morning and then set off to Stratford races, which was the pipe opener for the festival. In those times the Festival lasted just three days. We would call at Wolverhampton races on the way back on Friday and Uttoxeter on the Saturday in order to make a week of it before returning to our normal lives.

You had to be fit to survive Cheltenham week in those days. You had to survive 5 days without sleep, as most nights there were spent drinking and playing darts, dominos or cards. You had also to be able to bet effectively through the daytime and to perform in the mega snooker tournament that lasted all week, Hundreds of pounds changed hands each night but I can honestly say that other than verbal batterings which were par for the course for anyone who ever took themselves seriously, no one ever fell out within the group.

There are so many stories to tell from this era but I will dwell on two. One year Barry brought a friend with him, Gornall who was a policeman. We were all standing ready to go in on Gold Cup day when it was announced that the day was a sell out and we would not be able to get in. Quick as a flash, Gornall said to get behind him and get our credit card wallets out. He marched up to the entry gate and got his warrant card out and said to the doorman " Pickpocket squad" to which the door opened and seven of us marched in!

Another event worth recalling occurred one year when the betting had not been going well. Usually some of our group would be winning and they would act as bankers over the week for those who were not so fortunate but this year we had made a very bad start and it looked as if we would be heading home on the Thursday, when Barry came up with an idea. Off we trooped to the Guiness tent at the end of

Wednesday's racing which was dominated by the Irish contingent. We all had our Guiness in hand when Mike got on a table and shouted " £20 for anyone who can name a horse running today that Keith cannot describe the form of its last three races" What a night that was, Mike nearly got knocked over in the rush but although I failed on one or two of the Irish horses we made enough profit to fill up the betting banks for the rest of the week.

These were fantastic days. I can still remember the killer and cricket darts games being played with over 50 people at the hotel we stayed at in the village of Northleach, with over £500 going to the winner. I was useless at darts and soon realised that there was more money to be made in acting as the darts bookie. I made a fair bit of money at this by always keeping Rod on the side of the book .He was a fantastic thrower and won most games of cricket, despite giving away big starts.

The snooker tournaments were just as exciting. We played a game called Chase The Green, where you had all the colours except the blue and black on the playing surface plus two reds, which were non-scoring and a foul if the white touched them. The aim of the game was to score 51 points by potting the colours or scoring cannons off two colours, which scored 2 points. If you went in off or played a foul shot or touched a red your score was wiped out and you had to pay a fine into the ever -accumulating pot. You could only win if you potted the green, which was the only odd number score and you had to nominate the pocket you were going to pot it in. Chase The Green would often last the whole week as the other players always ganged up on whoever was leading and it was a great leveller as the better players were for ever going for their shots and touching a red which meant another £10 in the kitty.

Barry and Rodney were party to two of the worst pieces of luck I experienced in my gambling career. The first was during my stag party before my wedding to Hazel in 1987. I had, with Hazel's permission, decided to make it a stag week and got the Cheltenham gang together to go for a weeks racing at Newbury, and Aintree.

We all stayed at Manchester on the first evening and set off for Newbury the following morning after breakfast, there were 6 of us. At breakfast we formulated our jackpot and placepot perm for the day. There were six of us and as usual we each picked two horses in each race, the aim being to end up with perms being completed with two entries in each race using the most popular selections. As it transpired that morning, in two of the races three horses tied as the most popular. That would not have been a problem normally, we would have just increased the perm but Barry D'Arcy's business was in trouble at the time and it was a struggle for him to come for the week .He asked if we could draw lots in the two races and drop a selection in both.

No prizes for guessing what came next, we had the winner in 5 of the 6 races including two big price selections and in the sixth race the horse that we dropped won. The jackpot was not won and £117,000 was carried forward, Barry's decision had cost us £19,500 each, which in 1987 was a lot of money. It was difficult to raise spirits that evening and in the morning Barry had gone.

The second occasion occurred much later, just after Centaur had started in 2000. I was working night and day to get things going and Hazel suggested I take a few days off and go racing. Andrew could not make it so I rang Rod and he was up for it and we had three days racing at Salisbury, Fontwell and Brighton. On the first day we were in high spirits, Rod had brought with him a ten-pound note attached to a thin piece of elastic and we spent the morning in a supermarket standing around with the £10 pound note lying on the floor behind us. Just as well or other meaning people reached down to pick it up Rod pressed a button and it shot up his trouser leg. Watching the shocked look on the "victims" was a real Candid Camera experience!

We were not laughing later that afternoon however. We got to Salisbury early and did our usual jackpot and placepot perms with us both picking a horse in each race giving us two selections per race. I was hopeless and did not select a winner but Rod was in tremendous form. He had the first three winners including one big price winner and the last two winners. In the fourth race his selection was a non-runner, which means that we went on the favourite for the race. We were delighted when the joint favourite won the race and when the sixth winner cruised home we were off to the champagne bar for some bubbly.

After a celebratory drink we went to the nearest tote window to find out how much we had won, over £10,000 had been carried forward from the previous day so we were anticipating a share of a pool exceeding £20,000. Rod handed his ticket over and confusion reigned when the tote operative told us the jackpot had not been won. Eventually the Tote manager came over and scrutinised our ticket. He then informed us we had been very unlucky, as when a selection is a non- runner and there are joint favourites, the selection transfers to the joint favourite that is the lowest number on the racecard. On this occasion we went on to number 1 who was second! The jackpot pool carried forward to the next day was £26,000.

I think I am fated never to win a jackpot or scoop six as on several occasions I have had 5 winners and a second when entering a perm with friends. It looks as if I am the jinx.

Barry and Rodney and Doreen and Cindy travelled up several times from Manchester to see Pat when she was ill in hospital and attended her funeral. In the year after Pat's death I found it hard to visit family and close friends in Penrith but took Chris and Darren for a week's holiday on Anglesey with Barry and Doreen and their children and this was a key step in my getting started on the next part of my life. Although I do not see them as often today Barry, Doreen and Rodney remain close friends.

If my meeting with Barrie Mitchell and Ivan in Tenerife was remarkable, the start of my friendship with Barry Eggo was even more so. In 1972 Pat and I were living in Cramlington in our new ground floor flat with our first-born Christopher. Cramlington was a new town and we lived on the edge of one of the large private estates opposite the start of a large estate of new council houses. One Saturday afternoon I was sitting in our lounge watching the horse racing when I could not happen but notice a young child, no older than 3, who was opening his first-floor bedroom window and starting to climb out.

I did not wait to see what was going to happen, I ran out of the front door and sprinted across the broad expanse of grass and concrete between our two houses. I arrived under his window just as he took flight and fortunately I was able to catch him. Some other neighbours had watched what was happening and came over and the noise alerted the young birdman's mum who had been hovering inside the house. Maureen was clearly shocked by events but all's well that ends well. Later that evening she came over to our house with her husband Barry to say thank you and thus started my closest friendship until I met Andrew Cork and we started Centaur.

Over the next three years Barry and i were inseparable and spent many many nights together, either as a foursome with our wives or on boys and girls days and night outs. The friendship carried on after we moved to Penrith in 1974 until Pats death in 1984. Afterward I found it difficult to spend time with Maureen and Barry as it felt that Pat was always there with us and we drifted apart when Hazel and I got together and moved to London.

There were many many memorable moments I shared with Barry, both gambling and otherwise. I have already mentioned his part in the annual Cheltenham expeditions, however undoubtedly the most entertaining, and profitable part of our friendship came when Barry got a job at the Empress Bingo hall in Whitley Bay. Before then Barry and I used to go out for a drink to the local social club one evening a week and play darts and snooker and we would usually go to the betting shop on a Saturday and write out some mixed bets which we joint funded. Barry was a Fraud Officer for the Department of Social Security so we always had a lot to talk about with my job in audit often bringing to light frauds.

Times were hard for both of us in 1972, Barry had three young children and neither Pat nor Maureen worked. I had a mortgage to pay on a part qualified salary and Barry ran a car. I can remember one evening we were watching the nine o clock news when a news item came up saying that Lord Vestey, one of the Queen's cousins, had been arrested for tax evasion. This really struck a chord with Barry who said, there he was involved in persecuting and punishing the least well off in society and yet people at the top of society were robbing the country of millions in tax revenues. In other words " One law for the rich and one law for the poor.

Not long afterwards Barry told me to come to the bingo hall he worked at in the evenings and although I said that bingo was not for me he insisted and said I had to wear a jacket with big pockets. I duly turned up and he told me how to play and went 50/50 with me on some tickets but said that I must go to the large horseshoe table at the side of the room at the half time break.

No luck on the bingo although it was amazing watching some women keep a dozen cards going effortlessly while I struggled to keep up with two. Half time arrived so I trooped over to the horseshoe table. It had 50 metal plates laid out in the horseshoe shape, each with three numbers written on between 1 and 50. Customers were invited to place fifty pence on each of the three numbers, a dealer then dealt cards numbered between one and fifty face up. If your number came out you took a 50p off your plate and if you were the first to pocket all three numbers you shouted "house" and you won all of the 50pences left on the table less the house's cut.

This game was extremely popular and if I had not arrived at the table early I would not have been able to play. After a minute or two in came the dealer, Barry! The intermission lasted 30 minutes in that time there were about 20 games played. Much to my surprise I won twice toward the end of the session winning about £50 and then £40. Afterward Barry and I went for a drink and a third man, Charlie who I had noticed from the horseshoe table joined us, Charlie had also won twice.

It was then that I realised that Barry was manipulating the cards when he collected them in after each game. It took him a few games to recognise Charlie and my cards and to place them close together. He had mastered a shuffle, which looked impressive but failed to disturb the cards a great deal. Over the weeks he had come to know the regular players and how they cut the deck of cards, some cut very thin, others very thick, Barry would get our cards toward the top of the pack and give the pack to a thin cutter or towards the bottom of the pack and give the pack to a thick cutter. While this routine was pretty much infallible,on some occasions another players three cards would get placed in front of ours in the pack and they would win. However, over the next year I was able to pay my mortgage in fifty pence pieces!

One of the funniest things I have ever witnessed occurred after I had been going for about six months. One of the regulars shouted out "fix" after I had won yet again. Barry asked her what she meant and she said that I was always winning and that I was his friend and that something crooked was happening. Barry remained calm and went over to her with the pack of the cards and told her if she felt that way why didn't she cut the cards. She took the pack and cut them several times and mixed the cards up and then handed the pack back to him. Then, as Barry turned to go back to his station, quick as a flash he substituted another pack of cards. which he had given to her ,which he had "sorted". After less than 20 numbers I had won again to which the woman remarked" Well I guess he must just be really lucky! "It is just as well I was not having a drink at the time or I am sure I would have choked.

The other event, which was also remarkable, occurred on Grand National day in 1979. Pat and I were living in Penrith then and Barry and Maureen had come over for the weekend with their children Dawn, Robin and Neil. On Grand National day the plan was for the girls to go out shopping in the morning and for Barry and I to take the kids down to Lake Ullswater for a play and then study the form and put our bets on and the girls and kids grand national bets on and we would all watch the races on the TV in the afternoon.

Barry and l both fancied Rubstic for the Grand National, who was ridden by a local jockey, Maurice Barnes. We had backed the horse in the ante-post market. We did our studying of the form and came up with 7 horses which meant 114 bets if we placed a full cover each way perm on. After much discussion we decided to drop it to 6 horses, which meant only 57 units and as we had already backed Rubstic and the national was such a competitive race, he was the one to go.

That afternoon was one of the most exciting afternoons I have spent watching horseracing and also one of the most frustrating. Over the course of the afternoon, five of our 6 horses won and of course Rubstic was a convincing winner of the Grand National. The winnings from our mixed bet came to £7,000, which meant £3,500 each, which was more than enough to buy a new car at that time. Had we put the original bet on and left Rubstic in the combination we would have won £175,000 although Ladbroke's maximum payout in those days was £100,000, a truly life changing win.

Barry was with me at Cheltenham in 1984 when I did enjoy a life changing win but more about that later.

My friendship with John and Joan Carruthers came about through Pat who met Joan playing squash at the new Penrith courts I had managed to get built through Sports Council sponsorship. They played in the same team together and travelled to play matches around Cumbria. From the moment John and I met at one of the regular parties he and Joan held at their beautiful farmhouse home in Clifton Village near Penrith, we hit it off and I have never laughed as much in my life as in the five years we socialised before Pat's untimely death.

I fell victim to John's wicked sense of humour on the very first night we met. There must have been thirty people at the party that night and as usual John was a genial and attentive host, getting drinks for anyone who had an empty glass. For those who knew John like our other friends John and Sandra and John and Jennifer, that was something you never let happen, but unsuspecting me allowed three or four refills of my pint glass to take place. At about midnight I did start to feel a bit groggy but thought to myself that I would just limit further drinks. I was standing against a doorway at the time, which unbeknown to me led down to the cellar, and I leaned back for support. The next thing I knew I was looking up at a sea of faces and I was lying on the stone cellar floor. Apparently what had happened was that I had fallen back on the cellar door and it had opened, resulting in my tumbling backward down a flight of stairs. If I had not been totally inebriated due to John's doctoring of my drink I would have probably broken my back but I must have relaxed as I was falling and amazingly my pint glass was still in my hand at the bottom half full!

Over the next few years I saw the same thing happen to many innocent victims. Rod came up one year at New Year when he was going through a difficult divorce with his wife Cindy and I took him to a New Years Eve party at John's to cheer him up. My abiding memory of this visit was a very hung over Rod tramping around the Lake District on the New Year's Day fox hunt in a designer suit which was soaking wet up to the thighs! It took us two days to thaw him out!

John and I were even more dangerous when we got together. I can still remember the Christmas Eve when we visited our friend John Siddle's fancy goods store in the centre of Penrith and started to hold an impromptu auction of John's most expensive paintings. On another occasion a bus lost control and crashed into John's display window. Within 30 minutes he received a call from John and I purporting to be his insurance company letting him know his policy had lapsed as he had not renewed his premium.!

Despite this tendency towards wickedness, as I commented on earlier, John was the most dependable person I have ever met. Whoever found themselves in difficulty in John's village or among his friends, John was there to lend a hand. His devotion to Joan was another constant feature and it is a tragedy that Joan contracted Alzheimer's soon after she retired.

By the time I married Hazel in 1987, I had deliberately let most of the close friendships I had when I was married to Pat slip. Hazel had one or two close friends but was more family –orientated. She was and still is very close with her sisters Ann and Lily and her brother George. It was not long after we got married that we moved to London due to my career with the Audit Commission.

Hazel is a contradiction in many ways, an intensely shy person until she gets to know people she is an absolutely fantastic hostess. Our dinner parties and house parties became things of legend within the London and South East region and we would often have over a hundred people in fancy dress at our annual Christmas Party. This featured a one -mile long conga chain down Southgate High Street. So much for boring boring auditors!

Our life in London was one long social whirl as Hazel developed a lot of friends at C and A , where she worked as a Senior Payroll Administrator . I developed a wide circle of friends too, mostly within the Audit Commission as they moved me around London a lot. It was quite a wrench for me when we moved back up North in 2001 and although I worked in London again, heading Centaur from 2009 to 2012, we never revived the social scene again. I was too busy working flat out to develop Centaur and Hazel lived most of the time at our house in Seahouses close to her two sisters.

Although we got to know and socialised with a lot of people, the only close friendships that Hazel and I developed from the Centaur years other than Andrew Cork, who I will conclude this chapter with, were with Ian and Dawn Craig and Demetris Tackshoudis.

I first met Ian and Dawn at Kelso races in February 2005. Ian was IT Director for Bank of America at the time and had joined Centaur the previous year as an alternative investment. He had made good profits and decided to branch out into bloodstock shares with us and bought shares in three horses including Crathorne.

Crathorne ran at Kelso on 3rd February finishing third and Ian, Dawn and I had a good chat over the famous Kelso owners' tea later that afternoon. Ian's father had been a bookmaker and he was a keen horseracing aficionado although the demands of his job kept him in the USA for most of the year and limited his racing.

Over the next 7 years a firm friendship grew from that original meeting resulting in us going on holiday together regularly and meeting up as often as Ian and I could afford to let the girls go shopping! Seriously, Dawn and Hazel are among the most dedicated shoppers I have ever come across, we had 5 houses at one stage and it still was not enough to store the results of Hazel's shopping. I seriously thought of launching a series of Shopping Seminars with Dawn and Hazel as lecturers, there is no one better at answering the question " That dress looks new darling, where did you buy it?" with at least ten different responses, none of which agree with the questioner.

Ian backed up his friendship by becoming one of the partners in Centaur Greyhounds and he got a lot of enjoyment from those three years as well as developing a budget model, which helped the partnership enormously. One memorable moment stands out from this time, which I describe later in the Greyhound Bloodstock chapter. Ian was listening to my telephone commentary from Walthamstow greyhound stadium when Centaur Decree won The Arc Final, while in the middle of a Bank of America Board Meeting!

Another key moment, which cemented our friendship, occurred in 2008 when Ian was at a crossroads in his life. Although he was hugely successful in his banking career with a multi billion world wide budget responsibility, the flipside was that he was seeing less and less of his wife Dawn and young son Jack.The same thing had contributed to the break up of his first marriage several years before from which he had another son Scott. Ian had a classic decision to make family or career.

This process was occupying much of his thought process when he and Dawn came to stay for a weekend with us at our house in the Lake District near to Lake Bassenthwaite. Ian is partial to a nice bottle of wine and after Dawn and Hazel went to bed on the Friday night we worked away through most of my stock of Rioja, and Barolo. I remained in listening mode but I think that the evening must have helped

Ian to make the decision because shortly afterwards he resigned his post.

Things worked out brilliantly for him however as the Bank did not want to lose him and gave him the job of Head of European Credit Card business based in Chester, only 30 minutes drive from his home. That all night session almost took its toll on me when I dozed off in the morning and missed the appointed time for the Centaur message to be sent out, however a quick cold shower and I was back in action.

I am quite proud that in the 12 years I was at the helm of Centaur and acted as the main horse racing analyst, I never failed to send out a message or do the necessary underlying form analysis,.The nearest I ever came to failing came about in April 2004 when Andrew and I went to the Grand National meeting at Aintree.

When I knew we were going I rang Rodney and he agreed to meet up with us and he said he would sort the accommodation. He rang me later to tell me we were booked into the Adelphi, Liverpool's premier hotel where a mutual friend Dave Smith was executive chef. Dave had been part of our Cheltenham festival group on a couple of occasions but mostly worked abroad so I had not seen him for about ten years.

The Adelphi should strike a chord with many of you. It was the subject of one of the first and most successful TV Reality Shows on BBC. Dave became a media star overnight because of his running battle with hotel management, particularly the ferocious hotel manager Eileen Downey.

Eileen terrorised the rest of the hotel and fired a number of staff on the spot as the first two episodes featured her rampaging around the hotel. Then in episode three she had to go down to the kitchen to deliver a change in the planned menus and we saw a different side to Eileen. She tiptoed up to the kitchen door and did not storm in but knocked on the door three times to be met by a hail of abuse from the chef, Dave. It was absolutely hilarious. Everyone who had been watching the show thought that Dave's days were numbered, however he was just too good an executive chef for the hotel to lose.

Dave had asked Rod for us to go up to his office on the Thursday evening The hotel was hosting a massive charity dinner that night connected to racing with several hundred guests but Dave said we could all dine and have a drink in his office while he managed the main event. Everything went to plan that evening and we ate and drank like kings, courtesy of Dave.

 It was eventually six o clock in the morning when Andrew and I staggered up to our rooms, very much the worse for wear and collapsed face down on our beds fully clothed. The next thing I can remember was a ringing noise in my head that went on and on and on. I eventually managed to roll over and realised it was my mobile phone ringing and with a supreme effort managed to answer it. It was the Seahouses office saying that it was 9.30 and it was bedlam there, as the nine a.m message had not gone on line!

After telling the office to put a holding message on line I started to go downstairs but had to abort this in favour of a kissing the porcelain session. Meanwhile Andrew had surfaced. He had a stronger constitution or had had less to drink than me and said he would go and get the Racing Post so we could do the tipping. I still have an abiding memory to this day of Andrew running across the main road in Liverpool in his tee shirt and pyjama bottoms to the newsagents-every minute was vital! Between us we managed to come up with a credible member and premium rate message in the next thirty minutes and even managed to deliver a profit for our clients on the day.

That was the last time that drink ever came between me and the Centaur clients. After Liverpool, our messages went out on time every day, seven days a week until the business stopped trading in 2012.

My friendship with Demetris Tackshoudis arose in unusual circumstances but showed that diffferent geographical locations are no hindrance to firm friendship. We first met in 2005, Maxnet was thriving and I received a telephone call from Cyprus one day from a gentleman named Demetris Tackshoudis from Cyprus who said that he had seen our advertisements in the Investors Chronicle and asked me to explain how the investment worked.

We spoke for some time and I arranged to send Demetris the detailed results for Maxnet since it began in 2004 and he agreed to fax me due diligence information about himself. When this came, it tied up our fax machine for 10 minutes! Demetris was a hugely successful international businessman who owned the Metro Group, which was the largest chain of supermarkets in Cyprus, a shipping line and a number of other businesses. He also had a large investment and property portfolio.

In our follow up conversation, Demetris let me know that he was so interested in Maxnet that he wanted to become an international distributor for the product. We both believed in doing business face to face and he said he would fly to Newcastle for a weekend and we could put together a business plan. A month later I met Demetris 's flight at Newcastle Airport, he brought with him his nephew Michael who was a senior business aide in his company and liked sports betting.

Demetris was expecting to be put up in a hotel in Newcastle but was genuinely overcome when I took him home for the weekend and Hazel cooked. We got on like a house on fire and he got me to give him a flipchart presentation of the Centaur business after dinner. I was expecting Demetris to invest a few million in Maxnet however at breakfast the following morning he came up with something different. He proposed setting up a new, jointly owned, company in Cyprus. He would guarantee investors an annual return of 10 per cent, tax free, and would invest the funds in Maxnet. We would share profits in excess of 10 per cent and he would underwrite any losses sustained by investors.

Demlink began trading in late 2005 via offices in Larnaca and Nicosia. It did well for the next two years and I came over regularly to Larnaca to meet Demetris to discuss progress and other putative business projects. He was without a doubt the most generous man I have ever met and always put Andrew and I up in top hotels for the duration of our stays. We had lunch and dinner with him and his family every day we were in Cyprus. He was also the only person I have ever met who worked harder than me. He was in his office in Larnaca before six in the morning and rarely finished work before 9 pm Monday to Saturday.

Demetris and i became friends as well as business colleagues and I also developed a firm friendship with Michael and his mother Elena who was Chief Executive of Demetris' business empire. We are still friends today although our business lives have drifted apart. Demlink closed after the Credit Crunch hit and Maxnet had two poor years and Demetris fared poorly with a major property investment scheme in Eastern Europe. He is currently setting up a chain of supermarkets in Iraq and Sudan.

Over the 16 years that Centaur and subsequently KSTIPS has operated, I have had lunch and coffees with mith many clients, several times these have led to long-term friendships.

Manesh Lakhani was one of the first 50 clients to join Centaur in 2000 and I am pleased to say that he is still with us today, even though he lives in Seattle and works at a senior level for Microsoft. Manesh gets up in the early hours of the morning to pick up his betting messages and goes on to work 16-20 hour days.

I used to go on racing trips 3to 4 times a year with Manesh when he was based in the UK. Andrew would often join us. Since moving to the USA, Manesh flies over to our villa in Tenerife to spend Chetenham week with me. As well as being a long-term friend, Manesh has often worked as an unpaid business consultant for Centaur and KSTIPS. He is one of the most knowledgeable individuals in global telecommunications in the world and saved Centaur over £100,000 by restructuring our telecommunications.

Manesh was an active member of our horse racing syndicates and was fortunate to own a share in Hasty Prince (more later). He is one of the most sophisticated bettors I know and was close to being appointed Head of Sports Betting by Ladbrokes. I always wanted him as a Director but could never afford him!

I came to know Gary Bell in 2006 when he became a significant Maxnet client. A successful solicitor and long term Chelsea fan, Gary liked the way Maxnet was structured and had a successful 4 years as a client. I got to know Gary better when he organised some client recruitment meetings for me in Northern Ireland.

We hit it off and have met regularly socially over the last 10 years. Gary was a confidante for me during the period things were not going well at Centaur and I hope that I returned the favour when he went through a painful divorce. It says something about both of us that we came through these events smiling on the other side. Gary has remarried and is so much happier with Cheryl.

They say that you can choose your friends in life but not your family.

I will finish this chapter on friendship by describing my friendship with Andrew Cork. We first met in 1994 when I was promoted from Audit Manager to Senior Manager of the Harrow Section with District Audit. Andrew was one of the two Audit Managers reporting to me. I cover this period in detail later in the book and will focus on Andrew and my personal relationship here.

Andrew and I hit it off immediately as friends. We are both gastronomeurs and Andrew is an expert on wine. We both have an extremely lively sense of humour, love music, quizzing and travelling but more importantly are both devoted to horseracing and gambling.

Over the last 18 years we have become more like brothers than friends and are extremely close. Since Centaur developed, we have visited all the racecourses in the United Kingdom and Ireland and others in the United States, France, Japan, Hong Kong, South Africa, Australia and New Zealand. We have also visited all four tennis majors and all of the greyhound tracks in the United Kingdom and Ireland.

In 2007 Andrew and I bought a horse with the idea of trying to win the Grand Pardubice chase in Czechslovakia, one of the most famous races in the World, run over a gruelling 4.5 mile cross country course. Flight Command had been previously trained by Peter Beaumont and was a good jumper if somewhat slow. We bought him at the May Doncaster sales and transferred him to Charlie Mann. Our plans were frustrated when Charlie ran him on ground that was too firm at Bangor and he went lame. Andrew and I and Ian Craig and Gavin Cheeseman, his two other owners had already booked hotels in Prague and then Pardubice so we decided to go ahead and travel and watch the race.

We spent the Saturday in Prague and in the evening I told the others that dinner was on Centaur as a thank you for buying the shares. Unfortunately Andrew was feeling ill and remained in his hotel room but Ian, Gavin and I ventured out as planned. We looked around the main square and surrounding streets and settled on what appeared to be the top fish restaurant.

We settled down and had our pre dinner drinks and the waiter bought the menu and wine list. I then ordered champagne to go with the dinner. All of a sudden the level of service improved and we were particularly well attended by the wine waiter. It was touch and go whether we ordered a second bottle of champagne as the pink champagne I ordered, thinking it was the equivalent of £45 per bottle, was delicious. Thankfully we were in so much of a hurry to get to Darling's , a famous club in Prague, that we left it at one bottle. Although I am an accountant and a gambler I have to say I have a real issue with numbers and figures and when the waiter gave me the bill my eyes nearly popped out of my head when I realised that the bottle of champagne had cost £450,twice the cost of the meal! No wonder the waiter was so attentive.

This would never have happened had Andrew been with us as he would have known that we would not have been able to buy a bottle of Louis Roederer Crystal Champagne for that price. This incident caused much merriment on the night as Ian and Gavin said they wished they had taken a picture of my face when I read the bill! Next June on my sixtieth birthday a courier arrived wih a bottle from Andrew –no prizes for guessing which champagne was inside.

Perhaps the most amusing gambling story involving Andrew and I occurred when we were working for the Audit Commission in the late 1990's. At that time we were betting professionally using a combined betting bank and would have been one of the largest bettors in the UK. Because there was betting tax of 9% at the time we had to travel to the racecourse if we were having a big bet to avoid the tax penalty. If you looked at our annual leave card for 1996/1997 and 1998 you would have seen that a lot of our annual leave was taken in half days.! We would have been well overdrawn for annual leave had I not been able to authorise flexi-time as Senior Manager, this mounted up as Andrew and I both worked near 80 hours a week running the most successful Audit Section in London.

One Friday in the summer I had spotted a horse I had been waiting to back engaged in a selling handicap at Haydock Park's evening card. For anyone who knows the M6 Motorway, which Haydock abuts, Friday is not the day you would want to use it. Undeterred, we booked the afternoon off and made the journey from Central London. What was normally a four- hour journey took six due to the weight of traffic however we arrived at the course in good time.

The horse in question was trained by Cliff Hill, a West Country trainer/farmer/butcher,who kept a small string and specialised in landing gambles in lower grade races. Andrew and I were lined up ready to go and the plan was to check the horse out as soon as it came in the paddock and go straight to back it with the bookmakers. We planned to try to get £2,000 each way on and expected to get between 8 /1 and 10/1.

We were watching the horses come into the paddock when this grey horse came in sweating profusely and walking as if it was on three legs. To our horror, it was the horse we intended to back. Mission aborted, we checked the ring and it was drifting from 8to1 to 12/1 and we went for a drink to drown the sorrow of a ten hour wasted drive. We came out of the bar just before the race was off to see that Cliff's horse was no longer 12/1 it was 9/4 favourite! The race started and it came back as if it had five legs not three winning by eight lengths! It was a long journey back to London that night.

I have selected just four of the hundreds of amusing incidents we were involved in for description, however if you are ever following a vehicle on the Motorway and happen to see two figures apparently head banging to the Kings of Leon or Thin Lizzy, look no further!

We do not often get a chance to catch up with old friends en masse but that opportunity was afforded to me at my sixtieth birthday party. I was expecting something special to happen as it had for my 50th and 40th birthdays but thought that when a limousine turned up with Ian Craig, Andrew and Steve Taylor to take me to Hexham races for the afternoon that that was it, especially as Hazel had arranged for one of the races to be sponsored in my name. We had a great afternoon and returned home at about six o clock on a glorious summer evening.

I opened the gate to the front of the house and was greeted by the sight of a gazebo and about 50 of my lifelong friends who Hazel had traced. She had even arranged for one of my long term clients Tim Melton who fronted up a popular band in London to travel the 300 miles and play. It was pretty hard fighting back the tears and we had a great night. The party went on until the early hours, the highlight was undoubtedly an impromptu rendition of the Blues Brothers by Andrew Cork and Ian Craig.

I first met Andrew in 1993 when I took over as the Senior Manager of the West London District Audit team in 1993. Andrew was one of the two audit managers working in that team. Over the next 7 years Andrew was my right hand man as I turned round the performance of first that team and then the East London and Lewisham teams. More importantly though, through our shared love of horse racing,, Andrew helped me to develop the betting system which has made us both and Centaur clients many millions of pounds. More about this later, he also was instrumental in his role as Finance Director in the success of Centaur between 2000 and 2011.

We are extremely close and share a wicked sense of humour that quite often has each other in tears. Since Centaur became a big business we have gone on holiday together many many times in our quest to see racing take place around the world. Since we met we have also seen each other through some difficult times, Andrew has stumped up the necessary cash to kick start most of the business ventures we have operated since we left the Audit Commission.

Centaur gave us both the chance to acquire a team of racehorses and greyhounds and Andrew got immense pleasure from the management and day to involvement with these wonderful animals. We had many many spectacular moments such as when Hasty Prince ran away with the Tote Silver Trophy at Chepstow and when Centaur Corker annihilated the opposition in his brief but stellar careeer. The greatest tribute that I can pay to Andrew is that all of our former trainers and jockey contacts in racing still ask after him regularly with genuine affection.

Since the end of Centaur, Andrew has helped me overcome the depression that I felt and throughout the time I have known him he has been the best friend anyone could have asked for. Other firm friendships with long- term clients, which I should mention are with Bob Evans, Anthony Hammick, Jonathan Cope, Gavin Cheeseman etc etc.

Climbing The Greasy Pole

A Life In Public Service

The next two chapters deal with the thirty years I spent working in the public sector from 1969 to 1999.

My first two jobs on leaving school were, as a junior claims assistant with Refuge Assurance and as a trainee area manager with Corals Bookmakers. I may well have made a career in the bookmaking industry, however as a trainee area manager I was principally used as leave/holiday relief for shop managers and was sent to all parts of Northumberland and Durham.

This would have been alright if I had had a car but I was still learning to drive and spent many nights walking home from Newcastle to Wallsend having missed the last bus or train. Jobs were plentiful at the time as the economy was booming and, as Pat and I were thinking of getting married, I decided after three months to try for a job, which would ideally lead me to a professional qualification.

I started as a Junior Finance Trainee with Northumberland County Council in late 1966. After a qualification period I would be able to take the Institute of Municipal Treasurers and Accountants exams and hopefully become a qualified Public Sector Accountant. Trainees were initially posted to the Internal Audit section as that gave us a good grounding in the work of the County Council as a whole. In my first year I undertook Cardiff checks on creditor payments for the Finance, Education, Social Services and Planning Departments. This meant selecting a sample of payments and tracing them back to source in order to verify the service or goods purchased. Interesting work and my ground -work did lead to a fraud being discovered. We also travelled the County cashing up imprest holders.

The Chief Internal Auditor at the time was a hard - nosed Scot called Joe Bishop who ran the section of 20 or so with an iron fist. I will never forget the day I was allowed as part of my training to prepare a file for a fraud interview and sit in on the interview. The miscreant started off as a confident individual who had brought his trade union representative along to assist in his defence. After an hour of questioning he was a jibbering wreck who was advised to sign a confession there and then.

After a year, I was moved to the general office where my duties included paying jurors expenses at the County Court, which was adjacent to County Hall near the Tyne Bridge in Newcastle. This was a fantastic job as you got to listen in on some of the juicy trials that were taking place. I also learnt the delights of reconciling the Council's many bank accounts to the Cash Book.

I was due to move on to the Accountancy Section in 1969 in order to assist my training for sitting the IMTA intermediate exam that year. However I had noticed an advertisement for the District Audit service, a branch of the Civil Service that was responsible for the external audit of Local Government on behalf of taxpayers, in the press offering a better salary than I was on at present. I enjoyed auditing because of the constant variety of subject areas and decided to apply. After an extensive interview process I was successful and took up the post of Audit Examiner based in Manchester in 1969.

Before I go on to describe my job with District Audit, I should not leave the section on Northumberland County Council without describing a highlight that occurred when I was there.

The Computer section was the hub of County Hall with several offices being taken up by the IBM mainframe and associated data entry. It was also the location of a ferocious three- card brag card school twice a week on a Tuesday and Thursday. Most of the senior management took part in the card school including John Duncan the Assistant Treasurer who went on to be a very able County Treasurer. I got on famously with John who had a great sense of humour but also was a keen horse-racing fan and we often went racing with two or three of the finance staff notably Chief Cashier David Wood who was on the board at Hexham Racecourse.

As a parting gift I decided to rig the cards and see what happened, Frankie Wilson, who went on to be

Treasurer at Bedlington Council, was my accomplice and we sat in the adjacent room watching with a few of the data input girls who were in on the set up. The next 15 minutes were hilarious, the three players who had been "dealt" priles started playing very confidently, leaning back in their chairs After 5 minutes the player with a prile of Queens was getting a tad nervous but there was no question of stacking. After ten minutes and over £2,000 in the kitty all three were perspiring. That's when I stepped in and stopped the torture, fortunately I had already obtained a reference for my new job or I do not think one would have been forthcoming!

I took my Intermediate IMTA exam, shortly after joining District Audit,in the Guild Hall on Newcastle Quayside and shortly after I got married. In those days there was no professional study, everyone learnt by correspondence course. I was not that confident as I had not scored that well in the mock examinations I had sent in and the two my Senior Manager, Reg Harris, had made me take after work in the Town Hall in Manchester. However at least I had prepared, unlike many of my fellow examinees. There were about 400 students sitting the three- day exam and it was a major boost to my confidence to see over100 leave the exam on each of the first two days. By my maths I had a good chance of being one of the top scoring 33% who the Institute passed, if the Guildhall proved typical and I was proved right a couple of months later.

The two years I spent with District Audit in Manchester were pretty unremarkable. My time was spent partly at the mammoth audit of Manchester Borough Council and part auditing some of the surrounding district councils in the beautiful Peak District such as Bakewell (Of tart fame) and Buxton.

From a learning perspective the smaller councils were the best as they still kept manual ledgers and all of the bookkeeping entries could be traced, unlike Manchester where the ledgers were computerised with the files holding millions of transactions. From a personal perspective Pat and I made good friends with my Audit Manager Colin Ashworth and his family and Colin got me started playing tennis again. I maintained my betting interests by getting a job with a local bookmakers on Saturday which was pretty boring but paid well, I had less than 300 bets to settle compared to the 1000 or more I was capable of when managing for Coral's so I had plenty of time to listen to the commentaries.

My father's untimely death in 1971 brought to an end my spell with the Manchester Section of District Audit. I applied for a transfer back to the North East and the transfer was granted. There were two audit teams operating out of Newcastle at the time and I was an Audit Examiner in the team, which undertook the audits north of the River Tyne.

During this period I uncovered a major capital expenditure fraud involving a local firm of builders that knocked on into the famous Poulson corruption enquiry. This was extremely exciting and led to my following the audit trail around other local authorities where the firm had carried out work. I left District Audit before enquiries were finalised but many councillors were surcharged and there were also some custodial sentences. I was also given my own audit to manage for the first time, Bedlington Borough Council where my friend from Northumberland County Council days, Frankie Wilson was Treasurer.

During this period, Pat and I bought a new two bedroomed flat in Cramlington New Town with my mum's assistance and moved in with our new baby, Christopher, in October 1971. I also met and became friendly with Barry Eggo and his wife Maureen, which I describe in the chapter on friendship above.

We upgraded in 1972 to a three- bedroomed terraced house on the basis that Pat would start working and place Christopher with a child minder.and we would have two incomes coming in. However, this did not work out as Pat found she could not cope emotionally with leaving Christopher. On top of this I failed the first part of my final IMTA examination, I passed all the local government subjects but in District Audit we had to take a separate paper entitled District Audit Law and Procedure instead of Economics and although my assignment marks and mock exam marks were good I was marked a fail in the exam.

I did not take this too kindly, as passing the exam would have improved my salary. Things were pretty tight at home. So tight that when we went to do a stay away audit at Berwick-Upon-Tweed, I slept for a fortnight in our car, an Austin 1100, in order to make a profit on our overnight allowance. Something I would never wish to do again. I asked to see the District Auditor, John Spiers, to discuss retaking the paper. I showed him all of my assignments and my mock exam papers, which had been marked positively. He said that the actual exam papers were farmed out to District Auditors in the field for marking and he would make enquiries. In the meantime he drew my case to the attention of Cliff Nicholson the Head of the Distrit Audit Service.

Cliff asked me to go and see him in London and gently probed my knowledge of District Audit Law and Procedure. He was clearly satisfied because he said that District Audit could not afford to lose someone with my qualities and he offered to mark my course work personally. All of this gave me a considerable boost but in life I have learnt that highs quite frequently are followed by lows. Six months later, I opened my post to read that for the second time in a year I had passed all three local government papers but had failed District Audit Law and Procedure again!

All of this stress and continuing financial pressures caused by increasing interest rates led to the most significant poor performing period in my betting career and I am ashamed to say thst I took out a £2,000 personal loan and used it to fund my betting.

One of my main characteristics is that I am a decision maker. I believe in taking control of my life and not in letting events dictate. Within three months I had applied for and had been appointed Chief Internal Auditor at Eden District Council, one of the new local authorities created by Local Government Reorganisation in 1974. More remarkably I had sat and passed Economics in the IMTA final, which I was allowed to take instead of District Audil Law and Procedure, as I was now a local government employee. This involved learning the whole syllabus and revising for the exam in a period of less than 4 weeks. However, I locked my self away in a hotel at Preston for the three days leading up to the exam and swotted like mad. This worked despite the fact that on one of the three evenings there was a knock on the door and when I opened it there was Pat wearing only a raincoat!

That left only the second part of the final examination to take, which constituted a major case study/thesis plus a paper on management. However after taking up my post I soon learned that there was so much work to do that it would be at least a year before I would be in a position to start my studies. That soon became two years when we had our second child, Darren.

Work was also different to anything I had experienced previously as none of the three constituent authorities of Eden District Council had previously maintained an internal audit function. This meant that I and my two assistants had to spend the first two years documenting all of the authorities systems, then assessing the strength of the internal control environment and designing a range of tests to test their integrity and look for error and fraud. Hence, I had little or no time for study.

I did have time for betting however and I had one of my biggest wins ever from a multiple bet during this period. I can remember that Pat and I had gone to Lancaster shopping one Saturday afternoon. Knowing that I would not be able to watch the racing as we had the children with us I placed a £0.50p each way Canadian bet at the Ladbrokes shop in Lancaster, which cost £26. After two hours shopping and lunch, which those of you with small children will know was far more exhausting than the shopping, I popped back to watch the last horse to run. This was called Willy What and was making its debut for Stan Mellor over hurdles. I was excited as I had three winners at good prices and a second. I was a lot more excited ten minutes later when Willy What won at 33/1 giving me a payout of over £5700, equivalent to around £100,000 in today's money.

This was pretty much a life-changing win for us at the time. We had been living in a new council house provided by Eden under the terms of my appointment until our house in Cramlington had sold. That eventually happened and we used my winnings to put down a deposit on a new four-bedroom detached Barratt house in Penrith. I sent Pat shopping for furniture and carpets over the next month with her mum and Maureen. I have learnt over time that there is nothing most women love more than home making and it is just as well that we had taken a decision that I would have a vasectomy or we would have had all four bedrooms occupied in no time!

Unsurprisingly we found some pretty startling errors during the early days of our initial audits at Eden. One of the authorities had employed a local firm of Quantity Surveyors to manage their capital programme. A review of those contracts found a large number of significant overcharges by both the contractor and the Quantity Surveyor. The recoveries made from this audit paid for the cost of our section for nearly ten years and helped to increase the profile of Internal Audit within the Authority. The annual external audit report also helped with this as it made some extremely favourable comments about the effectiveness of the internal audit function that had been established.

At the time I managed just two staff, Norman Lothian who was my deputy and Tony Smith who was an audit assistant. After two years Norman moved to the accountancy section and Tony stepped up to be replaced by a young female trainee Janet. I have to say that it is just as well that political correctness had not arrived in the 1970's as Tony and I had a bit of good- natured fun at Janet's expense, such as when asking her to take stock of the body parts in the Mortuary.

The most amusing moment of my career in audit also happened when I worked at Eden. Penrith is adjacent to the M6 Motorway and the authority developed a lorry park in the mid 1970's. The lorry park became a huge success and the Council collected considerable income from overnight parking fees. Much of this income was in cash and this meant that the system was classified as high risk and required periodic spot checks and cash ups. On our very first spot check, Tony, Janet and I met outside the lorry park at 9pm one winter evening. We would note the registration numbers of 100 lorries and then visit the attendant's huts in the morning to ensure that there were ticket stubs or accounts for each of the 100 numbers.

We had been creeping around and recording the numbers for about 15 minutes when a breathless Janet came running up to me " Mr Sobey, you need to come quick, someone is being murdered in one of the lorries!" I stopped what I was doing immediately and followed Janet and she pointed out the lorry in question. I crept up to the lorry ready to wrench open the cab door when I heard the screams. They were certainly loud however I don't think that someone who was being murdered would have been calling out "Yes" "Yes" "Oh Yes!"

The rest of the 1970's flew by. Eden decided to computerise its major systems and entered into an agreement with Wakefield Borough Council for them to design and provide continuous service delivery. This took about a year to implement and I was heavily involved in the redesign of most of the systems. At the end of this project I was promoted to Assistant Director of Finance in 1978 and was given responsibility for the Organisational Development function as well as Internal Audit. During this period the Institute of Municipal Treasurers had become the Chartered Institute of Public Finance and I was told that I had until 1982 to pass my final examination part 2 under the old syllabus.

The constant travelling back and forward from Penrith to Eden almost cost me my life. On one such journey, I was travelling west on the M62 in pouring rain and poor visibility. I was in the outside lane overtaking when all of a sudden my engine cut out and I had no power. There was nothing I could do but indicate left and close my eyes! There was total mayhem behind me as lorries and cars braked or swerved as I made my leisurely drift across to the breakdown lane. Later it transpired that a wrong part, fitted at a recent service, was the cause of what was a truly frightening incident.

Back at Eden, I discussed my position with the Chief Executive and the Director of Finance, Peter Farmer. The latter said that it was essential that I obtained the final qualification as he was thinking of retiring within the next five years and saw me as his successor. The problem was that to take the final part 2 required 12 weeks full time study and there was no way that Eden could spare me for that length of time.

I eventually managed to agree a compromise at 2 days per week and enrolled at Preston College. I had a result in that the Case Study I put forward was privatisation of a local authority stores depot, something I was looking to review at Eden. Everything went swimmingly and I passed the examination in November 1992 and became a fully qualified member of CIPFA. Not only this but my case study was widely published and used as a blueprint by many local authorities. I was also asked to lecture on the topic at several venues.

The articles undoubtedly raised my personal profile and I was headhunted by several firms and approached by two or three local authorities offering a more senior position. Pat and I talked things over at length and we decided to stay in Penrith, where we had an excellent family and social life and where I would probably step into the Treasurers job in a few years time. The kids were growing up now and she was keen on us buying a rural sub post office, which she would run, something our friends Jennifer and John were doing successfully. We bid on a couple of rural sub post- offices, which came on the market unsuccessfully but then were successful in acquiring Castletown Sub Post Office.

Castletown could hardly be described as rural. It was a densely populated suburb of Penrith with about 3,000 inhabitants mainly living in Victorian housing.and with a rapidly expanding industrial estate at its western edge. The sub post office had been owned and run by an elderly couple. It had been allowed to run down and the shop area was used mainly for selling wool and other craft materials with turnover of less than £20,000per annum. The living area above the shop and the cellar below it required a lot of work.

Leaving our lovely four bedroom detached house to live above the shop was quite a wrench. However Pat threw her-self into our new venture with a vengeance and we achieved remarkable progress over the next two years. Pat had the house completely re-furbished and then set about improving and fitting out the shop premises and cellar. She also set about boosting the post office business. She realised the potential of the industrial estate, who were all taking their outgoing post and buying their stamps from the main post office, bypassing our Post Office to do so.

By the end of 1983 we were providing a separate counter for industrial estate customers and had seen a massive increase in turnover almost doubling our Post Office salary. The refitting of the shop was also paying dividends and we were competing effectively with a VG shop some 400 yards away in providing a general dealer/off licence and news service. We had increased our mortgage in order to refurbish the house and shop but the increased turnover meant that this would soon be repaid. Als, I had been told by my boss that he was going to retire in the spring of 1984, and that he would recommend that I should succeed him as Treasurer.

Life seemed to be going extremely well in early 1984. Then my whole world was shattered;

- I lost my wife and the mother of my children when Pat died in March 1984.
- I had to turn down the offer of the post of Treasurer at Eden for which I had waited in the wings for five years.
- Despite a campaign by local residents to save it, the Post Office closed our sub post office as part of a national rationalisation of urban post offices.
- My mother in law who was helping to look after the children died in our flat from a heart attack

Unsurprisingly it took me quite a while to recover and to get my life back on track. I could not have done it without my mother who came over from Newcastle one month in two and ran the shop and pretty much kept domestic life on track. My mum died at the ripe old age of ninety- two, shortly before this book was published. The selflessness, which she showed in helping me, and my sisters, has hopefully guaranteed her a reward in the after life.

I found that I could not sleep for almost a year after Pat's death and started on a fitness campaign in order to tire myself out and induce sleep. I began running and exercising hard, resulting in a weight loss of four stone by the end of 1984 but it had nil impact upon my sleeplessness.

I had kept in touch with Barry Eggo after we left Cramlington in 1973 and he persuaded me to start playing Saturday morning football in a veteran's league in the North East. The standard was high with a lot of former Sunderland and Newcastle players taking part and I thoroughly enjoyed it. Barry was very fit and was heavily into road running. He suggested that I should take part in a 10 kilometre run at Killingworth as his running club was taking part en masse.

When we lined up at the start I had not told Barry how hard I had been pushing myself and he suggested that I set off doing seven- minute miles and look to gradually build up from there. I tried this for a mile but found that I was used to running much faster and despite him urging caution when I passed him I was soon up with the leading twenty or so out of an entry of 1,200 and stayed on to be a very creditable 18th. I could have probably been 17th but with a mile to go I was tracking a very very attractive female runner and I thought that it would be much more enjoyable to follow her for the last mile than bust a gut and finish one place higher!

Sport helped me to get a grip back on my life as I am an extremely competitive person and my improved fitness levels helped me get into the county tennis team and to play in the top division at squash. I ran competitively until 1988 and completed two marathons and several half marathons. My best performance came in the Geordie Run in 1985, a competitive half marathon with an entry of round about 1,000. I was pretty much at peak fitness when I entered this race and had decided to go out and run as fast as I could right from the start. The first 5 miles of the Geordie Run are steadily downhill and then there is a very long stiff climb from the river at Wallsend up to the main Coast motorway and then a three -mile flat run back into the City Centre.

I was running well and when we got to the start of the climb I was in the first thirty runners. The climb was tailor-made for me as I did a lot of running in the hills in the Lake District. Over the next two- mile uphill pull I passed runner after runner so that when the climb plateaued out I was up to fourth place and I still felt as if I had running in my legs. Then it happened –I stopped at a drinks station to take on some water when I was grabbed by two of the first aid attendants and told to sit down. I had not noticed that my tee shirt was covered in blood from a burst blood vessel in my nose. This would have sorted itself out, I had had it happen before but before I could convince the first aiders I had lost over one hundred places.

As well as taking up sport on a grand scale, I had a phase of doing the things that I had always wanted to do. I learnt to swim and ski and I also did a parachute jump for charity. This was extremely entertaining. I had only put my name down in the first place to impress a woman whom I had started dating. Pat was a local hairdresser and her local pub was organising the event. I persuaded her that she should do it with me but left out that it meant staying overnight in a hotel near Grange -In -Furness.

The organisation that managed the jumps had everyone present training all day Saturday practising falling backwards and forwards from objects at various heights. We were all pretty sore at the end of the day and being the chivalrous gentleman that I am I felt it only right to offer Pat an all over body massage. This gradually eliminated her stiffness but seemed to add to mine!

D Day dawned the following morning and we were all taken to the airstrip and segregated into groups of 8 and kitted up including parachutes. As luck would have it Pat and I were in the group that was scheduled to jump first. By the time we had to board however she had backed out together with two others, probably a wise decision as things turned out.

The planes we used for the jump were small and had a rail in the middle that we hooked up to as the eight of us who were jumping sat down four on each side. I was to jump first from the right hand group. The plane taxied up and then took off. Not long afterward the co pilot stepped into the main body of the plane and grabbed part of the open doorway. For the next five minutes, unsuited, he pointed out all of the local landmarks we should look out for on the way down, especially Morecambe Bay, which he told us we should take care to steer away from.

I would like you all to use your imagination at this point. Imagine the plane with its 8 intrepid would be parachutists all pressing their fully kitted bodies hard back against the side of the plane and doing their best not to look out of the open door. Meanwhile, the unsuited instructor is leaning out of the open door pointing out the landmarks! A moment of visual comedy that has stayed with me to this day.

The jump went pretty much as planned for me, I looked up and the parachute had opened. I navigated the chute to the main runway and executed my landing correctly. Not so some of my fellow jumpers however, one smashed into the buildings and broke a shoulder and another hit the actual runway hard and had to be helped away and driven to hospital. The jump was from 4,000 feet and was over very quickly as most of the time you were checking that you were drifting in the right direction. We were offered the chance of a second jump later in the day, which I was contemplating when Pat came up and whispered in my ear that she had booked the hotel for another night and with that in mind discretion was definitely the better part of valour.

The mid 1980's were pretty much a void in my work career. I carried on being Assistant Treasurer at Eden. I got along well with the new Treasurer Alan Ellison, who came to Eden from Farnham Borough Council and I helped him settle in effectively however there was no doubt I could have done with a new challenge and my entrepreneurial bent almost created one.

During the 1980's the social revolution that was taking place all over the country took part in the Castletown suburb, where I lived above our shop. Castletown became an extremely busy, densely populated, area of principally rented properties. Commercially, the area and the large industrial estate at its western perimeter were served by 3 general dealer/off-licence/retail outlets and a bakery shop. There was intense competition between these businesses and residents had to go into Penrith for other services such as hairdressing.

Although I had limited capital, operating a busy general dealer retail outlet meant that I was aware of the needs of Castletown residents and in 1985/6 I put together a plan to acquire the other three competing businesses. Iplanned to convert them into one hairdressing and beauty salon, one conversion into 8 bedsits and a fish and chip shop in the shop located on the main road running between Penrith and Greystoke on which several major camp sites were located. For this to succeed I needed a partner and Ken, a friend of Barry Eggo's who had just been made redundant, was keen to go into partnership with me with him running the Fish and Chip Shop and his wife managing the bedsit property with Pat running the hairdressers.

My proposals were going through the planning process when Ken had second thoughts and hard as I tried I could not get the project delivered. This was a big disappointment as It would undoubtedly have been successful and made Castletown a better place to live in. Worse, Alan took me to one side and said that I clearly was not fully focussed on Eden and that I should look to move. He was going to advertise a post of Deputy Treasurer which would in effect absorb my position-although I could do the job easily he let me know that I would not get the new job! No room for friendship in the business world.

Alan's motivation behind this was that the Chief Executive had retired and he wanted the new job. Having a Deputy Director of Finance meant that it would be possible for him to manage the two functions. All good in theory but Alan had serious internal competition for the CEO job in the shape of Eden's Director of Technical Services Ian Bruce. Ian had come to the lakes as Chief Architect several years previously and was very prominent in local circles being a team leader for the Mountain Rescue service and heavily involved in ecological matters.

I had known Ian for ten years and I think he had respect for the Internal Audit Service. We had carried out several capital expenditure reviews that led to major financial savings and the privatisation of the stores function raised his profile nationally. In my book Ian was a certainty for the CEO job not least because he was far more effective at member level than Alan but I was careful to avoid adding my support to his campaign.

Despite this when the campaign was over and Alan had lost, he accused me of helping Ian. The next two years were not pleasant for me. Alan became extremely bitter at not getting the CEO and foolishly tried to undermine Ian, with the help of his new Deputy Treasurer appointee Bill Philips. Ian prevented him getting rid of me citing the excellent work Internal Audit had produced for the Council and the many commendations we had received from the District Auditor

All of this made for an uncomfortable time for me at Eden. Whenever anything major was planned, the Chief Officer concerned would seek out my views, as after over ten years spent reviewing the Council 's procedures and financial systems I knew them inside out. Philips, who was a pompous bombast, did not and was essentially bypassed. He spent his whole time trying to undermine me or to get something on me. I had made up my mind to apply for a job with the Audit Commission but had three memorable moments before I left. The first was late in 1985 when I underwent a near death experience.

One morning in November 1985 I awoke at around 5am in the morning with an agonising pain in my side. I went down to the bathroom when a second attack came and the pain was so severe it threw me off my feet. After a gap of two to three minutes a third attack followed. I had never experienced pain like it before and decided to drive myself to Penrith Hospital, as it would probably take about 40 minutes for an ambulance to reach me. After waking Christopher and telling him to open the shop and work till I got back or the first member of staff came in I rang my mum in Newcastle and explained what was happening. I will never forget that drive to hospital, it was only a mile but I had two more spasms before I got there.

An hour later I was in an ambulance speeding into Carlisle Infirmary for an emergency operation for a kidney blockage. Fortunately this was a success but It almost wasn't as the following morning I was being wheeled down again to theatre for another op before I got through to the theatre nurse that they had got it wrong! I had already had my operation!

The second memorable event was in March 1986 when I had a massive betting win at Cheltenham. This could not have come at a better time as I was looking to expand the shop to install a video outlet and a hairdressers' salon in the cellar. My bank Barclays would not play ball and were putting pressure on me saying that I was in negative equity following the closure of the Post Office. I decided to go for it at

Cheltenham and borrowed significantly on my credit cards.

I met up with the two Barries and the rest of the crew at Stratford and also met some of our Irish friends who came over every year. As usual the Monday night at the pub in Northleach was abuzz with chatter about the impending festival. Everyone was exchanging naps and I let everyone know that my nap of the meeting was Cross Master in the Royal Sun Alliance Chase. Cross Master was 33/1. This was far too big a price for our Irish friends but not for our Cheltenham team who knew I had a fantastic record in this race.

One of the things I teach in my Professional Betting Courses is that you must have courage in your convictions. Mine were sorely put to the test when I went through the card on the first day of the festival without a single winner, losing heavily. Our daily routine was to go to the main William Hill shop in Cheltenham after an early breakfast and put on our daily mixed bets and try to steal any exceptional value in the morning prices and then go for a game of snooker for a couple of hours. That day I was the only one who placed multiple bets, everyone else wanted to try to recoup their losses by having two or three main bets at the festival. The bet I placed was a 50pence each wayHeinz, which covered six horses in a full perm, three at Cheltenham and three at Newton Abbott. I also had £15 each way on Cross Master at 40/1.

At around twenty past three I was involved in an agonising wait for the result of the RSA chase as Cross Master and Forgive and Forget, who went on to win the Gold Cup the following year, had crossed the line together. After what seemed like two hours rather than two minutes Cross Master was announced as the winner. My feet never touched the ground for the next thirty minutes as the boys hoisted me up and carried me round the racecourse, they had all won a lot of money and many like Barry and I had got the dual forecast up which paid £326 to a £1 stake several times.

The best was still to come however. About thirty minutes after the last race, Barry and I staggered into the Tote On Course betting shop a bit the worse for wear having consumed a couple of bottles of champers. I went to check the results of my mixed bet I knew I had Cross Master and a 10/1 winner at Cheltenham and a loser but did not know the results at Newton Abbott. Afterwards, Barry said he had never seen anyone sober up completely so quickly and he guessed what had happened when I started to do an Irish Jig in the middle of the betting shop. Yes, all three selections at Newton Abbott had won, the manager in the Tote Shop very kindly worked the bet out for me and it came to £81, 250.!

Once again betting had delivered a life changing moment for me. When I got back to Penrith I paid off my mortgage and told the bank manager at Barclays what he could do with his arrears letters. I then went a bit wild and bought a brand new BMW and took the kids on a big holiday. My betting suffered for a while afterward and I had a failed attempt at playing poker for big stakes but all in all I came out of 1986 with about £50,000 in net winnings.

Back at the Council, Philips was becoming even more nauseating. He had developed this habit of creeping up the stairs to my office and then bursting in trying to catch me on the telephone to my bookie. He had spread the word amongst the senior Members of the Council that I was a gambler and that this was inappropriate for a senior member of the Finance Department. However most of them told him that they were well aware of my hobby and that there was nothing wrong with it and had he not heard about my Cheltenham win!

Philips was nothing if not persistent and one week at the Departmental Management Team he brought the subject up and sought to get an assurance from me that I would stop betting. I listened to what he had to say and then at the end of his speech I said that I was thinking of suing him for discrimination. Taken aback he asked on what grounds and I told him that he and the Council's management team were gambling continuously via the Chief Officers Shares Club! There followed a 20 minute debate as to whether playing the stock market was gambling and I countered his attempts at legitimising the City by saying that the Royal Family were well known gambling participants.

The outcome of this meeting was a competition between my betting performance and the stock market. The relevant performance was a standing item on the weekly Finance Department management team for over a year until a certain Monday in October 1987. Strangely no one ever raised the subject of gambling again after Black Monday!

LIFE IN THE AUDIT COMMISSION

Do As We Say And Not As We Do

I finally decided to leave Eden District in 1988 and applied for a job with the Audit Commission. Following an initial interview for the post of Audit Manager I was told that there were no vacancies in the North of England but I could begin as an Auditor in the North or a Trainee Audit Manager in the South.

This was a difficult decision for me to take as it meant a considerable loss of status and salary. However, Safeway had opened a massive store some two hundred yards from our shop in Castletown and the writing was on the wall. Hazel agreed that it was time for a new start.

For those of you who don't know what the role of the Audit Commission was it was to carry out a continuous financial and value for money audit of local authorities on behalf of the taxpayer. It exercised this function via an in-house audit service, District Audit and by appointing a number of commercial accountancy firms to undertake audits.

The Commission had legal powers to surcharge councillors deemed to have acted unlawfully or fraudulently and also issued national value for money and fraud reports, which publicised issues relating to the provision of local government services. It was a high profile organisation and was given similar responsibility for the Health Service in 1990.

I reported for duty in my new job at the District Audit Office at Cumbria County Council in October 1988 and was met by the Senior Manager for the Cumbrian Team Bob Kitson and his Audit Manager Ray Morris. I was given copious reading material and told that this would serve me as on- site induction. I would go to a formal induction course at Warwick University during the next month.

I was told that later that day the Deputy District Auditor for Region1, Brian Wilmorr, would be arriving from his office in Middlesbrough to review the External Audit files with a view to signing off the 1987/8 annual audit for Cumbria County Council.This was real eye opener for me.

The review took place in the same office that the audit team were located in and it turned out to be an extremely embarrassing affair. Wilmorr was extremely critical of the audit work undertaken and humiliated Bob in front of his staff by the end of the process. This may have led to a better audit taking place but it was appalling man management, something that I was to learn ran right through the District Audit service at the time. At that time, the way to progress career wise in District Audit was very much to excel professionally rather than by being a good manager.

I was soon to get my turn at receiving the sharp end of Mr Wilmorr's tongue. After a week's background reading of the Audit Commission manuals, without any tutorials, I was despatched to carry out the annual audit of Allerdale District Council. I was told that I would have two support staff after two weeks but they never arrived and I eventually completed the whole audit on my own.

This was a good grounding as I undertook all of the relevant audit jobs relating to a borough or district council which started to build a solid foundation for me in external audit techniques, which were different in many respects from the internal audit approach which I was used to.

I started the audit on a Monday but the audit files did not arrive until the Thursday, so I decided it would be a good investment of time to read the Council Minutes for the last two years and to make a list of any major decisions which would have an impact on the accounts. As it happened this examination led to a major piece of District Audit case law. My reading of the minutes identified that Allerdale's Chief Executive had persuaded the Council to guarantee the costs of providing a timeshare development in Keswick in return for a leisure centre and swimming baths being built.

I was not aware of local government law covering this matter but thought it a highly unusual transaction and copied the relevant minutes and attached a briefing note covering the relevant facts and sent it to Bob Kitson. Within days, Brian Wilmorr was meeting the Council and telling them in no uncertain terms that he deemed their actions to be unlawful. This saga dragged on for years and went to the High Courts where the judges eventually confirmed the views of the District Auditor and surcharged individuals who had key responsibility.

I had made a high profile start to my career with the Audit Commission but the result was that Brian Wilmorr took me under his wing and reviewed all of my work personally. After a year of his swinging criticisms made in writing without any verbal feedback and the absence of any plaudits for good work, which led to major financial savings I had pretty much had enough. I was thinking of starting to apply for Treasurers jobs with local authorities when the District Auditor for Number 1 Region John Spiers called me in to his office. Much to my amazement he told me that his Deputy, Brian Wilmorr, had spoken highly of me and recommended me for promotion to Audit Manager. There would not be any vacancies in Number 1 Region for over a year but I could go and work in the London Region on full manager pay for a year and then transfer back after a year and take up the post in number 1 Region if I wished.

I discussed this with Hazel and she said I should take up the post as she had not been able to get a job in Carlisle and money was tight as interest rates had rocketed up, pretty much doubling our mortgage. I planned on travelling back to Carlisle on a Friday evening and driving back down to London on a Monday morning.

The London District Auditor was Jim Mcwhirr, a Scot who remarkably had been the Senior Manager for the Eden District Audit for a few years when I had been Assistant Director of Finance there. Jim suggested that I should spend the first year auditing some of the small and medium size District Councils located in Essex, as they would be the type of audit I was used to and I could develop my audit management skills ready to take on some of the larger audits. He posted me to the Essex and East Anglian region where the District Auditor was Neil Childs.

The year I spent as one of Neil's Audit Managers was one of the most enjoyable of my professional life. Neil was the youngest District Auditor in the District Audit Service and was being groomed for a top post when he developed cancer of the lymph nodes. I went to work for him when he was just emerging from a successful year of chemotherapy. My first audit as an Audit Manager was Maldon District Council in Essex.

Maldon was a well-run authority but, as I had nothing to do in the evenings, I spent a lot of extra time at the audit working on additional projects not in the audit plan. One of these identified a major saving if the council were to reorganise its refuse collection service. The Director of Finance cooperated with me on this review and he passed on some favourable comments about the quality of this year's audit to Neil and Jim Mcwhirr.

I met some extremely intelligent people during the course of my twelve years with District Audit. Brian Wilmorr was definitely in that category however no one could hold a candle to Neil and the fact that he was also a brilliant coach who got great pleasure out of developing his staff was another reason why I was so lucky to have had him as a mentor. Neil quickly sussed out that I had a real talent for value for money audit and management consultancy but that my knowledge of accountancy, particularly local authority capital accounting and housing subsidy was weak. Without making me feel uncomfortable, as I was a few years older than him, he used his reviews to make me ask myself the questions I needed to ask in these areas so that I fully understood all the intricacies. At first I was very apprehensive of Neil's file reviews due to my experience with Wilmorr but I soon began to welcome them and after six months more than held my own.

Travelling back and forward to Cumbria at weekends was a nightmare and sometimes resulted in twelve-hour journeys. When the summer came Hazel took to coming down and staying for a couple of weeks, which was excellent as we toured the area including Central London. Then in mid 1990 I had a mega decision to make.

The London Borough of Haringey audit was the most difficult external audit in the UK. In 1990 the Council was over ten years behind with its accounts and there was a major legal issue over fire damage at Alexandra

Palace, which was dragging on and constituted a massive contingent liability for the Council. The Audit Manager for the audit was Mick West, a protégé of Neil Childs who had just been promoted to Senior Manager. Jim Mcwhirr called me into his office one day in June 1990 and when I got there Neil Childs was with him.

Jim liked to have a bit of fun and he started by telling me that John Spiers was on the phone every week telling him that the vacancy in number one region was now open and that I should come back I assumed that this was going to happen when out of the blue he said that at the last meeting of District Auditors, the Haringey audit had cropped up and Neil Childs had suggested that I should be given what was probably the highest profile audit job in England.

Jim asked me what I thought and I said truthfully that I was nervous in taking on an audit of this size and complexity after only nine months as an audit manager. Neil then said some very nice things about my commitment and tenacity and that in his view Mick West and I could sort this audit out for once and all. I told them I needed to talk this over with Hazel but to my surprise she was happy to move to London even though it would mean she would be a long way away from her family.

I took over the Haringey audit in September 1990 and after settling in for a month and getting to know Mick West, we worked out a strategy to tackle what was a nine- year backlog in the final accounts. This involved giving the regularity audit a clear priority over value for money and fraud work and recruiting a large number of contract staff to resource what was over 2000 days in budget terms.

Three years later when I left, after being promoted to become the Senior Manager responsible for the West London team, we had reduced the deficit to three years and had established a clear process for eliminating the remaining deficit. It sounds easy when you put it down on paper but it was anything but I assure you and my health suffered badly from drinking percolated coffee for 16 hours a day 5 days a week and from a series of extremely heated meetings with the Haringey Director of Finance John Pirie.

Pirie was one of the biggest bullies I have met in life. He was a big name in CIPFA and ran the Finance Department with a rod of iron, regularly promoting his favourites to important posts even though they were incapable in many instances of meeting the jobs requirements. He had been used to getting his way with a succession of District Audit Senior Managers through sheer obstinacy however he had met his match when it came to Mick and I.

One of the reasons for the unacceptable delay in the audited final accounts was Pirie's refusal to accept any audit qualifications. Imagine the situation then when I had completed the 1981/2 annual audit and my opinion was a disclaimer in that every single balance sheet balance and the Revenue Account were materially misstated. Mick was pretty gobsmacked when he read my report on the final accounts audit but I have to say that after he had carried out a detailed review himself and confirmed my findings he backed me up 100 per cent against considerable pressure from the District Auditor and the Audit Commission who were dead set against a disclaimer.

I can still remember the meeting with Pirie to discuss my report. Mick and I were summoned into to his office to find his whole management team plus others sat around the long table with two seats at the far end for "The Christians". As soon as we were seated, Pirie launched into a vitriolic rant for at least ten minutes culminating with a theatrical tearing up of the report and throwing it the full length of the table with a promise to have Mick and I removed from the audit. I don't know what he was used to previously but Mick never blanched and replied that he had personally discussed the report and underlying audit work with the Audit Commission's Accounting Practice Department and that they were in agreement with the findings but that he was happy to go through our findings balance by balance.

This was a big test for me but four hours later the rest of the table was notably subdued, it was then that Mick played his trump card. He acknowledged that receiving a disclaimer opinion would be a major embarrassment for most authorities but if Haringey were to accept it, we could quickly agree balances for the following and subsequent years and significantly recovery the backlog , which was even more embarrassing. After a gap of a few weeks in which Pirie tried to use his influence against us he conceded. We then recruited some 20 contractors, mostly well- qualified South Africans, Australians and New Zealanders and pushed on recovering the backlog.

Normally an annual audit at a London Borough like Haringey would take around 900 audit days plus some 300 days for grant claim certification. This would involve a full time team of 6 or 7. During 1990 to 1993 we had on average 15 people working full time. A typical day for me was;

Arrive at 6 am –make sure job sheets were written out to keep team occupied for the current day. More importantly put the 4 coffee percolators on.

8am -6pm Supervise the contract staff, facilitate access to working papers for them and deal with the hundreds of queries that arose each day. Hold closure meetings with authority staff.

6pm – 8pm Have team meetings or management meetings with Mick, often in the pub. These were invaluable for retention of sanity, particularly because of the non stop banter and humour which Mick encouraged. He was aided and abetted by our Housing Account supremo Dave Palmer, a contractor who was so talented that we signed him up for a number of years.

8pm -11pm Occasional meetings with the Council.

Most days I finished the day feeling like a ping- pong ball after dealing with a constant stream of questions about local government accounting and statutory powers. However the other feature of the Haringey audit , which made it the most enjoyable of my professional life was our tennis nights during the summer.

At first these happened by chance when I noticed that a number of our international contractors played tennis. We started playing ourselves and then against local authority teams (cricket and football too) By the time summer 1992 it became a feature of our recruitment process that you needed to be able to play tennis to succeed in getting a trainee or contractor post.

The standard of the tennis played was extremely high and I could only squeeze into the team at number four or five but putting this into perspective, one of our South African contractors was in their Davis Cup squad. We played mostly at Enfield and regularly attracted a good crowd.

My time at Haringey included a second near life and death experience. On November 20th 1992 I met Hazel after work and we went in to London for a meal and to watch Sunset Boulevard in order to celebrate our fifth wedding anniversary. Half way through the show I had a sharp pain in my lower right side. It became so frequent that we had to leave before the end of the show. The following morning I was in constant pain and unable to walk any distance so Hazel called out our GP. As usual a locum turned up who examined me and said that I had gastro enteritis.

Two days later I was in agony, sweating profusely and had not eaten for two days. Hazel took it into her own hands and drove me to Casualty at Chase Farm Hospital at Enfield. I was seen relatively quickly and the A and E doctor said that she was pretty sure that I had a burst appendix but needed to rule out a severe kidney infection due to my previous medical history. She said I needed to pass water so they could test my urine. It took over an hour but I eventually passed water only for the junior doctor who arrived to drop the receptacle and spill the contents! Fortunately the consultant decided to send me straight to theatre.

Twenty hours later I was still being operated on for peritonitis. I eventually was wheeled out into intensive care where I spent the next four weeks, before the risk of infection reduced to a non- critical level. I thought then that the worst was over and Hazel went back to work, then one evening at visiting time I was chatting to a friend Roger when my stomach started to swell up dramatically and turn purple. The ward sister took one look and summoned the registrar. By the time he arrived, things looked really bad and they had pulled the curtains round the bed and got rid of all of the visitors on the ward. The registrar took one look and asked me how much pain I could take, as he needed to cut me open there and then to let the poison come out. I gripped the headboard and told him to get on with it. When he cut me open it was like a volcano erupting but thank goodness it worked. I was left with a scar right across my stomach but hopely little or no residual infection.

I remained in hospital for a further three weeks and then had to undergo a further six weeks convalescence. I would have gone back earlier but Mick simply would not let me, he said that he would never forget seeing me in intensive care shortly after my operation and that there was no way I was going to put myself at risk. Shortly after returning to work I received some very good news, I had been promoted to Senior Manager, at the same time Mick had been promoted to District Auditor, clearly our efforts at Haringey had been recognised.

I had really missed the buzz and the incredible humour that percolated the audit office daily with Mick and Dave Palmer, both notorious practical jokers. Dave was a full time contractor who had established himself as the national expert on the audit of grant claims especially Housing Subsidy,he had worked for Mick for several years. At first I was a little uneasy with Dave's sarcasm and overtly sexist humour, however eventually like everyone including the female trainees I came to love him. Dave would not play tennis as he was on the verge of the England badminton squad but he eventually taunted me so much that I agreed to play him at badminton if he would return the complement by playing me at squash.

The courts were full of District Audit spectators for both matches with quite a bit of betting on the score. I was a pretty fit guy at the time but after playing for an hour and not winning a point at badminton I had to surrender. I was no duffer and the rallies went on and on but I simply could not finish the point off and mentally Dave was two strokes ahead of me during each rally. So a week of torment ensued, before the return game was played. I heard that Dave had been practising every night but it did him no good and I was in no mood for charity and reversed the scoreline, which stopped the taunting pretty quickly.

Mick left pretty soon after my return to take up his post but I was to remain at Haringey for six months to allow the new senior manager Jagat Chatrath to settle in. Before he left though he played what was probably his greatest practical joke. Everybody knew I was a workaholic and every night I used to stagger out of the audit office to walk the four hundred yards to the city centre car park laden with audit files to review in the early hours of the morning. This one evening I staggered uphill to the car park only to find that I could not find my Golf anywhere. What was puzzling me was that if anyone had stolen it they would have had to know the keycode to exit the barrier.

After half an hour or so, I trudged back to the audit office reconciled to the fact that I would need to report the theft and get the tube home. I decided to ring Mick first and tell him before I left the office as occasionally I had lent the car to an insured member of staff to visit an audit site. He listened to me and said that before I rang the police I should go back and have one last check. There was something in his voice that raised a question in my head, but how could they have got the keys? To this day I don't know how they did it but when I went back to the car park, there was my car in its original location! The following day there was silence in the audit office until Dave asked if I had worked late last night when the whole office burst into laughter.

Getting used to Jagat after Mick was quite a challenge. He was a completely self centred popinjay who spent most of his time getting his staff to write articles, which he then published in his own name in CIPFA and Audit Commission journals. All of this work was done at the client's expense. Despite all of this "glory" Jagat had remained at Senior Manager level for many years and had continually failed District Auditor selection boards. Thich led to him carrying around a big chip on his shoulder.

A defining moment in mine and the client's relationship with Jagat , came when I drafted the 2004/5 Audit Planning Memo. Over the last two years we had obtained the respect of the Haringey management team by carrying out a series of well received Value for Money projects and these had helped to isolate John Pirie who remained an intransigent enemy. The highlight was a review of Haringey's Capital Programme which I had carried out which identified over £3million per annum benefits to the Council if they restructured their programme.

I remember this project well as Dave Palmer and I did most of the work in our own time using knowledge obtained by carrying out the main audit. The end product was an 80- page audit report, which we presented to the Council with the press and local radio present. It was nice to receive a thank you from the Leader of the Council and the Chief Executive for our work. Our reward from Jim Mcwhirr was to be told that there were two missing apostrophes in the report! This pretty much typified the management style of District Audit at the time.

I drafted the Audit Planning Memo using the format that had worked well in the two previous years with the client. When I showed it to Jagat he had a fit and said it was far too brief and that the purpose of the Audit Planning Memo was to demonstrate compliance with the Audit Code of Practice, I explained that I used an Internal Planning Memo on the Audit File for this purpose but who was I to question the mighty Jagat. On we went to the Audit Planning Memo discussion with John Pirrie. I introduced Jagat to Pirrie and he was his usual obsequious self. I could see Pirrie thinking that he could not believe his luck to be rid of Mick and I and he decided to have some fun straight away. He waited till we were seated and then threw the APM across the table and asked us "What is this jibberish?" Jagat tried to justify his masterpiece but the meeting ended with him jabbering away and walking backwards through the entrance to Pirie's office.

LIFE AT THE TOP

The End Of My Public Service Career

I could not wait to get away from Haringey and take up my new role as a Senior Manager and eventually I started in charge of the West London Team based at Harrow in March 1994. This was the largest District Audit team in London and had eight constituent audits and an annual budget of 2800 days or so plus government grant claim certification. The major audits were the London Boroughs of Harrow and Hillingdon plus the Health audits of North East Thames Health Authority, Hillingdon Health Authority and Hillingdon Hospital Trust. The staffing budget provided for three audit managers but there were only two in situ, Andrew Cork and Irving Pascal who had joined District Audit from a private accountancty firm two years previously.

My arrival at the Harrow office created a shock on both sides. Part of the Audit Commission's role was to review and advise on local authority and health authority's management arrangements however I was already aware that they certainly came nowhere near practising what they preached. I could not believe my eyes when I walked into the audit room at Harrow. The staff tables were arranged in a vertical line based upon hierarchy, pretty much Victorian stuff.

 I spent an hour with each member of the team on my first day and it became obvious that they had been encouraged to know their place and that they should only communicate any ideas they had with their immediate senior. The former Senior Manager Sheila Hill while a very bright and committed auditor certainly did not believe in open management and staff meetings were virtually non-existent.

I spent my first three months taking stock of the section, its staff and the audits including a full review of the previous year's audit files.. I found some good things, some bad and some truly appalling. My major discovery was that there had been an accumulated, budget overspend of some 1200 days on previous year's audits. This had been disclosed to District Audit Senior Management at the time of handover only and had not been disclosed to the clients. This behaviour verged upon fraudulent in my view.

The District Auditor for West London was Mike Robinson, a real high flyer who often led national value for money projects. He and Jim Mcwhirr had me in and explained the situation with regard to the over-spend and said that I had been brought in because of my previous record in running audits and that my primary target was to eliminate the overspend over the next 5 years. I said that I would take on board that target and would also improve the quality of the audits, which was abysmal if I was left to get on with it and did not have interference at District auditor level. Mike Robinson tried to bluster his way out of the situation but there was little he could do.

So began a management revolution as far as District Audit were concerned. I created a totally open team management system in the West London Team. We had a weekly meeting each Friday afternoon to discuss the progress of each audit at which anyone could contribute and everyone had to speak for five minutes about their personal contribution to the audit that week. I changed the Value For Money policy to use specialists to carry out most of the studies, particularly in health.

This brought about an immediate improvement in quality and in client relations. The Clients appreciated the views of expert practitioners rather than plain accountants/auditors and soon began to buy additional audit days for local projects. The Value for Money experts also attended the weekly audit team meetings to talk about their projects and to assimilate knowledge about the Client from the Audit Team.

After just two years, West London went from being the worst performing team in the London and South East Region to the best by far in all of the main performance indicators.;

- External quality review marks
- Timeliness of audit opinions
- Timeliness of Management Letters
- Additional Audit Days sold

This remarkable gain was not accomplished without corresponding pain. My initial review of the audit files which I completed by working seven days a week for the first two months in post disclosed two main facts. Ihad been told previously by Mike Robinson, that management were trying to get rid of Andrew Cork who, lo and behold, was prone to spending the odd half an hour in betting shops in the afternoon! However my review found that Andrew's audits were extremely well run and were on budget. In contrast, the other manager Irving Pascal's audits were massively overspent and the audit product was poor.

Mike Robinson had told me when I started that Irving needed to be handled with kid gloves as he was the chairman of a local housing association and could be instrumental in the Audit Commission gaining work in that sector. Mike was not best pleased when I asked to see him after three months and told him that there was little or no evidence of supervision by Pascal on any of his audits. More worryingly two of his staff, encouraged by the different atmosphere in the section, had come to see me to say that he spent most of the day on the telephone to what seemed to be persons paying him to be their accountant. Mike tried to fob me off by saying he would talk to Irving about his lack of productivity.

I found Mike's attitude dumbfounding. The Audit Commision had just issued a national paper on countering fraud and yet here was a serious situation in- house that apparently did not merit proper investigation. I pointed out that we were already one audit manager post under budget and with Pascal's behaviour things would never improve with the audit overspend not to mention that, if he was carrying out fee earning work in District Audit time,he was committing fraud.

This situation was creating intolerable pressure on me and I went to see Mick West for advice. Mick listened and said that all of this was creating a lot of embarrassment for Mike Robinson as he had been District Auditor for that team for several years and he was pretty powerful in District Audit. However, Mick like me felt that if Irving was guilty it was fraud. He said that I needed to collect enough evidence to give Mike Robinson no room for manoevre.

So, I enlisted the Head of Computer Audit's assistance. She produced downloads of the Audit Room's telephone calls and then one afternoon,while I kept Pascal in a manager meeting all afternoon, she downloaded his District Audit computer onto a key and took it away for analysis. Glynis rang me the next week to say that there was overwhelming evidence of private work being carried out with District Audit and the Client having to foot the bill for this and for Pascal's extensive private business calls.

I went to see Mike Robinson two weeks later with my Evidence Files. The meeting did not go well, especially when I refused to hand over the files unless

Jim Mcwhirr was present. This happened and after a couple of days Jim rang me and told me I had to interview Pascal and, unless he could produce counter evidence, i was to suspend him for gross misconduct. This meeting, at which I was accompanied by the trusty Andrew , went well. Irving, who was well over 6 foot tall and quite often adopted aggressive body postures in conflict situations, had the wind taken completely out of his sails and at the end of the meeting asked if he could resign rather than be suspended. I told him that decision was in the hands of the Regional Director but escorted him off the premises.

I had done what needed to be done but like many others in my position I was to come to wish I hadn't over the next two years. Pascal employed a top barrister who soon had the Commission running for cover by filing a countersuit for racial discrimination. This hung over me for over two years until the tribunal took place and I received little or no counselling or support from senior management during this time. To make matters worse Robinson did not replace Pascal's post as he said he was suspended not dismissed which meant that I had to run a three- manager team with a huge backlog with just one manager. Eventually the tribunal took place and it did not take them long to rule out any trace of racial discrimination on my part. Pascal's suspension was upheld but he was not dismissed. He was transferred to Mick West's team but he resigned shortly afterwards.

These two years took their toll on my health and I developed major problems with my stomach and aesophagus. However one of my health Chief Executives, Phil Brown gave me some good advice on treatment and I eventually got the problems under control via a combination of drugs and Chinese medicine. I should also give fulsome praise to Andrew. He and I worked solidly every Saturday and Sunday in the Harrow office for two years, except for holidays, developing and implementing a strategy to claw back the deficit and at the end of year setting up a Management Letter "factory".

Praise is also due to Andrew Chappell who was a field auditor who I used to manage Pascal's audits. Andrew was someone else who had been written off by the Robinson/Hill management. However although Andrew had his faults like everyone, he was extremely ambitious and worked exceptionally hard over the next two years in which he developed enormously. During this period I ensured he was appropriately rewarded, by paying him the maximum performance bonus payable and when the Pascal situation was resolved he got his well- deserved promotion. Mick also loaned me David Palmer for two years to carry out our grant claim and Housing Revenue work, which gave me major assurance and even got us grudging praise from Harrow, who were notoriously critical of District Audit.

The way I managed the Harrow team began to create waves in the region as word spread and even Jim bit his tongue when he rang on a Friday afternoon and there was nobody present in the audit office. This was because we were following up our weekly team meeting with our weekly Dim Sum meeting in the Golden Palace in Harrow! After one year, every member of the team would work flexibly for as long as I wished to meet any urgent deadline trusting in Andrew and I to ensure they were repaid in time or financially.

My management philosophy has always been to get to know the people I manage, identify their strengths and weaknesses try to use the former to best effect and to work to eliminate the latter. I have to say that the Audit Commission, while publicly espousing staff development in the 1990's practised self -fulfilling prophecy far too often when evaluating staff.

Perhaps my outstanding success at West London was Attul Sharma. Attul was an extremely amiable young Asian man whom we recruited in 1994. Although diligent, Attul proved to be incapable of handling responsibility for individual audits, as he could not handle the closure discussions effectively. I identified this through our internal development programme and arranged for him to go on relevant development courses. The two Andrews considered him to be a risk as he often failed to carry out key tasks on the opinion audit effectively and wanted to transfer him. However I had reviewed his work and in my view the work he did do was presented more effectively than any other more member of the team. Henceforward I used Attul to carry out file reviews and leave the managers to sample check his work. The outcome was that at both the External Quality Control Reviews we underwent,we received a rare excellent rating.

By 1996 I was able to tell Jim Mcwhirr and Mike Robinson that the deficit I inherited had been recovered almost three years early. Jim was already delighted by our QCR marks and told me that I would be considered for promotion to District Auditor at the next promotion board. At the same time he let me know that he wanted me to move from West London to take over the audits at the London Boroughs of Tower Hamlets and Lewisham. Lewisham was a Labour flagship authority and had recently asked for District Audit to be removed from their external audit.

My switch to North and South East London was to end in the finish of my career with District Audit. Everything started extremely well, The three key officers at Tower Hamlets were all women, Sylvie Pearce the Chief Executive was a diminutive powerhouse, Eleanor Kelly the Director of Finance was a new recruit formerly a senior partner of a private firm and Christine Gilbert the Director of Education went on to hold several national positions in Education. The Borough had massive problems with a huge Asian population, many of whom were relatively new immigrants. This led to severe pressure on resources, which was made worse due to inefficient financial management over a number of years. Lewisham was completely different. It saw itself as a well-run authority keen to develop best practice in managing services.

After I had settled in at Tower Hamlets, Eleanor and Sylvie asked to have a meeting with me. Eleanor had certainly done her homework on me and she said that what she had heard about me was positive. The previous Directors of Finance at Hillingdon and Harrow had said that I had made a real difference during my stay without compromising my independence in the slightest. Eleanor said that she and Sylvie had a huge task that would probably take over ten years to restore Tower Hamlets to the status of a well managed authority but that she would like to use the external audit process to flag up the areas than needed "surgery". Findings brought to light would be acted upon swiftly and she intended to set up a special Audit Committee.

For my part I agreed that, whenever I reported my findings I would put the findings in context as it was inequitable in my view comparing Tower Hamlets with any but a few local authorities who faced similar challenges. This reporting style had brought me criticism from the desk jockeys in the Audit Commission before. They believed in using comparator performance indicators as a sledgehammer to batter authorities. This style was widely adopted by Senior Managers in their reporting and in my view was misleading and point scoring to say the least and could irreparably damage client relations. Our statutory remit was to engineer change for the better and to improve services and the accuracy of financial reporting. This could be achieved far more effectively in my view by creating the right climate for change within client authorities.

My 1996/7 Management Letter at Tower Hamlets was the most difficult to write in my career with District Audit but in my view was my best piece of work ever. It was certainly my longest ever management letter at over 200 pages, compared to the 60 pages I had been used to writing at Hillingdon and Harrow. The Letter did not hang fire in flagging up major and serious weaknesses in services and qualifications of the financial statements but everything I said was put in context and set out a clear route for monitoring progress in future years.

Although I got a lot of criticism at District Auditor level in London and South East saying that the Letter was far too long, this was because many of them rarely flagged up any key issues in their annual audit and carried out the minimum work possible under the Audit Code of Practice. What really mattered to me was the personal letter of congratulations I received from Andrew Foster at the Audit Commission and Sylvie Pearce thanked me at the Audit Committee meeting at which the Letter was presented to Members saying that the Management Team would use the document as an agenda for change over the next 5 years.

Eleanor and Sylvie were two of the most able people I have met and certainly among the toughest. I can still recall the events of an ugly strike by the refuse collection staff at Tower Hamlets. The audit office was on the ground floor at Mulberry Place, the Council's Headquarters. On one day in 1997, the area outside the entrance door was virtually obscured by several hundred large and threatening refuse collection operatives and supporters singing raucous songs about the failures of management. Visitors and staff were very apprehensive about entering or leaving the building. After about 30 minutes, the throng parted and in the middle was the diminutive figure of Sylvie Pearce. I could not hear what she was saying but I could see her pointing her finger several times. After five minutes of Sylvie's harangue, the throng melted away. I am sure that dealing with critical audit reports made Sylvie quake in her boots!

Lewisham was a completely different kettle of fish to audit. As I mentioned previously, the Chief Executive Barry Quirk had complained to the Audit Commission about what he considered to be a poor quality external audit, which he felt did not challenge officers sufficiently. I went to meet Barry to introduce myself as soon as I heard I had been transferred and at that no holds barred meeting I invited him to ring the CEO's at my former audits. I guaranteed him that I would use the most talented staff in LASER to carry out work at Lewisham over the next year if he would delay the application for change. He agreed at our next meeting and suggested that I started to sit in on their weekly management team meetings so that I could quickly identify with the key issues the Council had to face.

After a year we had secured a sound footing mainly thanks to the work of Barbara Gowland who in my mind was the best management arrangements consultant anywhere and who wowed Lewisham with her work. I was extremely fortunate that Barbara liked working with me and would not take on any other work annually until I had agreed her programme at my audits. Also, Dave Palmer showed them what it was like to have a proper Housing Subsidy and Housing Benefit Audit. He found that they had been massively overclaiming Housing Benefit for several years but identified some major counter savings on Housing Subsidy. The 1997/8 Management Letter was a lot different to that which Lewisham had been used to receiving!

The next three years seemed to fly by and we had continuous excellent feedback from both authorities. During this time I went for my promotion board for District Auditor. It was a case of bad timing for me. Jim Mcwhirr had announced his retirement as Regional Director and his replacement Brian Wilmorr, of previous note, was pretty keen on ensuring a "take over" from his previous South London domain in the LASER hierarchy . For whatever reason, "too useful in the field", age, I was 49, and a failure to play internal politics, I was rarely sighted at corporate headquarters while other candidates virtually lived there,I did not get the job that I felt I was best qualified for.

Jim was clearly worried that I may leave as he fixed up for me to go on an extremely expensive management development course at Ashbourne. I found this very interesting, most of the delegates were from commercial organisations and were climbing their way up the greasy pole and a lot of the lectures were based upon American management theory about how to align management and coal face priorities with corporate objectives. The technical content was pretty boring to me as I had been to many such courses over the last 15 years however observing behaviour during the group sessions was fascinating and I have to admit to being a bit mischievous and stirring things up.

The diamond of the course for me was a session run by the then England cricket coach Phil Neal on balanced lifestyle. This session bypassed a lot of the delegates who were still on the 100 hours a week corporate input track but it struck a major chord with me. Phil used a tool called the Value Circle as a means of self- evaluation of how effective your whole life is, not just your work life which tends to dominate most successful people's thinking. The Value Circle completely changed my life and has changed the life of several family members and close friends when I have sat down with them and gone through it. I even amended it and used it in the advanced Professional Betting Courses that I ran at Centaur for ten years.

Perhaps the most dramatic illustration of how it can trigger change was when Hazel and I did it with her sister Ann who shortly afterward divorced her husband of 27 years.

When I returned from Ashbourne I asked Hazel if she would sit down one evening and go through the Value Circle process with me. It took a while to convince her but the results were both startling and worthwhile. The Value circle technique showed conclusively that I had been sacrificing the most important personal relationships in my life with my wife and sons for an overwhelming career drive. Hazel, who is a very private person, confessed that she was really worried that I would end up killing myself due to the pressures I was putting on myself and it became obvious that I spent little or no real quality time with my two sons. The outcome of our discussion was that we agreed that I would take early retirement as soon as we had established sufficient financial resources to support this decision.

An equally significant event occurred during this time. Andrew and I devised a betting system, which was to revolutionise our own income and was to do the same for a generation of Centaur clients. Andrew had followed me to Tower Hamlets as part of one of the countless internal reorganisations that took place in District Audit. While there we had an awful lot of Council meetings to attend. We usually took a break between 4 and 8 before going back to work, no prizes for guessing where we spent most of this time!

During this period we had some spectacular wins and, after we got back to the Audit Office one evening in 1996, Andrew said we should spend some time analysing what we did that was successful and what was not with a view to setting up a betting bank to bet all year round. We both knew that we were successful bettors but as auditors, what was clear that we were betting for entertainment purposes as an escape from the considerable pressures at work and not betting systematically. We carried on discussing things over the next two weeks and came up with the following conclusions.

Key success factors;

- Keith's race reading abilities which flagged up a lot of big priced future winners
- Value based betting worked for us –never bet below 5/2
- Do multiple bets wherever possible
- Do forecasts and tricasts when particular races appeal.
- Follow Andrew on the all weather tracks and in sprint handicaps.

Problem areas

- We bet too often, mostly out of boredom
- We were guilty of chasing our losses on occasion

- Lack of time, being at work often cost us winning bets.

The most difficult area was to arrive at a commonly agreed staking system. We did not have the ability to go back and analyse our past results, as we had not recorded our betting. Eventually we decided that we would both put £10,000 into a joint betting bank and agreed on a value-based matrix/algorithm (See Appendix1) to allocate funds from the bank. We decided to stake £500 or 2.5% of bank per point staked with a maximum bet of 4 points or £2000. The process we adopted was;

Night before

1. Review the following days racing independently
2. Come up with a list of horses that we thought would win
3. Run the list against our matrix
4. Agree qualifiers/no bets
5. Decide on bet stake.
6. Fix base price or SP we use to vary betting stake
7. Decide which one of us was going to the track, which we did where possible as this saved 9% betting tax on winnings payable in betting shops.

Day of Race

8. Check for non -runners/going changes that might affect selection.
9. Check price available in early morning market.
10. Adjust stake of bet to comparison of actual price with base price. For example if we had decided to stake 1 point at a value price of 2/1, if we could get 3/1 we would stake 1.5pts and if only 6/4 we would stake 0.75 pts.

We also had a £5,000 bank for multiple bets and forecasts both of which had delivered us big wins over the previous ten years.

By the end of our first twelve months, our betting bank had grown to over £40,000 and by the time I left the Audit Commission it was over £120,000 and had paid for some expensive racing holidays for Andrew, Hazel and I.

Our multiple betting very nearly delivered early retirement for us. One day we were on holiday in the North East and were travelling to Hexham races. We had decided to have a multiple bet and I rang it in to Corals. We had our wives in the car and they were busy talking so I was not concentrating too hard after I had rung in the bet, which was six horses permed in each way trebles, fourtimers, five timers and an accumulator. I staked the bet to a 2£ unit so the total cost was £146 but the telephone operator mistook 20x £2 each way trebles for £22 each way trebles. It was only when she read the bet back to me that I noticed the mistake, which I then corrected. Andrew said at the time that we should maybe have let it ride and he was right. All six of our selections won and the bet returned £180,000!

That day was definitely my best ever days betting. Ascot was the main meeting that day and between us we had 5 bets at each meeting, all won. The day started when we backed a horse I had had my eyes on in the first race at Hexham, Salvo, which went off at 50/1. We backed it with the bookmakers and the Tote and also had the dual forecast up. By the end of the afternoon we had cleaned the racecourse betting shop out and several bookmakers. All in all we won some £30,000 in cash excluding the multiplier. Hexham continued to be a really lucky racecourse for Centaur clients over the next few years and I tipped up Salvo when it won its only other race at Taunton a few years later at 25/1.

The fact that we had become one of if not the most successful betting fund in the UK had a material effect upon the events that saw me leave the Audit Commission in 1999 . That year Brian Wilmorr had carried out a reorganisation in LASER. This saw most of his former associates in the southern part of the region assume the positions of power and eventually the northern part of the region's administrative office at Stevenage and services were centralised at Millbank in the same building as the Labour Party offices. As part of this, the District Auditor responsible for my audits, Chris Koehli was replaced by Les Kidner, who was one of Wilmorr's key District Auditors .

In the past , Kidner's wife Monica had worked for me as an auditor at Harrow. She was a lovely woman who had a great sense of humour. However, tragically, she died of cancer not long after I left West London. Over the last few years I had been left alone to run Lewisham and Tower Hamlets. Both councils continually spoke positively about the audit to Andrew Foster the Controller of the Audit Commission. I was happy and enjoyed the relationship I had developed with both CEOs.Before Jim Mcwhirr retired in 1999 I asked him to promise me that he would let me see out my time at these audits as I intended to go at 55 in 2003.

Kidner was a notorious meddler who spent 95% of his time playing internal politics, and who who was an advocate of doing the minimum work possible at his audits. He was shocked when he visited Tower Hamlets and Lewisham and saw the amount of audit work that we carried out, much of it paid for by the client as voluntary extra projects. He told me he disagreed with my approach but had no answer when I said did he want me to lose the Commission the considerable extra fee income I delivered each year.

The next time he came he said he wanted to move me out of the audits to audit some major health authorities and he wanted to replace me with two young female audit managers who would each manage one of the boroughs. I told him in no uncertain terms that I would not do this and reminded him of the promise Jim Mcwhirr had given me. Kidner was far too crafty to not get his way however, he waited until I took a 5 week holiday in summer 1998 to celebrate my 50th birthday touring the west coast of America. When I was away he went to see Sylvie Pearce and Barry Quirk and told them that I had asked to be moved from their audit for a new challenge and by the time I returned he had moved his two protégés in.

In life I have learnt it is often that when things are going swimmingly well and you are on a high that it pays to watch out. There I was having just had the best holiday of my life and thinking that life was great in that my two clients really appreciated what I had done at the audits and that given Jim Mcwhirr's promise I could look forward to a very enjoyable last 5 years or so at the Commission before retiring early. But it was not to be

It was almost not to be on our holiday. Hazel and I spent 4 days in Las Vegas. It was our first visit and like most tourists we were gobsmacked by the sheer scale of the entertainment and the surrounding countryside. Before we knew it we were due to move on having marvelled at the sunset over the Grand Canyon, when Hazel pointed out that we had not yet played the tables or the slots. It was the day of my 50th birthday so we decided to have an evening gambling. Firstly Hazel played the slots for a couple of hours while I wandered around observing.

I should point out here that I have never been a casino gambler as I don't like betting against overwhelming odds and like to feel in control of my gambling, reasoning that the research I put in to horseracing and my accumulative knowledge gives me an edge. Hazel came back winning fifty dollars so we decided we would try roulette next, and cashed in two hundred dollars.

We decided we would play our lucky numbers 17,7,4 and 10 and looked for a table where none of these had come up in the last 20 spins. We found our goal after about five minutes walking around and placed ten- dollar chips on each of our four numbers. No luck in the first three spins then, just as I was thinking that we had blown two hundred dollars, in came number 17. We had just won three hundred and fifty dollars. That was enough for me, mission accomplished and I went to leave the table with our winning chips when the croupier pointed out that it was house custom that the winner left a chip on the winning number for the next spin. That showed our naivety in casino etiquette but there was no naivety and a lot of jigging when in came number 17 again!

We eventually cashed out our chips and were over six hundred dollars in profit. On the way out we noticed the keno outlet and Hazel persuaded me to stake one hundred dollars. After watching the first few numbers we were already winning at least one hundred and fifty dollars. It was clearly one of those lucky days that every gambler enjoys once in a while, however there was no way the casino was getting back our winnings and we set off to go back to our room.

On the way out we passed one of the mega jackpot slots, which had a $50,000 jackpot. I told Hazel that as everything we had done we had won on we should risk ten dollars. She needed no persuading as she loved playing the slots and came back with forty quarters, I asked her why she had not got ten one dollar tokens but she replied that she was the slots expert and we had a much better chance of an overall win with 40 tries instead of ten. Imagine our faces when on the eigth spin we landed the five jackpot reels, I was waiting for the bell to ring but nothing happened. I told her to guard the machine with her life and ran off to get a floor supervisor. I duly returned with the supervisor who appeared perplexed but as soon as he saw the machine he knew what had happened we had indeed won the jackpot prize but it was not a jackpot for quarters but dollars!

As you can imagine there were not many words spoken in the Sobey household that night however the mood lightened when we found out we had won twelve hundred dollars on the keno overnight. We ended up, staying an extra three nights in Vegas but there were no more visits to the casinos as I reasoned our moment had come and gone.

Kidner clearly thought I would give in, faced with the fait accompli he presented me with on my return. However, he had picked the wrong person to use his bullyboy tactics on. I rang my union immediately and explained the situation and brought up my medical record. Their advice was to go on sick leave quoting aggravated stress immediately and they soon obtained supporting letters from the two consultants I had been seeing over the last 5 years. My next action was to ring Sylvie, Eleanor and Barry and let them know what had happened, they were not best pleased and wrote to Andrew Foster telling him so.

District Audit's personnel policies entitled individuals to receive full pay for up to six months absence if supported by doctors certificate. A further 6 months could be paid at either 50% or 100% pay at the discretion of the Commission. After three months absence during which I had received a letter from Andrew Foster saying that he did not want to lose me and that he was sure something could be worked out to allow me to continue with the Commission, I had a visit from Kidner and the Head of Personnel.

At this meeting Kidner carried on with his bullyboy tactics and said in management speak that it would be his decision as to whether payments continued after my six months were up and that he would be able also to influence the early retirement decision. He was looking pretty pleased with himself when he finished. Less so when I pulled the tape recorder out of my pocket!

I am never one to leave attacks on my person or family unanswered and several years later when I began to run Centaur greyhounds at Walthamstow, the first two to run I named ThankyouLesK and ThankyouBriWil. I let the District Audit staff magazine know and there was much hilarity among the ranks, unfortunately, the two dogs had about as much ability as their namesakes and failed to win races.

Lo and behold my early retirement went through double quick and so came to an end 34 years of public service. I have to say that although it took up a major part of my life I have never looked back thanks to the amazing time Andrew and I had with Centaur.

PART 2

THE RISE AND FALL OF THE CENTAUR EMPIRE

THE EARLY DAYS OF CENTAUR

Fantastic Forecasts Conquers The Tipping Market

Many of you reading this book will have read publicity about Centaur or our tipping, investment and education adverts and thought that we were a typical one or two man horseracing tipping service. Nothing could be further from the truth. Ask yourself has any other tipping service in history;

- Met the demands of the investment market and managed investor funds of up to £7million for 6 years.
- Operated a horseracing and greyhound bloodstock management service that won 11 Category 1 and 2 races.
- Written the first Professional Gambling degree in the world and operated a Sports Trading Academy in the heart of the City of London
- Been able to use Arsenal and Manchester United's facilities free of charge on a regular basis to carry out Sports Trading Courses.
- Employ 25 staff with an annual salary bill approaching £1 million.

We were probably the largest horseracing telephone tipping service ever too when we operated solely in that area with over 2000 paying clients in 2003/4, but what is that well known saying again" The bigger they are…………"

It all started one Saturday morning in early 2000. Andrew had come over to our house in Southgate for a morning of form analysis before we went off to do battle with the bookmakers. We both had a copy of the Racing Post and he commented that there were more racing tipsters in the paper than horses and it would be interesting to find out what would happen if we put our selections out via a tipping service.

This struck a chord with me. I had just heard that the Audit Commission had granted my request for early retirement so that after nine months sitting at home I could go and do something else. I had been writing in order to keep myself occupied and was half way through a novel and of course had been running our betting fund which continued to do really well. I asked Andrew, what he felt about setting up a tipping service as a joint business venture and after going through a business plan approach we decided to give it a go.

At that time there were probably twenty tipping services operating in the Racing Post, the largest of which seemed to be Henry Rix, The Winning Line, Isiris, Mark Holder, Steve Hamilton Lewis and Clive Holt. Their adverts all said the same thing basically " I tipped you a 5/1 winner last week aren't I great!" there was no meaningful information as to long term profit record or any evidence of independent verification of performance claims. We decided that we would try to break the mould;

- We would aim for a niche in the market by providing forecast selections as well as single bets. After much deliberation we came up with Fantastic Forecasts as a brand name, pretty naff when you look back but surprisingly effective as we did what it said on the tin.
- If we could gain a foothold in the market we would supply our results to date on demand and provide independently audited long term results in our advertisements.

We put £10,000 into a business account at Barclays in Southgate and set up a company, Centaur Tipping Services Ltd. to run the tipping service. We would do the tipping jointly and I would carry out the necessary marketing and client administration. Andrew would act as Finance Director and run the bank account.

We encountered our first setback almost immediately. The Racing Post had received a lot of criticism about its tipping adverts from the Advertising Standards Authority. Accordingly they had instituted a procedure whereby would be tipsters had to proof their results to the paper for three months and show they could make a profit before they were allowed to start placing advertisements. This meant a minimum delay of three months before we could start advertising in the Post.

Undaunted, we turned our attentions to Teletext who televised about 30 pages daily with horseracing results, declarations for the next days racing and tipster adverts. I made contact with their marketing department and we were invited to present our ideas for Fantastic Forecasts to the Head of Marketing at their Fulham headquarters.

Andrew and I spent the two days before the meeting sketching out our ideas for the adverts but when we got there, the meeting centred on our credibility in racing. There was a large degree of scepticism that tipping winning forecasts consistently was possible and we were asked for three selections for the current day that we duly provided. We explained that our tipping strategy was to look for three forecasts a day, one a banker involving two favourites and the other two in races where the selections were close to being joint top rated in our analysis.

After twenty minutes we were off to the pub with the whole racing marketing section for lunch, an extremely wet lunch as it turned out. There was a Jim Thompson Thai pub/restaurant nearby and we ensconced ourselves there at about 12.30. By 2 pm the meal had been consumed and the wine had started to flow. It was explained to us that they would have to consider our proposal and,if it was approved, they would call us back to discuss payment/revenue terms. At 3 pm one of their colleagues came running in to the lounge and came up to the table we were sitting at. He was clearly excited and told the ensemble that our first forecast had won at Windsor at 23/1, the banker had lost but the third had won at 279/1 at Hamilton. A £10 reverse forecast on all three selections costing £60 returned £3,020. A gasp went up from our hosts and we were certainly looked upon in a different light when Andrew and I produced our Wiliam Hill betting slips in which we had staked £50 on each of the forecasts.

It was after nine o clock when we left Jim Thompson's, something our hosts were clearly used to but not Andrew and I and we both needed to get taxis all the way home. Needless to say Fantastic Forecasts tips were up on the Teletext screens pretty quick. This genre proved unsatisfactory for us however as we did not have control of our service and were not provided with the telephone numbers of clients ringing in to pick up the tips. We also only had Teletext's word for the volumes of business so we decided to serve a months notice as per our agreement after 3 months, when we heard that we had been accepted to advertise in the Racing Post in July. All in all we made about £5,000 profit from the three months on Teletext, clearly not enough for us to make a living as tipsters although we did enjoy several extremely enjoyable lunches during this time.

Our first Fantastic Forecasts adverts went into the Racing Post in the first week of July 2000. We had to spend a bit of money setting up a business infrastructure with a new personal computer and a small switchboard that handled up to 6 calls at once.

We decided to advertise both a member service for £15 per month or £149 per annum and a premium rate service where clients paid £1 per minute to receive our views on that days racing. We signed up with a telephone management business Greenland Interactive to manage our premium rate lines.

When we met the Racing Post advertising manager Mike Griffin, a hardened racing aficianado who had seen it all before, dealing with some of the colourful characters who had set themselves up as racing tipsters, he was pleasantly surprised to meet two former senior government auditors who were entering the arena. Mike was quite paternalistic towards us in that first year and told us which adverts in his view were likely to work and which locations in the paper were likely to work. His view was that we had a chance of surviving and eventually prospering if we could stay in the paper each week for a year. Depending on the size of the adverts we used and, whether we used colour or black and white, this would cost us anything between £30,000 and £100,000.

Centaur Tipping Services Ltd was not our only entrepreneurial venture at that time, we also ran Centaur Competitions Limited who promoted the One In A Hundred Racing Challenge. This came about when we went to see the Marketing Director of Greenland Interactive about our premium rate racing service. Greenland's main business was to run telephone competitions for ITV and the Daily Mail for which they needed a network providing thousands of telephone lines. In my writing phase while I was waiting for the retirement decision from the Audit Commission I had a brief phase of designing competitions which I sent off to the main television games companies such as Celador, several of these had a horseracing theme.

At the meeting with Greenland I mentioned this in passing and the marketing manager said I should come back to see her with my designs. I thought at the time she was just being polite but she followed up with a call the following week and I took my prototypes to Camden for a meeting. I had designed three horseracing- based games/competitions but the one she really liked was " The One in A Hundred Racing Challenge". I had created this to fill a void between the two successful racing competitions that were in existence, The Tote Ten To Follow competition raised over £1million in entries annually and The Top Tipster competition run by Channel 4 as part of their Morning Line TV programme every Saturday morning, which I had won twice personally. Channel 4 never published the income raised from this competition but the fact that it was long running suggested that it was lucrative.

The Ten- to- Follow competition cost £5 per entry and the two annual competitions covered the duration of the National Hunt Season and Flat Season. Contestants picked entry lines of 10 horses, which accumulated points over the whole season. The

Channel 4 competition asked contestants to nominate 3 selections in several televised races on the day of the broadcast and clients rang a designated telephone number paying so much per minute while they spoke their entry.

The One In A Hundred Racing Challenge, which we set up, was a monthly competition. Clients were required to ring in three selections each day of a calendar month and paid £5 per day. They were grouped together in pools of 100, so the odds against winning the group prize of £10,000 were only 99/1. Other prizes were provided to keep those not doing well interested in ringing in till the end of the month. Winners of the monthly group prizes were put forward to an annual competition for group winners in which the first prize was £100,000.

Our competition concept gained significant momentum when Greenland committed to run it and went into a partnership with a major call centre Dataforce, based in Northampton, to act as administrator. They estimated that running costs for the first year would be circa £1,million and set targets of 2,000 clients by the end of month1, 10,000 clients by the end of Q1 and 20,000 by month 6, some 2% of the Ten to Follow entry. Greenland /Dataforce said that they were prepared to put up £800,000 of the costs but Andrew and I would have to contribute the remaining £200,000. This was a major decision for me and we talked it over several times with Hazel. She was happy for us to commit and uttered the immortal words " If it fails I will always be able to support you as I have a job for life at C and A." Within 12 months, C and A had closed their UK operations. These had played a major role on UK high streets for 80 years.

A considerable part of the budget for our competition was for marketing. Our strategy was to market at racecourses via sponsorship and distribution of our brochures, which I have to say were fantastic and easily fit into recipients' pockets. More importantly we planned a major campaign in the Racing Post and occasional credit card size adverts on the racing pages of the national dailies. All of this was designed to raise awareness of our brand. However, we suffered a major blow in the week leading up to go live when the Racing Post said it would not carry our adverts. They would not give a reason but the expensive legal advice we sought confirmed that they did not have to. We found out later that they had connections to both of the existing competitions and clearly felt that three was a crowd.

The Racing Post decision led to a last minute crisis meeting between Greenland and Dataforce to decide whether or not to go ahead. I can remember that afternoon sitting at home with Andrew and a friend Bob Green who we had appointed as Sales and Marketing Manager tensely waiting for the decision. After what seemed a day, not two hours, the phone call came giving the project the go- ahead. There was much whooping and cheering in the Sobey household and the champagne was brought out to toast the venture. Looking back now it would have saved a lot of effort and money if the answer had been no.

The launch of the Marketing campaign for The One In A Hundred Racing Challenge came in March 2000 when our marketing team descended on Chepstow Races. We had signed up with Richard Dunwoody's marketing agency and he had signed up Jenny Pitman as an ambassador. Jenny and Bob were to be interviewed on the Racing Channel by Miriam Francome to talk about the competition. Everything went extremely well on the day and we handed out over 600 brochures, very few were left lying around after racing which suggested that most people had taken them home to read and hopefully to enter.

Our brochure distributors were all friends of Hazel and mine and it is only right to pay tribute to the fantastic efforts that they put in over the next 3 months. Lee Jenkins and her husband Steve and Lisa Woodhouse from C and A and Ged and Anna Tyson and their children Matt and Lizzie all worked extremely hard alongside Andrew, Hazel and I on a commission only basis. However, despite this and an advertising campaign in the nationals we did not secure the necessary number of entries to meet our targets. We received only 600 entries in month 1 and less than 2000 by the end of month three. The one bright spot was that we did sign up a number of personalities including Sir Bobby Robson.

Looking back, the failure to advertise the competition in the Racing Post and on Channel 4 was critical but it may also be true that the competition could have been overly complex. Whatever the reasons, it failed and we ceased trading in July 2000. We had very few creditors and none of them took any formal action to achieve recovery. The one thing that Andrew and I took away from this project was a much better understanding of the punter's mentality as we spent many hours discussing racing with racegoers while we were marketing the competition. This was to help marketing Centaur although it was an expensive lesson.

It was now up to Centaur to provide me with a living wage. Andrew decided to stay on at the Audit Commission until things picked up as he was 12 years younger than me and well away from an early retirement package. For the rest of 2000 we tried every form of marketing from handing out marketing fliers and putting them on car windscreens at race meetings to advertising in the Racing Post, national and regional newspapers. Despite this and some excellent tipping, we had 6 profitable months in a row from July 2000, we had a membership of less than one hundred with few clients taking out annual memberships. Nearly all of the income we had raised had to be ploughed back into advertising.

Shortly before Christmas, Andrew and I took stock. If things stayed as they were there was no basis for carrying on as a tipping service. What was making matters worse was that our own betting was suffering as I had less time for tax- free betting, as I needed to be at home to take calls. We decided to give it one last go and took out four full page ads in the Racing Post in the second half of December 2000 advertising Fantastic Forecasts and quoting some of our winning forecasts with headlines like " Give Your Bookie The Old 1 /2 with Fantastic Forecasts. Clients could have a membership till the end of February for just £10.

We had a tremendous response to these ads with over 400 people taking up the offer. What we needed now was a really profitable January. I have learnt over the last 12 years that timing is everything in business and on this occasion I had got it spot on. I made a good start to January and when it got to Saturday the 13th of January, clients who bet £100 on my main bets were winning over £2,000.and the forecasts which we recommended betting to a £10 stake were £120 in profit.

Then came one of the many days that long-term Centaur clients will still remember. I only had one member bet that day £150 each way on Roman Uproar at 16/1 in a 3 mile staying handicap hurdle at Newcastle. I put out 3 forecasts, one of which was a reverse forecast on Roman Uproar and Pottofairies, who was priced up at 33/1 in the morning shows.

In those days I used to put the tips on a recorded, telephone message, which went out at 9am daily.

There was money for both horses, probably most from our clients but Roman Uproar drifted back to 16/1 just before the off. Andrew and I went to Ascot as usual as it was only an hour and a quarter drive for me. We listened to the 2.50 at Newcastle in the course betting shop. In those days there were commentaries only from other courses.

I will leave it to you to imagine what we were feeling when the commentary came on as they swung into the home straight at Newcastle with only two hurdles to jump and our two horses 10 lengths ahead of the field. It seemed to take an hour for the race to finish and the commentator kept saying that the third horse was finishing strongly and gaining rapidly on Pottofairies. however, at the finishing line we were first and second. Fantastic Forecasts clients won £2,120 for the £200 that they were recommended to stake on Roman Uproar and £2,330 for £20 with the forecast.

If you had been in the betting shop at Ascot that day you would have seen two rather portly gentlemen jigging for joy. One person who was there was the Daily Telegraph racing correspondent Tony Stafford. Tony came over and introduced himself and said that he had seen us regularly at the race courses over the last year or two but had never seen us display any emotion and it was difficult to tell if we were winners or losers. When we explained what had just happened he congratulated us and said he would watch Fantastic's adverts closely in future. This was apt as Tony came to work for Centaur a few years later.

There is no doubt about it this particular 13th was an unlucky day for the bookmakers.

I had a good idea what the result would do for our membership figures, but I was taken aback when I got home. The phone never stopped ringing that weekend and I got some great quotes to use as testimonials in future adverts. When you think about it some of our competitors like Isiris were bragging that they had a winning each way bet on a 9/4 shot and there we were quoting clients who had staked £260 on the day and won £4450!

I took the opportunity to revise our fees upwards to £695 for a year and £69 per month, which was quite a rise but we were still only a third of what Isiris was charging and half Henry Rix's fees. I continued in great form till the end of January and we went into February with over 400 clients over half of whom had paid for three months or more.

Over the next few years I learnt an awful lot about the tipping business and the fickle nature of punters and our policy of putting fees up when we delivered a big win or big winning year was definitely the right way to market. In the 12 years that we marketed Centaur, we had to put the fees down only twice. The first time in mid 2004 and then in 2007, the only year we made a loss on bank. We also never gave free trials. They cheapen the value of the service that you are offering clients in my view.

2001 turned out to be a mega year for us and it was not long before Andrew left the Audit Commission and began to work full time for Centaur. June 2001 saw Hazel and I relocate to Seahouses in Northumberland. This was quite a wrench for me leaving Andrew and my other friends in London and moving 350 miles north. I had been used to meeting prospective clients quite often before they joined as most new clients came from the south- east, but I need not have worried,

As I discovered, Royal Ascot was the best time of the year to advertise and Mike Griffin's advice to take out big adverts every day of the festival certainly paid off. We had a massive surge in premium rate income over the four days and 160 people took up quarterly or annual memberships. We certainly gave our clients an Ascot to remember. We started the meeting when one of our two member bets on the first day,Medicean won the Queen Anne Stakes for Michael Stoute at 11/2.

Our second recommended bet that day was £100 each way on First Ballot in the Ascot Stakes, a big field two and a half mile staying handicap. We also gave three forecast bets on the day one of which was a reverse forecast on First Ballot and Cover Up. First Ballot finished a close second to Cover Up after looking the likely winner, the forecast returned

£1610 for a £20 stake. Our clients ended up making a profit of £950 on the day to a £100 stake on our member bets and over £1700 on forecasts.

On the Wednesday of Royal Ascot our biggest bet to date in the history of Fantastic Forecasts, Nice One Clare, ran in the 30 -runner Wokingham Handicap over 6furlongs, a real cavalry charge. We had advised £100 ew as an ante post bet on this horse in March as soon as we heard that Jonny Murtagh had been booked to ride it and we doubled this bet on the day of the race. The winning margin was only a neck but the victory was far easier and after winning off a handicap mark of 98 this high class filly went on to win off 110 shortly afterwards.

The word was now rippling through the racing community about Fantastic Forecasts and many clients were referring friends or family. By the end of 2001 we still had not had a losing month for clients in the 20 months we had been operating. Our fees had gone up to £1195 for a year and we had over 1000 clients taking the service, over half for 12 months.

Until mid -2001, Hazel and I managed all of the administration. I maintained the client records and she made up the marketing and joining packs. We both manned the phones. Andrew looked after the finances and maintained the results records. The workload was huge and we had not had a day off for over 7 months when Hazel insisted that we were going to go to Newcastle for a meal and to watch

Sunset Boulevard for her birthday. All seemed to be working well when we had a nice meal at the best Indian restaurant in Newcastle but not so well when after 30 minutes of the musical we were tapped on the shoulder by an usher and told that we had been asleep for the last ten minutes and asked to leave!

That made up my mind. We had to get an office and recruit a couple of administration staff. Another reason was that as a gesture to show how reliable and honest we were, I had given my personal mobile number to clients. This was not so bad when we had 100 clients but I was getting a bit fed up of being rung by people working night shift in the middle of the night querying our latest published results!

One of the problems we faced was that there was very little office accommodation in Seahouses, which only had a population of around 1500 at the time. We were seriously thinking of opening the office in Alnwick, the nearest town some 15 miles away when Hazel heard that some offices above the Amusements in Seahouses had become vacant.

I still smile when I recall meeting the Landlord to discuss the rent. Although the location of the offices could have been better they were in good condition, carpeted and the three I was interested in came to about 1500 square feet. I met the landlord and when he said he wanted £1500, I thought that was at the top end of what I was prepared to pay per month. It was some while before it dawned on me that the

£1500 was an annual rent. However, when I realised, I managed to negotiate a 5- year lease without any breaks. Quite a contrast from the £30,000 per month rent Centaur paid for our Sports Trading Academy in London.

Next on the agenda was staff recruitment. I had decided that we would have two administration staff and a couple of part timers at weekends so that we could cover the telephones 7 days a week from 8am to 6pm. With most of the other tipping services you got an answering machine. Not so at Centaur where we provided a high level of customer service from the beginning. Customers calling could always talk to Andrew and I, the analysts, if they wished to and we often met groups of clients at the races,.

I was fortunate to recruit my eldest son Christopher as Office Manager. He had worked his way up to be Head of Purchasing at a 5 star hotel but was keen to move away from London and our other recruit Clare had a degree and a great personality. Over the next year Chris and Clare set up robust systems for client administration, results proofing and holiday deposit accounts and I was delighted that our customer service was matching our stellar tipping performance.

2002 was another eventful and hugely successful year for Centaur. We were now building up a significant balance in our business account and ,as I was still unsure how long we would be able to sustain the level of income I felt it wise to diversify. Hazel was very close to her sister Ann, who was Head of Maths at a large comprehensive school in Newcastle. Ann had been attacked and punched in the face twice in the last six months and I decided that we should help her to change career and at the same time diversify our business holdings. We therefore bought two sub post offices and general dealers and a Newsagent and off-licence shop in Seahouses and neighbouring Beadnell. Ann was charged with managing these and working the balance of her time at Centaur. I also looked at buying a couple of restaurants but decided against it due to the seasonal nature of trade in Seahouses.

There was no sign of things slowing down at Centaur now and we recruited three additional staff by the end of year to keep pace with the rapid expansion of the business. The cornerstone of growth was the remarkable success of the tipping. Unbielavably I went through the whole of 2002 without having a losing month, which made it over 30 winning months in a row. However I was keen to expand the business into other areas.

REBRANDING

Launch of The Centaur Group

In early 2002 Andrew and I carried out a complete review of the business and produced our first corporate plan. The main business aim was to become the largest and most successful tipping business in the UK. We felt there was also scope to branch out into bloodstock management, which had been our joint ambition when we started the tipping business. I was keen to establish the credibility and status of our brand and felt that to do this we should branch out into betting education as well as bloodstock management. We therefore formed two new companies, Centaur Bloodstock Management Ltd and Centaur Consultancy Limited to set up bloodstock partnerships and develop education products for the betting market.

The main finding of our review was that if we were to expand the brand and its products throughout the UK and Ireland that we should change the brand name away from Fantastic Forecasts which may have worked in the telephone tipping market but would not reflect the right image for the expanding nature of the business. Hence the Centaur Group was born in mid 2002.

There were a number of other businesses that used the title of Centaur. However, only one business was connected with racing and that had not filed accounts for several years. They eventually tried to blackmail us into paying them something to use the name but we just ignored them and they went away. We spent a lot of money re branding Fantastic Forecasts to Centaur and I think that the exercise was successful. However seven years later when we started delivering courses in London it was amazing the number of delegates who remembered us from our early days as Fantastic Forecasts.

The first course launched by Centaur Consultancy Limited was a one-day Professional Betting Seminar, which Andrew and I delivered. We started advertising the courses at £795 in the Racing Post once a fortnight. We were aware that the price was not cheap but felt that we needed to bring in £8,000 a weekend to make it worthwhile and to cover expenses. The agenda we delivered was;

- Developing a Winning Mentality
- Understanding the UK Handicapping System
- Race Reading
- Understanding Value
- Staking to win

These courses were well received and we got brilliant feedback. They were not at all about being talked to, we made them interactive and brought in guest bookmakers for the value session showing delegates how they priced up races and used hedging to reduce their overall risk. In the 18 months we delivered this programme we taught over 500 delegates at venues all over England, Scotland and Ireland. We also did two or three private courses for wealthy individuals. In addition to the courses we produced a number of themed DVD, which we sold at £49 and used as incentives for clients to join the tipping service.

A number of people connected to the racing media came on the course including Tanya Stephenson and Tony Stafford. I was often asked later why we stopped delivering them. The answer was that we had probably met demand and Andrew and I were becoming increasingly busy.

The second course we delivered was the real money-spinner however. Betting Exchanges had arrived on the scene in early 2002 and were creating a sensation. They probably split the racing fraternity down the middle. The middle- aged, died in the wool, punters were slow to see the benefits of laying horses and football teams and found the technology a barrier. Not so the " thinking" punters who realised that nirvana had arrived.

Two of my new members of staff, Craig Forsyth and Steve Taylor used the exchanges extensively and came to see me at the end of 2002 saying that they were pretty sure they could run seminars showing people how to use the Betting Exchanges effectively. Craig was extremely useful to the business as he was a computer programmer and network expert and the office systems developed considerably during his tenure and with the help of our external data base provider Dave Sedgwick.

We started running " Learn How to Use Betting Exchanges Effectively " courses in early 2003 priced at £495. The courses used a live link to Betfair to demonstrate;

- How to get started
- How to get best prices
- Hedging strategies
- Trading in running

These courses went like hot cakes. We learnt early on that we needed to provide courses for both beginners and more advanced exchange users, as it was difficult to meet the needs of both groups in a single course. Craig and Steve were working virtually full time on course marketing, administration and delivery and we gained a lot of plaudits from the post- course support they provided to delegates. Unbeknown to us, Betfair and Betdaq had been sending delegates to our courses and in mid 2003 I got an invitation from the Education Director at Betfair to come to see him to discuss marketing Centaur courses to the Betfair database, which was rapidly approaching 1 million registered users.

This was a massive opportunity for Centaur. Becoming Betfair's education partner would give us massive kudos and pave the way for international expansion of the education aspects of the business. After obtaining a non disclosure agreement we shared all of the details of our courses, the supporting manuals and speaking notes to help pave the way for an extensive delivery programme. As it turned out however we were done up like kippers! Two weeks into our series of meetings, Betfair full- page colour adverts started to appear in the Racing Post and on Betfair's websites advertising free betting exchange courses delivered by Betfair.

This was highly unethical and we had a solid case to take legal action but how would a small to medium business like ourselves take on a leviathan like Betfair in the courts. The whole episode left a bad taste but essentially we had to grin and bear it. Several years later Mark Davies, who was Betfair's Chief Executive at the time, did some PR work for Centaur. Mark confirmed to me that Betfair had stolen Centaur's material at the time and apologised. I have to say that his company developed a reputation for treating its suppliers poorly. Betfair's actions brought to an end our Betting Exchange courses and by the end of 2004, Centaur Consultancy ceased trading. Its net assets were transferred to Centaur Group Holdings Limited.

A portentous event for Centaur clients happened at the Goodwood festival in 2002. First of all I delivered two massive winning multipliers for our clients. On the Tuesday the four selections in the each way yankee which I advised clients to put on, all won. The bet won circa £5,000 for a £22 stake. Unbelievably I came within a short head of repeating the feat the following day when Waveney's narrow defeat at 20/1 cost clients nearly £30,000 for a £22 stake.

We were having a sensational summer. In early June I had tipped 9 winners in a row on our premium rate service at the Epsom Derby meeting and at Royal Ascot on the Tuesday I picked all 6 winners in a jackpot perm. One of our clients Andy Davidson sent us a photograph of himself receiving his cheque for £55,000 from Ladbrokes.

Following Goodwood I received many telephone calls and letters of congratulations. One of them was from a gentleman called Alan Moore. Alan explained that he had never backed horses before but had gone to Goodwood on the Tuesday and had seen Fantastic Forecasts advert in the Racing Post. Intrigued he rang the office number and took out a one- month membership, he put a £5 multiplier on our selections on the first day and won £25,000 and a £10 multiplier on the second day and won £12,000. He told me that in the past he had run one of the biggest investment companies in the UK, Burns Anderson, but he had sold it at the end of the 1980's to look after his daughter who was badly injured in a car accident. Since then he had not gone back into business but he said that Centaur was so amazing "it could take over the world". He asked if I could send him previous years results so he could do a full analysis.

I did my best to explain to Alan about the limitations of the betting market but he would not be deterred and a couple of weeks later he rang me back post analysis and asked if I would like to sell Centaur or take onboard another investor. I said no but he persuaded me that I had nothing to lose by meeting up to talk around the issue. I turned up at the meeting near Harrogate with Andrew. Alan was obviously out to impress us as he was accompanied at the meeting by a friend, who was Finance Director of Punch Taverns and whose house we met at. He owned six or seven motor cars which were parked in front of the house and must have been worth over one million pounds.

At the meeting, Alan had clearly learned from his friend Richard about the limitations of the betting market but said that he was convinced that, if we allowed him to become involved he could massively increase the value of the Company. He would not be drawn however on how much he thought Centaur could be sold for and he clearly was not willing to pay for equity. I thanked him for his interest but said that I was not interested because I thought that Andrew and I were doing pretty well. Our turnover for 2002/3 was likely to be well in excess of £0.5 million compared with £100,000 in 2000/1. Also we were expanding the company into a group structure with bloodstock management and education companies. Alan kept in touch however.

We closed out 2002 still not having had a losing month in 32 months for clients. Membership had increased to well over 2000 despite our taking measures to reduce it by putting up the annual fee to £2500, which was far higher than competitors and putting back the time of our message to 11am, which led to almost 500 clients leaving the service.

We delivered a massive Christmas present for clients in November 2002. At that time we still provided multiple bets as part of the main service. I put out a multiplier, centred on a major Newmarket meeting, which featured 6 horses in each way trebles and an accumulator. What an after-noon! The first 5 selections won including Lord Protector at 28/1 and the sixth was trotting in at Hereford when it slipped up on the flat! Clients who put the bet on as advised for a cost of £42 received over £14,000 back and several who extended the bet to a full cover Heinz collected over £110,000.

As you can imagine, the telephones never stopped ringing in the Centaur office for the next three days. However, while we collected a lot of additional fee income, surprisingly, despite taking out television adverts for two months, we failed to collect any major income to buy bloodstock. I will never forget talking to one client who had joined the previous month but had not renewed his subscription. I asked him if he had bet on the multiplier and he said yes he had won £114,000. I then asked if it was an oversight that he had not renewed his membership and he said no, he had won enough to pay his childrens public school fees for several years and that in his mind he did not want to risk any funds from a life changing win. I should not have been surprised as Andy Davidson also did not renew after his big win, he had just got married and the new wife banned him from betting after he had just won £55,000-that's women for you!

2002 saw Centaur diversify into bloodstock and at the same time we also launched a football betting service. This did not come about by design but because I was contacted in the spring of that year by Alan Bentley. Alan was an ex Sky football commentator who among various jobs was working for Talk Sport radio. Alan said that he had heard a lot about Centaur in his job and that it was all- positive. He asked why we had not branched out into other sports and I explained about our rapid growth and felt that it was not necessary but he said that he felt we were missing an opportunity and asked if we could meet up to discuss launching a football service we agreed to meet at a hotel near Doncaster as I was visiting the May sales to buy some horses.

My meeting with Alan was originally scheduled for dinner but he rang up an hour before and asked if we could put it back to 11pm as he had a media event to attend at Talk Sports headquarters in Leeds. By midnight there was no show so I went to bed, Andrew is a late night bird and he stayed up for a while. He came down to breakfast the following morning and told me that the only person to arrive after I had gone to bed was a guy in his thirties who was very drunk and who had two women draped all over him. Imagine our surprise when as we were finishing up our breakfast over came a guy in his thirties looking pretty much the worse for wear who introduced himself as Alan Bentley.

They often say that first impressions are the best and I wished plenty of times over the next year that I had followed those negative instincts. Over the next two days at the sales Bentley made a good impression, he clearly was very well known in football circles and I overheard a number of telephone calls with prominent agents and players. He also seemed to have a good knowledge of football tipping saying that his strategy would be to find out major injuries not yet announced in the lower divisions and look to oppose favourites who were likely to be missing key players. In normal circumstances I would have carried out a personal background check but decided not to given his obvious credentials as a football expert, big mistake.

Before the start of the 2002/3 football season, I spent £50,000 advertising Centaur's exciting new football service headed by Alan Bentley. This campaign was successful and Alan started with 250 clients, a mixture of current Centaur clients and new clients responding to our adverts in various publications. Alan was the first example of many that proved to me that media experts are completely useless at operating a profitable tipping service. Although he was knowledgable he had absolutely no regard for the clients money and chased losses outrageously, something completely foreign to Centaur values. By the end of the football season he had lost a betting bank and most of his clients. I was about to terminate our agreement when he came to me and said he had an opportunity to start working for ESPN in Asia and that would be a fantastic opportunity to launch a Centaur football service in the far east.

Although I had already found out that Alan was a prior bankrupt and a confessed sexaholic, who had several failed marriages behind him and a string of liaisons with porn actresses, he had actually made Centaur a profit from the football venture and I was attracted by the opportunity for global expansion. I therefore funded the £50,000 his business plan required. Much of it involved working with a media consultant who had managed Victor Chandler's expansion in the far- east. After Alan had been in Hong Kong for 3 months and there was no sign of progress or any client income, I received a request for a further £100,000. This started the alarm bells ringing and I used a private detective agency to investigate what was happening. I was waiting for their report when Craig and Steve my two senior office staff came to see me and told me that Alan had rung them offering them both jobs with the Alan Bentley Sports Betting Service that he would be launching soon in the UK and Asia. He had used the money I had given him to betray me and despite tight internal security had managed to steal the Centaur client database.

This was the first of many recruitment mistakes I made at Centaur, however all were driven by the opportunity for commercial advantage. This one was particularly hard to take as I had allowed Alan to live with Hazel and I for three months due to his financial situation. I may be a half glass full person in my attitude to recruitment however I am ruthless when it comes to retribution. As soon as I had finished hearing Craig and Steve's story I cut off Alan's company credit card and closed the Centaur Asia Bank Account leaving him stranded in the far -east. I also wrote to all Centaur clients and his former employers setting out what had happened.

It still hurts when I look back on this episode but I have to say that Bentley did provide me with one of the funniest moments of my years at Centaur. He had used his connections in the porn industry to get funding for a porn movie based upon a fictional England Women's Football Team who had a wide range of talents including excellent ball control! We had a board meeting scheduled and as I was down in London we held it at Andrew's house.

We were extremely busy at the time and I was keen to complete the board meeting as early as possible. Alan arrived and said he had just finished his movie and had the demo tape and wanted to show us it. I wasn't interested but said he could put on on the video in the background while we went through the agenda. Porn has never held any attraction for me but what should have been a one hour meeting took almost twice that time due to the fact that Andrew and I were sat opposite the TV screen and kept losing our place when discussing the managed accounts!

Bentley's departure left me with a dilemma. Did I keep the football service on or let it go. I was loathe to do the latter as it would probably hand clients and income to Bentley. So I looked for another high profile football expert and it was not long before one landed in my lap. Tony Stafford had been the main sportswriter for the Daily Telegraph for 25 years and was also a broadcaster on the newly launched Racing Channel on Sky TV speciailsing in American Racing. I was watching the evening racing from Windsor on TV one evening and Tony was the guest tipster. In a fantastic piece of tipping he went through the card in the televised races.

I was on the phone to Tony the next day. My timing could not have been better from his point of view as the Daily Telegraph had dispensed with his services. After a couple of meetings in which we thrashed out a commercial deal, Tony took over running the Centaur football service and we launched The Tony Stafford Racing Service via a sustained advertising campaign in the Daily Telegraph and the Racing Post.

This arrangement lasted two years, Tony's racing service broke even in this time and we covered expenses but income was declining and we did not renew the agreement. His performance as football selector was nothing short of disastrous however and after only a month, Steve and I took over. The football service ticked over for the next two years making a small profit but never built on its promising start. I tried a similar concept with greyhound tipping using a Racing Post expert but this was also unsuccessful due to the "expert's" inability to treat clients' money as if it was his own and his habit of continually chasing losses.

Tony Stafford was the most knowledgable person about horseracing i have ever met. He has encyclapedic knowledge of breeding and the history of racing and has a massive range of contacts from his journalistic days. However, despite this and like many other people who I met during my Centaur days he was a chronic losing gambler.

 He simply could not understand that you may have an opinion on a lot of races but you cannot win backing in every race without a differential staking system. Despite being racing manager for several years for one of the major Arab owners and more recently for Raymond Tooth and having many other sources of income, Tony was always short of money. His Centaur salary of £50,000 per annum was usually lost in the first two or three days of each month spent in the Centaur office gambling frantically on Betfair. Andrew and I had our suspicions about the reason behind the naming of a successful handicap sprinter trained by Noel Callaghan called Tonythetap!

Tony was responsible for one of my most satisfying moments in dealing with course bookmakers in 2002. He was staying at mine for a few days while we created some marketing literature for Tony Stafford Racing and we went to Brough Park with Andrew to watch two of my greyhounds run. We were standing in front of the stands watching the first greyhound being walked, when his trainer Jimmy Fenwick came up to us and we started chatting. I asked Tony if he would put £200 on for Andrew and I and gave him £100 to bet for himself. I thought nothing more of it when the dog who was drawn in trap 3 made all to win comfortably at 5to2. However when Tony went down to the bookmaker to collect he told him that he had backed trap 4 –he had not given Tony a ticket, which is a common practice with bigger bets.

A minor scene ensued and one or two of the Brough Park regulars chipped in that this was not the first time that this bookmaker had done this. We were getting knowhere and I was resigned to losing our money when Tony arrived with William Hill's track manager. The track manager asked to speak privately with the bookmaker and then came back with our winnings. Apparently Tony had told him the next time he was broadcasting on the Racing Channel he would mention the dodgy bookmaking practices at Brough Park. Such is the power of the Media.

No one can ever accuse me of sitting on my laurels and at the end of 2002 we tried another new venture, Centaur Hospitality Services. We had started the Centaur News in 2001, a monthly colour magazine distributed free to clients, it contained details of the performance of our services and bloodstock and future events such as stable visits, celebrity quizzes etc that we put on for clients. I came up with the idea that we should see if there was any appetite for golf/racing trips to Ireland and the Arc De Triomphe in November.

There was little demand for the former but our planned October trip to Paris was sold out very quickly. My son Chris organised the weekend trip and we all met at the Eurostar station at Waterloo early afternoon on the Friday before the Arc. Nineteen of the twenty travellers were pretty much on time but one looked like a no show and we were just heading off to board the train when a diminutive figure with Billy Connolly hair came running toward us. This turned out to be Pat Shearer, a Glaswegian with a broad accent who went on to make the weekend one of the most memorable of my life.

We arrived in Paris safely and then underwent the traditional nightmare taxi journey to our hotel, which put everyone in the frame of mind for a drink to steady our nerves and it was not long before we were all out enjoying the Paris nightlife. I suggested that we all go for a meal together and then people could go their separate ways and meet up at 10am for breakfast in the morning. Andrew and I joined a small group for a couple of drinks after dinner before we returned to the hotel to do our analysis for the following day's racing. This group included Pat who had had everyone in stiches at dinner telling us of some of his experiences and also Mel Turner whom I had recruited as a Centaur Sales/Administration executive some three months previously. Mel's job was to act as Tour Leader and to take away the daily shepherding responsibility away from Andrew and i.

Ten am arrived in the morning and eighteen of us were present, no sign of Mel or Pat. Ten minutes later Pat arrived with not one but two females and sat down to have his breakfast. I asked him if he knew where Mel was and he told me that he had left him pretty much the worse for wear at about 3am having come out a very poor second in a drinking contest with Pat. I went up to Mel's room and could hear a series of loud groans, he eventually arrived at the door in a terrible state and that was all we saw of him until we caught the Eurostar back to England on Monday morning. As you could imagine,I was not best pleased by this, particularly as he had apparently been telling all and sundry that he was the driving force behind Centaur and would soon be taking over from me on the tipping!

The Saturday was the first day of the two-day fixture at Longchamp and consisted of a large number of group 2 races and a couple of handicaps at the end of the card. Amazingly there was hardly anyone there but British tourists. Chris had done Centaur proud and as part of the package he had created, he had got the rent of a long table immediately adjacent to Longchamps magnificent leafy paddock for both days. The day started with buckets of Heineken but after news came through mid afternoon that both of Centaur's member bets had won these swiftly changed to buckets of champagne.

During the course of the afternoon we were joined at the table by a number of famous British and French trainers and owners, all invited by Pat who you could simply not say no to. The price of a seat was a bottle of champagne. Tablemates for the afternoon included Marcus Tregonning, Richard Hannon Junior and David Nicholls but the most popular guest was a French Trainer whose name I cannot recall who tipped everyone his horse in the last race, which duly won at 16/1!

This was a fantastic day of non- stop laughter and banter and it was quite late when some of our celebrity guests departed. My abiding memory is that when Andrew and I left at 10pm to start work on the next days cards, looking back to the racecourse, it was in total darkness except for this one brightly lit area in the paddock in which waiters were still scurrying back and forwards with bottles of champagne.

The big day arrived on the Sunday without any additional drama other than that one of our clients who had gone drinking afterwards with Pat had arrived back at the hotel minus his shoes and had to go out and buy a new pair. We arrived at the course in good time and took up our table and pretty much enjoyed a repeat of the day before although without the success on the betting front. Longchamp on the Sunday is a complete contrast to the Saturday. Having said that, our French trainer had said for us to back an outsider called Falbrav in the Arc. Although it didn't win the Arc it went on to win the Eclipse at Sandown the following year when trained by Luca Cumani, delivering a maximum bet for Centaur clients.

Pat was again the undoubted star of the show and achieved a remarkable feat on the day when he was dared to produce a photograph of himself with the Aga Khan. This he duly delivered after chatting up one of the prominent French lady owners who took him up to the Aga Khan's box.

Most of our guests were completely exhausted when we met up to board the Eurostar on Monday morning except for Pat who seemed as fresh as a daisy. The drama of the weekend was not over however, Andrew and I stayed back to escort everyone through passport control, which went smoothly until two gendarmes appeared and seized Pat at the window – he had a long out of date passport! For a while it looked as if Pat was going to have a much -extended stay in France but Andrew and I managed to intervene successfully on his behalf and we just managed to board the train on time.

Taking stock after the weekend we had, with the exception of Mel, one of the best weekends of our lives. However our venture into the hospitality industry had not been a financial success and despite the many many requests for a repeat Longchamp visit the following year we called it quits. I met Pat socially in Edinburgh a couple of times over the next few years but he dropped out of Centaur in 2005.

Before I sign off for 2002 I should mention that this year saw the start of Centaur Managed Betting Accounts, which were to become a major factor in our business over the next 10 years. They came about as a result of many of our clients contacting the office saying that they were going on holiday but did not want to miss our selections when they were away. Remember there was no roaming function on mobiles at that time and few if any bookmakers had international dial up numbers or offered Internet betting.

 After discussing the pros and cons of managed accounts at a Board Meeting we decided that we would draw up a scheme for operating managed betting accounts and refer it to the FSA for their approval and would procede if that approval was given. We had a meeting with the FSA and they replied following the meeting saying that although

Betting was outside their scope that the scheme we had drawn up met best practice.

So, Centaur Managed Betting Accounts began in mid 2002. We were taken aback by the huge demand for them and we had to make good some £10,000 in administration errors, which occurred due to deactivation dates not being administered correctly. Another problem was that we had to place the money for managed account clients ourselves. I had to set up trade accounts with several major bookmakers, more about this later.

On to 2003 and in the April of that year we recorded our biggest winning month to date. I achieved a strike rate of over 60 per cent in that month and it seemed as if I was reading the following days' newspaper each morning. Clients betting to a level £100 won just over £11,000. We reached the peak of our membership that month at around 2600. We had also made a spectacular start to our bloodstock management business with early purchases Hasty Prince and Overstrand winning big races and Centaur Corker proving to be the most exciting greyhound on the scene. Things could not be better, however the storm clouds were brewing.

Firstly we were prevented from advertising in our normal way in the Racing Post, when all of the other advertisers ganged up against us and pressurised the Racing Post to only accept adverts quoting winners in the last 14 days and not detailed audited results over a period of time. This was a commercial decision for the Post but removed a major advantage for us and it was not long before our advertising income began to drop significantly.

That and the start of racing TV on Sky television where punters had accesss to free tips had a significant impact upon advertising income for us in 2003/4. We spent around £150,000 in the Racing Post in 2002/3 and collected some £400,000 in new memberships linked to these adverts. In 2003/4 we collected only £100,000 from a similar spend.

Then, for the first time ever we failed to deliver a profit for our members in the 12 months from May 2003, ending up level for that period. The principal reason for this was that we had recruited too many members and were "smashing" the betting market when we released our bets. Typically if we recommended a £100 each way bet on a 10/1 shot at a midweek meeting, it would be as low as 3/1 after 10 minutes.

No other racing service had terrorised the betting market like this before, however it was not good for business as few clients were getting good value prices and the lower starting prices of winners led to a decline in profits recorded In our published results. The outstanding example of how tipping a horse at a big price can actually work against a successful tipster was when I tipped Michigan Blue in a 2mile3 furlong, claiming, chase at Hereford in May 2001.

There were 18 runners in the race and the Racing Post completely dismissed the chances of Michigan Blue and priced it at 66/1. When I looked at the race in detail however I considered Michigan Blue to be one of only four horses that would stay the distance. It was also dropped in class and although trained by a new stable, they had shown promise and were based close to Hereford.

I put out a message for clients to have a £100 each way bet on Michigan Blue at 10am,when 66/1 was available with both Paddy Power and Sean Graham and 40/1 with some of the larger bookmakers. By 10.30 am, 14/1 was the best price anywhere and when the race started that had reduced to 7/1. Although some of our savvy clients got between 33/1 and 66/1 for the horse, the great majority got between 10/1 and 20/1. Michigan Blue slaughtered the opposition winning in a canter by 20 lengths and went on to win his next three races. Although I made a lot of clients very happy that day, many were disappointed with their returns.

As 2003 progressed and results flattened out I decided to see if Alan Moore could do anything to maintain Centaur's financial impetus. We had kept in touch since our meeting in Yorkshire. Alan said that he was convinced he could derive considerable income from our database because Centaur had never operated a telesales function and had just sent out written reminders when subscriptions lapsed and written marketing flyers.

Alan was not cheap. He wanted £5,000 to ring 100 clients over a two- day period. He said that when he had finished I would be convinced of the need to operate a telesales function. I will never forget those days, it was really sunny weather and Alan sat in my back garden with me and a continuous supply of coffee then wine and rang the 100 former Centaur clients. Alan told me that before he set up Burns Anderson he had been the top salesman nationally for Allied Dunbar and it was easy to see why. The clients he got through to, were like putty in his hands and at the end of the exercise he had signed up almost 70 of the clients he contacted for various membership periods.

The next three months were spent in hard business negotiations with Alan. The outcome was that we signed a two year agreement with him to operate a telesales function for Centaur in return for 35% of any income raised, with a monthly retainer of £5,000 to be paid in advance but to be set against his monthly commission. Alan was also convinced that he could get Centaur sold for at least £6 million and was given a deferred shareholding if he achieved this objective within the next two years.

As part of this process Alan introduced us to CLB Coopers a leading firm of accountants based in Manchester, who became Centaur's accountants and tax advisers and also began certifying our monthly performance via a continuous independent review. Alan was confident that Centaur could start to move toward the Investment Fund market and CLB would provide the necessary due diligence for Investors.

He was largely responsible for Centaur's best -ever trading year in 2003/4. He came up with the idea that we should no longer include system bets, information bets and multiple bets in one horseracing service. Although I was nervous about doing this, Alan's sales results soon dispersed the nerves. In 2003/4 we more than doubled our previous best annual turnover raising over £1.5 million over the three services with Alan earning himself £350,000 in commission. We also launched a new horseracing service called The Bismark, which was the first commercial horseracing laying service.

One of the things that continually distinguished Centaur from our competitors was our continual programme of events for clients. These were entertaining in themselves, such as visits to major stables, pre-Cheltenham celebrity panels and big prize quiz nights, but also gave clients a chance to meet Andrew and I and the analysts and raise anything they wished to discuss with us. Perhaps the best example of this was our annual client day, which we held at Worcester races in 2003. For this event we hired a marquee and sponsored the whole televised card. We also hired Tony McCoy to give a run through of the days racing with me.

Things could not have gone better. It was a fantastic sunny day and over 200 Centaur clients and their guests enjoyed a great day out. The highlight of the afternoon for everyone was when our horse Unsigned, ridden by Tony McCoy and trained by Bob Buckler brought off a massive gamble from 6/1 to 11/8 when winning the 2.5mile novice hurdle. We had hoped to follow up with our French horse Monzon in the last race and incurred significant costs in bringing him over to Worcester, however the ground proved too firm for him to run.

That night, long after the racecourse had emptied, the lights were on at our marquee and many guests were dancing to one of my client's band Zootgoose including Tony who had stayed on afterward and thoroughly enjoyed himself. Days like this do not come cheap. We spent about £20,000 on the Worcester event however it helped to brand Centaur as being in a completely different league within the tipster sector.

CENTAUR MOVES INTO THE INVESTOR MARKET

In 2004, the tipping market was beginning to implode. Free tipping on the Racing Channel and the start of hundreds of cheap email and direct mail tipsters on the web, were giving the industry a very bad name.

Despite Alan's best efforts, our client numbers were decreasing sharply and traditional and e- mail advertising was not halting the attrition rate. However, that Spring, an opportunity arose, which was to change the future direction of Centaur.

In early 2004 I was given an invitation to give a keynote address at the Alternative Investor Exhibition at the Excel Centre at Docklands. Alan and I discussed this and we saw it as an opportunity to introduce the Centaur brand to the investment market. I had tried advertising our horseracing services in the Investors Chronicle occasionally before but the stock market was doing well at the time and investors were not turned on by the image of horse racing despite the robust due diligence we could provide about our previous performance. Most investors looked at our adverts and thought"Too good to be true"

I invested £15,000 in attending the exhibition and we had one of the best stands and locations. My keynote address entitled " The Betting Market versus The

Stock Market, There is only one winner" proved a big success and provoked a lively debate in the nearly full auditorium. The key points I managed to deliver were that,what I did was no different to what stockbroker analysts did in that I analysed the sporting markets and made recommendations in the same way that they reviewed the performance of companies and commodities. I also drew attention to the susceptibility of the stock market to world events and the fact that profits made from the gambling/exchange markets were tax-free. I acknowledged the fact that there were many charlatans posing as profitable horse racing services but pointed out that investors could avoid them by doing proper due diligence on tipping firms.

We did excellent business at our stand at the exhibition and more than covered costs but I also learnt two very important messages. Horseracing was a definite turn off for traditional investors. Hundreds of delegates at the exhibition came and looked at our point of sale material and excellent visual marketing display but from those I spoke too most saw horseracing as being too volatile and risky.

The second message I learnt was that investors did not want to bet for themselves. Well over 90 per cent of the accounts we opened at the exhibition were managed accounts. The increase in managed account business we were experiencing meant that we had to develop some creative ways of getting client money on without having an adverse effect on prices. It also opened my eyes to the fact that commercially, a laying service could offer more scope as it was possible to lay a short priced favourite in a race on the betting exchanges for upwards of £100,000 while getting £20,000 on in the win market was extremely difficult.

We had already found out that the investor market was not receptive to win betting on horses but Alan and I felt confident that we could work up some attractive advertising material for our laying service The Bismark. This had done very well in its first two years as a DIY product in the punter market and we were confident it could do as well as a managed account product in the investor market. We therefore began a major marketing campaign in the Investors Chronicle based upon the concept that with Centaur's Bismark Investment product you had 9 horses running for you in a 10- runner race.

Alan had been working hard to try to get an equity stakeholder or buyer for Centaur and for part of 2004 we were in extensive discussions for a flotation with a venture capital company, Zeus Capital of Manchester. One of the difficulties that surfaced was the lack of previous sales/purchases in our sector, the nearest being when the Winning Line sold its bloodstock operation to an Australian company for 2.5million. The deal originally put together by Zeus provided for the flotation to raise some £40 million and in time I would be able to take out between £6million and £10million for my shareholding.

Things were progressing well, when a change in the legislation involving tax allowances for charities scuppered the deal. During the remainder of 2004 our client numbers and income dropped by almost 50 per cent and this prevented any renewed equity interest over the next three years.

In the middle of drawing together this marketing campaign, I made a very big decision. The chronic aesophagus problems I had suffered when I was in London with the Audit Commission had resurfaced again and after a lot of thought and discussion with Hazel, I decided to move up to become Chairman of Centaur and leave the coal face.

The fact that I was Managing Director, Chairman and Senior Analyst had raised major concerns during the flotation and Zeus were insistent upon me taking action to strengthen Centaur's management framework. Given that Centaur's annual turnover exceeded £1.5 million in the previous year we now had to have our accounts independently audited and I felt that the time was right to start moving us away from a small private company to a corporate structure.

These factors, combined with my previous experience in management consultancy led to a change in my overall outlook, When Andrew and I had started Centaur Tipping Service in 2000, our entire focus was on tipping horses. However four years later we were running a million pound plus turnover business and my focus became increasingly targetted on the commercial development of that business. Yes of course the performance of our horseracing services was of critical importance but we also needed to develop a range of products for other markets if the business was to continue to expand.

The first important step to take was to recruit a capable Managing Director who could cement our position in the punter market and create a niche for us in the vastly bigger investor market. Alan Moore told me many times that he was that person, however having worked with him over the previous year I had decided that was not the case. Although Alan was a brilliant salesman, his management style was completely alien to me , in that he upset almost everyone who he came into contact with and was motivated solely by financial objectives. I realised the importance to Centaur of recruiting the right person and used headhunters to find me prospective candidates.

Three months and several unsuccessful interviews later and I was no further forward but was convinced that I should not rush the process. I had a bi- annual meeting coming up with Andy Mcinally the Managing Director of our telephone services provider, Greenland Interactive Services Limited. Over the last three years I had become friendly with Andy and we usually combined our meetings with lunch and an afternoon's racing. Andy had been CEO at Greenland for four years, he was a hard- nosed Scot with a dry sense of humour and I knew that he knew Centaur's business and was also interested in horse racing.

Over lunch I told Andy of my plans and my frustration at not being able to appoint a Managing Director. I was pretty surprised when he said that he was very interested in the job and that he agreed with me about Centaur's scope for expansion. The main difficulty from his perspective was whether Centaur would be able to match the salary /benefits package he had received at Greenland. After some weeks of negotiations we concluded a deal at £120,000 per annum plus a bonus linked to net profits and a new Mercedes plus first class travel.

In normal circumstances, I would have undertaken a detailed personal background check. However I had met Andy many times in a commercial setting over the last three years and felt this obviated the need for carrying out checks, particularly when a review of his CV showed that he had held a senior marketing position at Pepsi for several years. In view of the importance of this appointment, we used our retained lawyers, Hay and Kilner of Newcastle –On – Tyne to draft his contract on the basis of a three year contract with a 6 month notice period to apply for both parties.

Andy took up his role in September 2004 and Hazel and I moved into a beautiful house in the Lake District, which we had bought with my deferred salary . It was my intention to work one or two days a week in the Seahouses office and chair a monthly board meeting. As part of the deal with Andy I set out a range of performance indicators that we would discuss quarterly and they would form the basis of any bonus paid to him. After the first month Andy asked me to restrict my time in the Seahouses office as he felt it was undermining his ability to make major decisions, I agreed.

LIVING MY DREAMS

Centaur Bloodstock Syndicates-The Early Years

If someone had asked me back in 2000 "Why are you starting up a horseracing tipping service?" one of the reasons I would have given would have been" To make enough money to buy some racehorses."

Going back to my childhood, the thrill of seeing racehorses run and being close to these marvellous animals when they walked round the paddock, whenever my father took me to the races, still featured regularly in my memory.

Now. here I was in the middle of 2002 with a rapidly expanding racing tipping service with over 1000 paying clients. Surely many of them would share the same dream as me!

Andrew had owned shares in a number of horses before we started up Centaur, most notably the super talented Teeton Mill who had been purchased from the hunter chasing field by the Winning Line and syndicated. Andrew had further success with horses such as Crocadee.

Excuse me if I wince here at the mention of Crocadee's name. Andrew and I have tried on hundreds of occasions to win the Scoop 6. The nearest we came to winning was in January 2001 when we had 5 winners plus Crocadee. He was 6to4 favourite for the grade 2 Dipper Novices Chase at Newcastle. Everything was going along swimmingly and he was cruising along 3 lengths clear of the field on the bridle when he suddenly darted left before the 10th fence and unseated Tony Dobbin, who was riding him for the first time. We would have probably won around £100,000 –as it was we did not even get the place dividend.

Andrew was confident that we could set up a successful racing partnership model and we agreed the following policy for Centaur Bloodstock at a Board Meeting.

Centaur Racing Partnership Model

- Centaur would look to buy dual purpose horses at the October and May Horses in Training Sales
- Our purchases would be value based
- We would not buy two year olds, which in our view represented a high cost/high risk model in that only one in 7 would ever win a race.
- Centaur analysts would make notes over the course of the racing year flagging up horses that would be of interest if they were put up for sale.
- We would operate a 12- share partnership model and Centaur would look to retain one share as a purchasing fee.

- Partners would have 1/12th shares in any prize money won and sale proceeds when the horse was sold.
- Partners would receive owner's badges whenever their horse ran and would have unrestricted access to the horse in training.
- Entertainment in the form of stable visits and meals and drinks at racecourses would be recharged at cost.

There was a considerable air of excitement in the Centaur Offices over the next two months in the lead up to the 2002 Newmarket October Horses in Training Sales as we produced the marketing brochures.

Andrew, Steve and I had several selection meetings going through the sales catalogue and reviewing videos of the contenders and we ended up with a list of around 20 horses to which we affixed our budget i.e what price we would consider bidding up to.

Everything was set. We had done well for the clients in 2002 winning them nearly £20,000 on a £5,000 betting bank and we sat back and waited for the phones to ring after our marketing brochures were delivered.

It proved to be a long wait!

We then tried calling the clients to hopefully give them a chance to realise their dreams and become a successful racehorse owner. Again disappointing, most of our clients were punters who might win money with us in a month but were quite capable of losing that by betting their own fancies too.

The end result was that Andrew and I set off to the Newmarket sales with purchase orders amounting to the princely sum of £30,000, Hardly competition for Sheikh Mohammed and JP Mcmanus.

At least Centaur Bloodstock had started. We came back from the sales the proud owner of a 3 year old maiden gelding Unsigned, previously trained by James Fanshawe, purchased for 16,000 guineas. We sent Unsigned to be trained by Bob Buckler in the West Country in a rural environment quite different to Newmarket. I had earmarked the horse as a sure fire future winner when watching his last two races before the sales.

We then broke our own newly laid down rules. We met Mark Brisbourne, a trainer who we thought highly of at the sales and were persuaded by him to purchase a horse he had been offered by successful trainer Michael Jarvis, a three- year old filly called Without Words. Although Without Words had no winning form, Mark had done very well with her full brother and was keen to find a buyer. Despite not having identified the horse our-selves , we followed Mark's advice and bought the filly for £5,000.

Both horses were put away for the winter and we were able to fill up the two partnerships. Over the winter we organised a couple of stable visits to see the horses which put an end to the constant questioning as to why the horses were not running (Managing racing syndicates is definitely not a fun activity!)

The horses were working well and I could not believe the physical improvement in Without Words, who looked to have really strengthened. Into spring and we managed to persuade Bob Buckler to run Unsigned on the flat instead of making his debut over hurdles. The horse was still qualified to run in maiden races and we targetted Wolverhampton on the basis that the opposition was unlikely to be strong.

Anyone who knows Bob Buckler knows that confidence is his middle name and although he had not yet trained a winner on the flat he told us that Unsigned was trained to the minute. A further bonus was that we were able to book Oscar Urbina who had ridden the horse regularly at previous trainer's James Fanshawe's.

3rd March 2002 was D Day for Centaur Bloodstock and Unsigned looked magnificent in the paddock, winning the best turned out prize. All of his owners were present, I had given them a very confident message re betting and the horse was backed in from 9/2 to 11/4. The office also contacted the owners of Without Words and told them to have a bet.

They were off and although I was normally emotionless when watching races in which we had tipped I had to admit to a surge of adrenalin on this occasion. I need not have worried, Unsigned travelled easily the whole race, cruised into the lead 3 furlongs out and won eased down by 1.5 lengths.

Scenes of much jubilation coupled with tears from one or two of our owners (male) who had owned horses for years but had never been in the winner's enclosure.

I can honestly say from a personal perspective as a $1/12^{th}$ owner that winning at Wolverhampton with our first horse was pretty much as special as winning big races such as the Tote Gold Trophy at Chepstow and the Summer Hurdle at Market Rasen.

So far so good but anyone who knows horse racing knows that when you are on top you are probably heading for a fall.

Unsigned's win triggered off a fantastic reaction from our data- base of clients. We had been pretty much walking on water with our tips clocking up 24 winning months out of 24 and now everyone thought we were going to do the same with our purchases. We had over £100,000 pledged from current and new owners to go to the Doncaster Sales in May.

There were tremendous expectations for Without Words on her debut for Centaur on 27th March at Lingfield. She had been putting in some stunning work at Mark's over the previous month working better than horses with a 10lb higher handicap mark. Without Words opened at 16/1 and was backed in to 11/2 by her and Unsigned's owners. All of her owners were present and we were having lunch in a private box as the horses were being loaded into the stalls. Without Words was loaded first-she had looked magnificent in the paddock –then disaster struck. Not one but 3 horses refused to go into the stalls without maximum assistance and over 5 minutes passed to the off. There was a stunned silence in the box as Without Words broke slowly trailed the field and came in last –what was worse she was bleeding from both nostrils having broke blood vessels during the race.

You have to think that Without Words was undone by being too keyed up and having an extraordinarily long wait during the stalls. However, despite all of Mark's considerable efforts he could not get her to win a race in the two years we owned her. The first and last time I would purchase a horse on trainer's advice.

CENTAUR BLOODSTOCK STARS

Over the next 9 years Centaur bought over 30 horses, almost all of them at the Newmarket October and Doncaster May and October sales. Our purchasing model was extremely successful and over a 9 -year period any one purchasing a share in all of our horses would have won over 60 races and made a profit.

How many bloodstock operations can claim a record like that? Favourites Racing, perhaps the best known dual purpose bloodstock firm , who took over the Winning Line's bloodstock operation, made significant losses for their clients over the same period, despite spending 10 times our budget.

Centaur's owners and Andrew and I enjoyed some fabulous racing moments in the 10 years we were running the Centaur bloodstock operation and I have described some of them below. However for me one of the most uplifting moments was going to see our horses work in the winter at fantastic locations such as the Lambourn Valley where Charlie Mann trained for us .

Hear are my top ten;

Seahouses Office Staff in 2009

Border Artist Winning at Musselburgh

	PURCHASE PRICE	RACES WON	PRIZE MONEY WON	SALE PRICE	PROFIT AFTER TRAINING EXPENSES
	£		£	£	£
HASTY PRINCE	17500	4	110,000	250,000	300,000
OVERSTRAND	21500	4	50,000	215000	193,000
TREATY FLYER	10,000	7	110,000	20,000	100,000
CRATHORNE	17,500	9	65000	RETIRED	5,000
BAGAN	27000	7	30000	RETIRED	(57,000)
BORDER ARTIST	2000	5	35000	6000	BROKE EVEN
OSTFANNI	12500	3	10000	30000	BRO5E EVEN
QUETZAL	14500	3	10000	12500	BROKE EVEN
ALFIE RICH	6000	2	3750	12500	7000
RIGHTFUL RULER	18000	2	15000	4000	(40,000)

Hasty Prince

Hasty Prince was undoubtedly the best example of the Centaur Bloodstock purchasing model. He was a very talented but somewhat inconsistent 4 year- old trained by Ben Hanbury when he went to the Newmarket October Sales in 2002 with a flat rating of 90.

The horse went straight into my purchase note- book when I saw him demolish a field of good handicappers at Haydock in July 2002 over 1mile and three furlongs. He failed to repeat this performance in three subsequent runs but I saw him as a lightly raced horse, which had not been knocked about in his races when his chance had gone.

That year he was my number one purchase choice at the sales with a budget of £45,000. I could not attend the sales that year as I was on holiday in Tenerife but Steve Taylor and Andrew Cork did the buying based upon the lists I had prepared, with me on the end of the phone giving instructions when bidding got near to my budget figure.

As it turned out I did not need to be involved with the bidding in Hasty Prince's case. We had an amazing piece of good fortune.

Hasty Prince was one of the last lots into the ring on the third day of the four- day sale at 8.30pm. Fortunately for us very few bidders had stayed the course.

After a speedy auction Hasty Prince was knocked down to us for 17,000 guineas, daylight robbery for a horse with a flat rating of 90

I sent Hasty Prince to Jonjo O Neill as I really rated one of his jockeys Liam Cooper and thought he would be perfect for the horse. I had known Jonjo for over 30 years from when I was Deputy Director of Finance at Eden District Council and he trained and lived in the area. Jonjo was one of the top trainers in the UK and a few years earlier had moved his training establishment from Cumbria to Jackdaws Cottage in the heart of the Cotswolds to be the main trainer for the legendary JP Mcmanus.

Jackdaws' was quite simply Hollywood for horses by the time JP had finished investing in the already superb facilities. The horses had access to solariums and swimming pools and the whole complex was floored with rubber so that horses did not run the risk of slipping on concrete or tarmac. The schooling grounds and gallops were magnificent , far better than most racecourses.

While most trainers had a room to meet owners or invited you into their kitchen, Jackdaws had a guest - house for owners with wall -to wall plasma televisions and teletext screens not to mention a permanent hot and cold buffet and free bar. I only had to mention these facilities in my daily telephone message to clients once and Hasty Prince was fully syndicated at £3500 per share plus £200 per month for training and running costs.

That investment turned out to be money extremely well spent. Hasty had a great career as a hurdler which saw him win The £70,000 Concept Hurdle at Sandown and The £50,000 Tote Trophy at Chepstow and finish placed in the £100,000 Greatwood and Bula Hurdles at Cheltenham. He also gave his owners two great days out in the special owners facilities when he took part in the English and Irish Champion Hurdles in 2004.

However, it so nearly did not happen!

Hasty started his hurdling career with an extremely promising second of fourteen runners in December

2003 at Uttoxeter. That day he was ridden by an amateur jockey as Liam Cooper had to ride for JP Mcmanus elsewhere. Mr R Flavin got the fright of his life when he let out an inch of reign as the horse entered the home straight in last place. Hasty simply cruised past the whole field and went into the lead approaching the last hurdle only to blunder and get caught near the line. This was a very promising introduction and he followed it up with a good win under Liam at Huntingdon.

By this time Jonjo had realised that he had a potential grade one or two performer on his hands. Our plan was to run him once more then to give him a short holiday, miss Cheltenham and go to Aintree for the grade 2 novice over 2.5 miles as a fresh horse.

Jonjo chose a novice hurdle at Newbury on February 8th for his third run. Once again I was in Tenerife avoiding the British winter, which played havoc with my chest. The race was a good contest but I was quite happy with that as we would get to see how good Hasty was. I was far less happy however when Jonjo rang me late morning to tell me that Liam had had to go to Haydock to ride for JP in order to ride a planned gamble and as he could not contact me he had put Tony Dobbin up.

This should not have raised any concerns, as Tony was a top jockey and the leading rider in the North of England, however, following the Crocadee incident with the Scoop 6 and several other unlucky losses when tipping for the clients I had come to regard him as a jinx. Let me say straight away that the jinx was well and truly laid in future years and Tony rode several winners for Centaur but when Jonjo gave me the news I had this awful premonition of doom.

There was nothing to be done however and when the race started I was sat anxiously watching in a front row seat in our favourite pub, Strikers in Puerto Colon in Tenerife. My fears seemed groundless as Hasty gave an exhibition round of jumping and was sat cruising just behind the front two horses as they swung into the home straight.

Then disaster struck!

At the third last hurdle the leading horse fell directly in Hasty's path and despite heroic efforts, Tony Dobbin was unable to avoid him and came out of the saddle. Hasty was really spooked by this, as nothing had ever happened to him like it in his racing life to date and he veered violently left and hurtled toward the running rail at tremendous speed. Hazel and I let out a gasp and she hid her head in my shoulder fearing the worst, however, Newbury were one of the first racecourses to replace the old concrete running rails with plastic and Hasty smashed through the rails without doing himself any real harm. He was eventually caught and returned safely home. Phew!

Hasty never got to Aintree that year as he picked up an infection however he entered the 2003/4 national hunt season with a handicap mark of 132. Jonjo knew what he had under wraps and the horses' first run was in the £50,000 Tote Gold Trophy at Chepstow. He turned this race into a procession winning on the bridle by 5 lengths under Liam Cooper after again coming from last to first. This performance showed how unlucky we were not to go to Aintree.

Next up was the £100,000 Greatwood Hurdle at Cheltenham and a major disagreement over riding tactics!

Hasty was a raging hot favourite at 10/11 for the feature race at Cheltenham's October Meeting. Jonjo contacted me midweek saying that as we were dropping back to 2 miles against some speedy top class handicap hurdlers he thought we should vary his usual tactics of coming late from the rear of the field and be ridden more positively. I disagreed strongly saying why change a proven winning formula.

We were still disagreeing about this issue as the horse was being saddled. As things turned out Hasty was ridden in 4th or 5th in a relatively small field for such a big handicap. He swept into the lead as they turned into the home straight but was passed after the last and finished third beaten by a hitherto disappointing horse of Paul Nicholls, Rigmarole. We will never know if he would have won if ridden differently.

To be fair to Jonjo he failed to win his next race, the Bula Hurdle at the December Cheltenham despite being ridden with exaggerated hold up tactics by Tony McCoy, although he was not beaten far in that category 1 hurdle by Rigmarole, Rooster Booster and Davenport Milennium.

2004 brought along disappointing runs in the Tote Gold Trophy, Champion Hurdle and Irish Champion Hurdle around a stunning win in the £70,000 Concept Hurdle at Sandown at the end of April, where he annihilated a strong field including several horses who had finished ahead of him in the Champion Hurdle.

The Irish Champion Hurdle for which he was sent off third favourite ended a busy year in which Hasty Prince's official rating had climbed from 132 to 157. He appeared to be around 7lb-10lb below the very top of the hurdling ranks but was well capable of winning Grade 2 contests.

I went to Jackdaws with Andrew in May 2004 to discuss Hasty's programme for the following year. Jonjo felt that the horse should go novice chasing, Andrew and I strongly disagreed. We thought that Hasty did not have the size to go chasing and his fast daisy cutting style of hurdling could cause real problems if he was to hit a fence. Our preferred option was to campaign in him in the two and a half mile category 2 and three hurdles in Ireland and England and think about the Stayers Hurdle at Aintree and Punchestown at the end of the 2004/5season.

We agreed to continue these discussions but I got a telephone call a week later from Jonjo saying that JP Mcmanus really admired our horse and would be prepared to buy him. I explained to Jonjo my position as Head of the Partnership that owned Hasty and said that we would have to get a majority vote to sell. JP was prepared to offer £250,000 and eventually there was a clear majority to accept the offer.

The deal was finalised before the start of the 2004/5 season and the syndicate owners ended up getting a return, including prize money won, of £23,000 each for an investment of £3500- a return of over 650% in less than three years not to mention the emotional and social return in being there when he ran in and won big races.

Hasty Prince went novice chasing the following year and a after an awful start, in which he gave Tony McCoy two crashing falls, he gradually got his act together and twice placed in handicap chases at the Cheltenham festival. However another crashing fall in 2007 proved fatal and ended the career of a much loved and talented racehorse.

I cannot leave the Hasty Prince section without mentioning two anecdotes

The first was one of the best moments of my bloodstock career. Shortly after his sale I received a really nice letter from JP Mcmanus thanking me for selling him a horse who he really admired and enclosing a gold pen, The pen still has pride of place on my work desk in my study today.

The second was to recount that, after we had syndicated Hasty back in November 2003 and were just waiting for the share cheques to come in, I got a telephone call from one of the people who had agreed verbally to purchase a share. He was an ex footballer from the west country who fancied himself as a bit of a racing expert .He told me that after looking at Hasty Prince's form and videos he had decided the horse would never make a hurdler and would not be sending me his payment. His share was taken up by an elderly couple from Watford who did not have a great deal of spare capital but never missed a race and it gave me a great deal of satisfaction over the next two years to see them live the Hasty Prince Dream!

Overstrand

We bought Overstrand at the same sale as Hasty Prince for 21,500 guineas. He was a lightly raced three- year old winner of a one and half mile handicap for Amanda Perrett. I sent him to be trained by Mary Reveley a veteran northern trainer who was undoubtedly one of the most able trainers in the country.

Mary was in the process of retiring and handing over the stable to her son Keith and both had a hand in training Overstrand. I went to see Mary in November after the horse had settled in and went to see him on the gallops. Afterwards in Mary's kitchen (Quite different to Jonjo's facilities!) she told me that they really liked the horse and said he would win me some good races but that she was a great believer in giving three year old hurdlers a quiet introduction in their first year over hurdles. Accordingly he ran three times without distinction including in The Triumph Hurdle at Cheltenham.

While we were at Cheltenham Mary guaranteed me that the horse would win his first race in his novice year after the 30th April. Mary did not make promises like that idly and the horse trotted in at Perth on the 3rd May, having been heavily backed from 9/2 to 11/4.

Overstrand had been syndicated at £3750 for a 1/12th share plus £200 per month for training and administration expenses. It took a while before we sold all the shares but running him at the Cheltenham Festival did the trick and he was fully syndicated by the time he ran at Perth. I rang all the owners and told them to back him to recoup the capital cost of the share. Most did which gave them a great start to ownership with us –two or three already had shares with Hasty Prince.

Overstrand won his next two novice hurdles at Market Rasen and Carlisle , without coming off the bridle, at short prices ridden by one of Mary's apprentices Owen Nelmes It was then that Mary informed me of her grand plan. She felt that

Overstrand was capable of producing form equivalent to an official rating of 140, which meant that he was currently some 20lb ahead of the handicapper. Against this, he had never run in a handicap and was inexperienced. She had targeted the £50,000 William Hill Handicap Hurdle at Sandown on the 3rd December and if he ran well there he would go to the £100,000 Ladbroke Handicap Hurdle at Ascot shortly before Christmas.

All of Overstrand's owners turned up at Sandown and we had a box booked for a private lunch. This turned out to be probably our best ever days' racing. The wine was already flowing freely by the time we went into the paddock before the race. The betting was also flowing and we had backed Overstrand from 12/1 into 9/1 by the time the race had started.

Mary had pulled off a coup by booking Ruby Walsh to ride Overstrand, as Paul Nicholls did not have a runner in the race. The plan was to hold Overstrand up at the back of the field then let him come with a steady run up the long home straight at Sandown. Ruby executed this to perfection. On turning for home he was in last place but travelling easily. Ruby pulled him out to the outside and let out an inch of rein. The response was electric Overstrand cruised past the field with Ruby still stood up in the stirrups making high class horses such as Our Vic and Monkerhostin look as if they were slow. He went on to win by an eased down 5 lengths.

Afterward, amid much jubilation in the winners' enclosure Ruby, who was extremely impressed by the horse, was telling the owners that they had a Cheltenham winner on their hands. It proved to be a very long day, and night! I can recall Andrew driving two or three of the owners' home in the early hours of the morning, in order to help them avoid the rolling pin!

A defining moment came next for the Overstrand Partnership. On the Monday after Sandown, Mary Reveley rang me to say that Ruby Walsh had been in contact with her and he had a group of Irish owners who were prepared to offer £225,000 for Overstrand. This meant that each of the owners in the Overstrand Partnership had to decide whether to take an immediate profit of almost £20,000 including prize money won or keep the horse with the prospects of the Ladbrokes Hurdle then Cheltenham, Aintree and Punchestown.

Andrew and I wrote to the other 10 owners explaining the options. To our amazement the voting came back 10 to nil in favour of keeping their shares. Andrew and I abstained from the voting but, having a commercial approach to racing and knowing the risks involved we would have sold.

Ascot came next for the Ladbrokes Hurdle day on Saturday 20th December. Once again we had a private box for lunch and a one hundred per cent attendance from our owners. The day started brilliantly,.

On my way up to the box in the morning I bumped into Francois Doumen. We were privileged to have a horse in training at the time with Francois who was probably the greatest trainer in the world. We talked for a while and he told me that he thought he had an up and coming star in his runner in the first race, a lightly raced novice named Krach.

When our box had filled about 30 minutes before the off I told the other owners of my encounter with Francois and asked for contributions toward a bet on the horse from those interested. I suggested that they should back the horse to win what they were going to put on Overstrand later. Five minutes later Andrew was sent down to the ring with £20,000 to invest.

Krach won pulling a cart by 10 lengths having been backed from 7to4 to 11 to10. He would have undoubtedly justified Francois's high opinion of him but was tragically fatally injured in a training accident shortly afterward. I went down to the ring to congratulate Francois and he said to me with that famous twinkle in his eye that he could not understand how the horse had started at such a short price, as the owners did not gamble!

Overstrand had been his usual demonic self in the saddling area that day and broke one of his stable girls ribs! He had settled down however when he came into the beautiful leafy paddock at Ascot. Mary had been unable to book Ruby Walsh for the ride as Paul Nicholls had a fancied runner in the race and had booked top Irish jockey Barry Geraghty. This seemed like a good move, however after only three hurdles we knew it was a mistake. Horse and rider did not get on at all and Overstrand made errors at two of the first three hurdles. He ran on to finish 7th of 17 but never travelled with any fluency.

From there on in it was downhill all the way for Overstrand in Centaur ownership. He went to Punchestown after a break in the spring and picked up a nasty abcess, which kept him off the course for a year. During this time Mary Reveley retired and handed over the reins to her son Keith. Overstrand did not recover his form for Keith or for Martin Todhunter, who took over training the horse in 2006.

The syndicate had become demoralised (Memories are short in racing!) with the lack of recent success and voted to sell the horse. Martin said that the best way financially would be to put the horse in a claimer with a high claiming price and go for a big bet. He executed this perfectly, the horse ran away with a claiming hurdle at Perth and was claimed for £16,000. The owners were told to put at least one years training fees on him to win and we took over £100,000 out of the ring.

That was not the end of the Overstrand story. He was eventually reclaimed, after dissappointing for Philip Gray, by a new trainer Dr Richard Newland. Richard is now a very successful trainer specialising in revitalising horses, which have lost their form. He really worked the oracle with Overstrand who won many races for him including the William Hill Hurdle at Sandown for a second time. I watched that race and have to confess there was a tear in my eye as he cruised past the opposition again.

Treaty Flyer

One of the major elements of Centaur's Professional Gambling course was to teach delegates my approach to race reading. Without giving the game away, this involved stopping the video of national hunt races at the third last and evaluating which horses were travelling the best but did not go on to finish in the first three.

Treaty Flyer caught my eye when running in two claimers in the summer of 2008 when travelling extremely well. But in my view she did not stay the trip of 2mile 4 furlongs and two mile 6 furlongs she was running over. She was a 7year old mare who had had useful form for Pat Murphy as a 5 year old but had a year off with tendon trouble. I thought she would be a good horse to claim and pull off a gamble back to two miles, then resell.

At the time I was extremely impressed by the abilities of a Welsh trainer Allison Thorpe, who seemed to have a real flair for training fillies and mares. I sent her Treaty Flyer in late summer 2008. Treaty had a couple of ok runs on soft ground but Allison said that in her view the horse would benefit from a winter at grass and would be better on good ground.

As I was looking for a quick turnaround I just brought in one owner to join Andrew and I, Peter Tosh who was a long term Centaur client and was also Allison's accountant. As it turned out how wrong could I have been!

Treaty made her reappearance in a claiming hurdle at Ludlow. Andrew, Peter and I went for a coup in the ring as Allison had told us the horse was jumping out of its skin. Treaty won easily by 9 lengths having been backed in from 7/1 to 11/4. Even better no claims.

The plan was to get in and out quickly so Allison entered her in a selling hurdle at Fakenham ten days later. Tony McCoy took the ride and she won straightforwardly, again heavily backed again there was no bid. Off to Plumpton next five days later for another seller this time Richard Johnson was on board.

Allison had convinced us by now that if she won we should keep her. She did by 15 lengths with Dickie stood up in the saddle from start to finish. We bought her in and I got a new partnership to buy her for £15,000 from the existing partnership. Andrew, Peter and I kept one share each.

Over the next six months Treaty ran another 11 times in Centaur colours winning four more times and placing 6 times. Wins included the valuable Summer Hurdle at Market Rasen and a £10,000 hurdle at Ffos LLas. Her handicap mark increased from 95 to 137, a tribute to the training skills of

Allison Thorpe, who sadly had to give up training due to lack of owner support in 2012.

Owners who bought in to Treaty after her first 3 wins at a $1/12^{th}$ share price of £2500 ended up with a profit of round about £4000 each after we sold her in October 2009 to Ron Huggins of Double Trigger fame, who was looking to acquire a nice national hunt mare for breeding purposes. They should have made massive profits on the gambling front too but I am afraid that for some reason I began to underestimate the mare and only small sums were punted on her when she won two three big hurdle races at 14/1 , 12/1 and then 5/1.

Ron's plan was to try to get some black type in Treaty's form- book by placing in a listed hurdle. She would undoubtedly have achieved this but for over-jumping and falling at Sandown and Kempton in 2010. Ron brought her back to go chasing as a 9 year old to my surprise but she looked a high- class recruit when winning easily first time over fences. She was then miles clear at the last fence at Perth when falling at the last fence and fatally breaking her shoulder.

Many tears were shed over Treaty's demise and I received hundreds of emails even though we did not own her any more. She really captured the heart of jump racing supporters.

Bagan

Bagan was a high-class hurdler and chaser who I bought from Henry Cecil as a 5 year old in 2004. He ended up winning three novice hurdles and 4 chases for Centaur and achieved a rating of 133 in both fields.

He was significant in that he was the focal point in what turned out to be a stormy relationship betwee trainer Charlie Mann and myself.

Things started with Charlie on a high note. I went to the 2004 October sales with a budget of round about £130,000. I had Bagan down as my number one choice having tried to buy him privately over the past two years. He had caught my eye when he made a delayed debut as a 3year old in July 2002 in a one and a half mile maiden at Beverley finishing third. I tried to buy him at the end of his three-year old career but unusually for Henry Cecil he kept the then maiden three year old in training as a four year old with a rating of just 79.

I took the hint and Centaur clients had a big win when Bagan won at York in summer 2003 at 50/1! Again he was retained at the end of his four-year old career, much to my disappointment. Still it would be third time lucky for us at Newmarket.

My plans were to acquire horses for Martin Todhunter who was Centaur's number one trainer at the time, Keith Reveley who had taken over from his mother Mary, Bob Buckler and Brendan Powell. What I usually did at the sales was to get the trainers to go and check out the horses I was interested in physically before I bid on them. Much to my surprise all four trainers went to see Bagan and came back advising me not to buy the horse on the grounds that his legs would not stand up to hurdling/chasing. Reluctantly I took their advice and did not bid on the horse.

The following morning I was having my breakfast with Andrew and reading the Newmarket Sales section of the Racing Post and noticed that Bagan had been bought by Charlie Mann, a well-known Lambourn Trainer, for 27,000 guineas. This aroused my curiosity and I made it my intention to talk to Charlie to see why he had bought a horse who appeared to be unsound.

As it happened I almost bumped into Charlie as soon as I arrived at Tattersalls. I introduced myself and asked him about Bagan. Charlie told me that he knew Henry Cecil's head lad well and had been told that the horse was fine despite looking off behind. Best to keep him away from good to firm/firm ground. Charlie looked at the horses's form, which was excellent, and decided to take the plunge.

Charlie did not have an owner for the horse and despite the fact that I had spent the Centaur budget I agreed to buy him giving Charlie a small profit. I publicised a champagne breakfast and stable tour/gallops outing at Charlie's state of the art training establishment in November in Centaur's client magazine. Over 50 people came and we had a great morning and I was able to fully syndicate Bagan.

Bagan had a good first season, looking to be a high-class novice. After an initial fourth behind a subsequent group 1 winner at Bangor he won his next three novice hurdles at Ludlow, Kempton and Doncaster impressively, the last less than 10 days before Cheltenham.

This is when the honeymoon period ended!

I had discussed Bagan's programme for 2004/5 with Charlie on several occasions. I had made it clear that I thought he was a horse who should be campaigned on flat tracks, as he had to have treatment to his legs after each race. However, Charlie was desperate for him to run at the Cheltenham Festival in March as he had never had a winner there and Bagan would have a chance in the 2mile 5 furlong grade 1 novice hurdle. I had made it clear to him before I went on holiday that I wanted Bagan to run at the Aintree Festival in April in the grade 2 novice hurdle as he would be going there as a fresh horse on a flat track.

When I got back from holiday I found out that Charlie had talked to the owners after the Doncaster race and persuaded them that the horse should run at Cheltenham. Bagan ran there and injured himself coming down the hill and he was never to win another hurdle race for us. He sustained a tendon injury shortly afterward that kept him off the course for over a year.

Bagan was eventually responsible for the split between Centaur and Charlie Mann in 2007, which I cover in the Centaur Trainer's chapter. He was a magnificent specimen of a horse who in my mind failed to achieve his true potential.

Crathorne

Crathorne was a multi -talented horse who won 8 races for Centaur in three years between 1994 and 1997, five hurdle races, two chases and 1 flat race. The horse was trained for us by Martin Todhunter for the first 4 years of his Centaur career and came back from a year off with leg problems to add a ninth win in his final race for Allison Thorpe.

The credit for buying Crathorne goes entirely to Steve Taylor. When entered in the 2004 October sales, Crathorne had won only one of 25 races on the flat for James Bethell. However Steve, one of our top racing analysts, saw something in the horse and told me I had to buy him. I felt a lot more confident about him when Martin Todhunter chose the horse to be trained by him even though he was our cheapest buy at 17,500 guineas at the sales.

Crathorne was syndicated at £2,500 per share and even though we were unable to sell him at the end of his racing career, he broke even in terms of prize money won and also landed some good bets. He was one of the gutsiest horses I have ever seen and liked nothing better than to get into a head to head scrap. Perhaps the greatest tribute to him was his win at Hexham over fences in 2007 in truly deplorable conditions, which he would have hated.

Before I leave Crathorne I will leave you with a quiz question. Which is the only horse to come over from Germany to win at Catterick? The answer is Beaney who was trained by Mario Hofer.

I remember this only too well as he foiled a first time out gamble by us when we backed Crathorne, who Martin had schooled very well, in from 12 to 1 to 8/1. Crathorne looked sure to win as he cruised past the other English horses and went clear as the horses came into the home straight only to be caught and passed in the final furlong by the invader.

Border Artist

When Steve and Andrew arrived at the October 2002 Newmarket Sales they used their initiative to the benefit of Centaur and its owners. It was announced at the Sales that morning that there had been a pile up on the A14 and that there would be considerable delays, nonetheless the sales would proceed on time.

Andrew and Steve soon twigged that there was hardly anyone in the ring and there were profits to be made. They bought three early lots even though they were not on my purchase list. They quickly sold two on at a profit to trainers who had been coming to buy the horses back in but decided to keep Border Artist a three year old trained by Michael Blanshard, as we had only paid 2,000 guineas for him which was way below market price.

I decided to send Border Artist to David Nicholls who was widely acknowledged as the top trainer of sprinters in the UK. Thus started a fascinating three-year spell, which ended in the horse winning 6 times for us before being resold for 6000 guineas. His syndicate owners ended up about even taking on board training fees of some £55,000 over the three-year period.

I would like to say that they supplemented their prize money with gambling winnings but that was not the case, as you will find out by reading the Centaur trainers paragraph.

Ostfanni

Ostfanni was an extremely well bought 3 -year old filly at 12,500 guineas at the October 2003 sales. She had previously won one race in Ireland when trained by Declan Gillespie. Tony Stafford who had been head racing journalist for the Daily Telegraph for over 20 years and worked for Centaur at the time knew Declan well and recommended the filly as a good value purchase.

We syndicated Ostfanni at £2000 per share and sent her to Martin Todhunter who also had Manoubi and

Crathorne at the time. One client Brian Dunn, who I had known since Centaur began, took a 50 per cent share.

Martin always takes his time to bring on flat horses and Ostfanni had a few quiet runs before she struck form. She then took off in 2005 winning 9 races including three on the flat before the end of her career in 2009.when she was sold to become a broodmare. Unfortunately for Centaur, Brian insisted on selling her to dissolve the partnership after her first three wins. She made 30,000 guineas and syndicate owners at least broke even. Had we kept her they would have turned a nice profit.

Alfy Rich

The most economic form of racehorse ownership is to claim a horse out of a selling or claiming race, win a race with it landing a gamble and sell it on immediately. If you can achieve this you avoid training fees of between £15,000 and £25,000 per annum.

Centaur achieved this with a horse called Alfy Rich. Alfy was a consistent but moderate novice hurdler whose hurdling was a weakness, for a small trainer, Paul Rich The horse had caught my eye as a future winner if transferred to a trainer who could improve his jumping.

I noticed the horse had been dropped to a selling hurdle for the first time at Chepstow in May 2005 and planned to claim him if he ran well. He finished second and the plan was put into action. We were successful with a £6,000 claim and straight after the race he was on his way up to Martin Todhunter's Lakeland yard.

Martin had some excellent schooling jockeys at the time in Graham Lee and Brian Harding and had just appointed a new apprentice jockey Douglas Costello who was also an extremely stylish rider.

Martin took an immediate shine to Alfy who was an extremely scopey individual. He wanted to run him in a novice hurdle and was confident the horse would win. However, like Ostfanni, Brian Dunn owned a half share in the horse and he wanted a big gamble with the least possible risk.

So, Alfy lined up for a selling hurdle at Hexham on the 20th June 2005. He looked magnificent and won pulling a cart by 15 lengths, ably ridden by Dougie having been heavily backed in the ring from 7/4 to 5/4. Then the fun and games started.

Martin grabbed me before the race ended and told me not to sell the horse as planned as he had a probable buyer at a good profit. I saw Brian and he agreed. The next thing we saw was Martin leading the horse into the winners 'enclosure with blood around his nostrils. It appeared that he had burst a blood vessel, which is what Martin told us rather loudly.

Surprisingly there were no bids for the horse despite one or two notorious bidders being present and we took the horse back home. I went to see him a couple of days later and asked Martin how long he would take to recover from his burst. A rare smile from Martin as he said " No time at all he is in at Perth next week" and he pulled out a bloodstained handkerchief from his pocket which he had used to rub around the horses nostrils to give the appearance of a burst!

Alfy did the business for us again at Perth landing the second part of a monster double with Manoubi, both being ridden by Dougie Costello and we sold him straight after the race for £12,500. A really good bit of business.

Rightful Ruler

I bought Rightful Ruler as a maiden three year old out of the Barry Hills stable for 14,000 guineas at the October 2005 Newmarket sales.

He ended up winning three hurdle races for Centaur but was of note more for featuring in our biggest losing and winning gambles.

Martin Todhunter trained the horse initially and gave him his usual quiet introduction in his first year, three runs finishing a remote third in his last run at Perth. Martin thought the horse had come on a lot over the winter and rated him on a par with

Crathorne which gave us at least 15 pounds in hand of the handicapper.

I was expecting a novice hurdle gamble as the horse was still a maiden but Martin, who is normally extremely risk averse, picked a competitive handicap at Carlisle in October 2006 for the big coup. We smashed the horse from 12/1 in the morning to 5/1 and when I went in to the betting ring before the race I noted several of the main on course representatives of the big six bookmakers present. They were obviously nervous of a landslide, which did not come as we had managed to get £50,000 each way on for the owners in the morning.

Things were not going well for Martin at the time, his yard had suffered from a virus for the past 2 years on and off and several owners had taken their horses elsewhere. Centaur had reduced our contingent too due to the wishes of our purchasing clients. I was hoping that a winning gamble for our clients immediately before the October sales would lead to a boost in purchasing funds and Martin would be a beneficiary from that process.

When your luck is out it usually stays out and that was the case with Rightful Ruler that day. He was held up by Dominic Elsworth who allowed Front Rank to get a decisive first run on him between the last two hurdles. Nevertheless he seemed certain to be second and land the each way part of our bets at the last hurdle, when clear of the third and fourth horses only for them to both finish strongly and deprive Ruler of a place near the line.

My humour was not improved when Ladbrokes on course representative came up to me and said to me " that's what you get for gambling on novices against seasoned handicappers!"

Rightful Ruler was moved to Noel Wilson's yard over the winter as part of a general reshuffle of our horses. Noel endorsed Martin's view of the horse and urged me to go for a gamble in a handicap off his current mark off 90. However I asked Noel to get the horse in top form for the Cartmel August bank holiday weekend. Hazel and I owned a house not too far from Cartmel and we organised a big on course party for the owners.

It was almost a year since Rightful's defeat at Carlisle and he was still a maiden. He was entered in a maiden hurdle and the best of the opposition was rated 103 but had not run to that mark for some time. Noel thought that Rightful was better than 110 and he went on to achieve a mark of 120.

Revenge is a dish best served cold and we organised a massive countrywide gamble on Rightful from 10/1 in the morning down to 7/2. I had engaged Graham Lee, who I rated as the best hurdles jockey in the UK, to ride the horse and I gave him clear instructions to kick clear at the second last hurdle and not to look back. In the end Graham did ease the horse up on the run in but he still won by 18 lengths!

After the race which won the 10 owners over £60,000 in betting winnings and Centaur Tipping's clients some £1.8 million I went up to the same Ladbroke's course representative and said " That's what you get for backing a well handicapped novice in a novice hurdle!

Quetzal

Quetzal was another example of the results of the Centaur Bloodstock purchasing model. I paid £14,500 guineas for him as a six year old maiden from Alan King's yard at the May 2011 Doncaster sales. The perceived wisdom was that the horse was a poor jumper of hurdles and fences.

However I had watched him and thought that he should be ridden from the front and that would improve his jumping. In any case sending him to Martin Todhunter would achieve this aim.

Martin assessed the horse and said he was extremely nervous and that his previous yard had not been able to fit him with rear shoes. We cured that by tranquilising the horse before fitting shoes and he began to gain confidence in his work.

Martin as usual gave the horse a quiet beginning, running him initially over too short a trip over fences. I can remember the Racing UK commentator saying on his debut at Cartmel " Centaur have certainly wasted their money paying £14,000 for that horse" when he finished last of 5.

Hopefully the same idiot ate his words when Quetzal jumped brilliantly from the front to win three staying chases in a row before early 2012. He was then put away for the 2012/13season with his main target to win a good staying handicap chase.

Author's Comment

Reading about Centaur's star horses may give the impression that we delivered unbridled success for our owners. Of course that was not the case. We bought the odd unsuccessful horse, three of the 31 horses that we bought were killed in action and several attempted gambles came unstuck.

Perhaps the best example of well laid plans going astray with tragic consequences was with Prince Holing who we purchased at the October 2003 Newmarket Sales from John Gosden for 26,000 guineas, almost £10,000 more than we paid for Hasty Prince the year before.

Prince Holing had an official flat rating of 89 and was hopefully a high -class hurdling recruit. We sent him to Venetia Williams with the intention of competing in the 2004 Triumph Hurdle.

However after three very disappointing runs over hurdles in which his jumping was seriously flawed I decided to move him to Martin Todhunter, who I hoped would eventually iron out the horse's jumping flaws.

After he had the horse for 3 months Martin said that we had something special if we were prepared to be patient. He first tried to get the horse's flat handicap down to a realistic level while all the time he was working on improving the horses jumping. After a series of very poor efforts his handicap mark had dropped to 65 on the flat and he was ready to go over the jumps.

Martin said that he aimed to win 3 races in a row over both codes and asked me did I want to go on the flat first or over hurdles. Unfortunately I chose hurdles. Prince Holing was entered in a novice hurdle at Sedgefield on the 4th August 2004 and we urged all of his owners, who had suffered a pretty disappointing time up until then, to attend. We went for a huge gamble shortening the horse from 20/1 to 7/2.

Everything seemed to be going swimmingly as they turned up the back straight for the final time with Prince cruising along in fourth place, having jumped really well. Then for no apparent reason the horse stumbled badly and dropped back through the field to finish 9th. I rushed to the unsaddling enclosure to see what had happened.

Martin told me that the horse had gone badly lame and wished he had not finished the race. Half an hour later and we had to call the veterinary surgeon in to put him down. As you can imagine there was a real air of despondency among the owners but Hazel as usual put things in perspective by saying that everyone should be thinking about the poor horse and should go to say their goodbyes. I would like to say that that was the case but I am afraid that few followed our lead.

My advice to all of you thinking about racehorse ownership is;

- Seek expert advice before buying
- Try to see the horse run as often as possible and visit in training
- Go for syndicate ownership, it is very cost effective compared to outright ownership
- Celebrate the good days

Although Centaur Bloodstock no longer exists I am willing to provide advice and management skills to anyone wishing to experience racehorse ownership or to extend their current portfolio. I can be contacted via <enquiries@kstips.co.uk></enquiries@kstips.co.uk>

CENTAUR BLOODSTOCK TRAINERS

Our dreams in their hands

Before I tell the tale of the trainers whom Centaur Bloodstock used between 2002 and 2012, let me start by saying that trainers in the UK face an extremely difficult task surviving. UK racing operates on ludicrously low prize money, one of the lowest on average in the world.

Prize money comes from an unsuccessful business model of a levy on bookmaker profits supplemented by sponsorship, which again comes mainly from bookmakers. It is not surprising therefore that the British Horse Racing Board bends over backwards to deliver a format of racing in the UK over a year that meets the bookmakers agenda with lots and lots of moderate races providing a continuing reason for betting shop punters to bet.

As a racehorse owner in the UK today you will regularly pick up less than £2,000 for winning a race, the equivalent of one months training fee. Contrast this with the tote monopoly systems in Australia, New Zealand and France where the average winning price is around 50 per cent of annual training expenses. Is it any wonder that UK racing is prone to horses being run other than on their merits, for gambling purposes.

I got my local MP Alan Beith, a fantastic constituency MP, to arrange a presentation by Andrew and I to the Parliamentary Select Committee on Horse Racing in 2007. We demonstrated that owners in the UK, who were responsible for putting the show on, got an unacceptably small slice of the cake. We urged the Committee to study the Australian model, which provided for on course bookmakers but an off course Tote Monopoly that included extremely well managed TAB outlets, the equivalent of our betting shops but much more family orientated. As I expected nothing happened, the Bookmakers have a very powerful political lobby operation!

Matching a horse with the right trainer is critical to achieving success in managing bloodstock. Another major factor to consider when you have built up a string of horses is to avoid the risk of the whole string being disabled if your main trainer's yard gets a virus, an increasingly common occurrence. As we built our string of horses up at Centaur we operated a policy of not having more than 4 horses with a single trainer.

We spent a lot of time deciding where our horses should be trained and over the 10 years we were in existence we used 20 separate trainers. We experienced both success and failure. A fundamental element of Centaur's bloodstock management policy was that we would move horses around if they were not achieving our aims. This was something new we brought to the table and although not popular with trainers, it was undoubtedly beneficial for our owners.

I will deal with our trainers in chronological order.

Bob Buckler

Bob Buckler was a trainer/farmer based in Somerset. He was a hands on trainer ably assisted by his then wife Nell, who had a show jumping and point to point background. Bob immediately impressed me when I met him at the 2002 October sales and was of considerable help in vetting my list of horses. Andrew and I decided to send him Unsigned, the first horse Centaur bought, as we thought the horse had the scope to develop into a chaser in the future.

Bob trained for us for three years and was a marvellous host for a number of social events we held at his yard. He also planned and landed a massive coup for Centaur at our annual open day in June 2004 at Worcester Racecourse where we sponsored the whole card. Our horse Unsigned won, having been backed in by our clients from 6/1 to 11/8.

However I was becoming increasingly worried about the condition of his gallops, and when one of our new horses Derwent had to be put down after a stable injury our association regretfully came to an end. Andrew and I had some marvellous days at the races with Bob and it is good to see him doing well since he moved his yard.

Mark Brisbourne

I mention earlier about Mark Brisbourne and Without Words. While this and a subsequent cheap buy we placed with Mark were unsuccessful, it does not diminish my admiration for Mark as a trainer. Mark has an extended history of turning cheaply bought sows ears into silk purses and is probably the hardest working man I have ever met.

Mary and Keith Reveley

Mary Reveley was the leading Northern trainer for many years from her Saltburn yard, which was close to the Cleveland Hills and the North Sea. She traditionally had a large number of horses and ran her own syndicate operation. She was well supported by her family including her husband George and her son Keith.

The story of our decision to place Overstrand with Mary is covered earlier. We enjoyed a fantastic two years. During this time Mary handed over the reins to her son Keith with whom we were unable to establish the same relationship before Overstrand was eventually transferred to Martin Todhunter in 2006.

My abiding memories of the time at Mary's was sitting in her kitchen talking for hours about greyhound racing, something that was more than a hobby for her as she was a successful breeder. The way I looked at things she was like me, everyone she met wanted to talk about horseracing and her horses it made a pleasant change to talk about something else.

Jonjo O Neill

Jonjo 0 Neill is one of the leading trainers in the UK and was in 2003 when we gave him Hasty Prince. He is a public trainer as well as acting as private trainer for JP Mcmanus the legendary Irish gambler and businessman. His yard, Jackdaws Castle in the heart of the Cotswolds is in my view the leading national hunt training establishment in the UK and Ireland.

I have known Jonjo since the 1980's when I was Deputy Director of Finance at Eden District Council in the Lake District. Jonjo was the top northern national hunt jockey and won the champion jockeys title twice in a career as a jockey, which stretched from 1970 to 1986. He rode 901 winners in a career that was dogged by a spate of serious injuries.

Jonjo was coming to the end of his riding career in 1986 when he was part of a hugely successful partnership with the mare Dawn Run. She had won the Champion Hurdle for Jonjo and Irish trainer Paddy Mullins in 1984 and she was being aimed at a history making victory in the Cheltenham Gold Cup. Dawn Run was Jonjo's ride but his place in history looked to have been denied him when he took a crashing fall in December and smashed his thigh.

The newspapers gave Jonjo little or no chance of taking the ride at Cheltenham with an injury that normally took a year to recover from. However they had reckoned without the strength of character and courage in adversity of the Irishman. I received a telephone call in early January asking if I could make Penrith's swimming baths and gymnasium available for Jonjo to work on his thigh out of hours. The Council agreed and Jonjo was to be seen swimming and working on the exercise bikes every day/night throughout January and February. The rest is history. Jonjo made the ride and rode Dawn Run to victory, the only horse ever to complete the Champion Hurdle and Gold Cup double. Jonjo retired from the saddle shortly after that epic victory.

When we sent him Hasty Prince, he had not been long at Jackdaws, having spent the first part of his training career in Cumbria. Moving to Jackdaws meant scope to train many more horses and JP had sent him some 50 horses shortly before Hasty arrived.

An amusing event occurred which brought home the challenges Jonjo had to cope with at the time. I had arranged for the Hasty Prince syndicate to have a morning at Jonjo's yard one Saturday before he had his first run for the stable. Everything went very well. We were welcomed by Jonjo's wife Jackie. She took us for some refreshment at the superb owners facility and then arranged transport for us to meet Jonjo on the gallops.

With some 130 horses to exercise, most of Jonjo's morning was spent driving up and down the uphill gallop watching the horses at work and looking for injuries or progress. We arrived at the foot of the gallops to be met by Jonjo coming down the hill backwards in his jeep at about 90 miles per hour!

He met us with his usual cheerful grin, probably the warmest smile I have ever encountered, and asked our owners to split into 3 groups in 3 jeeps as Hasty would be working in the next group to go up the gallops. There was an immediate rush for the other two jeeps!

Andrew and I settled in Jonjo's jeep with his Head Lad and one of our owners while the other two jeeps followed up the hill keeping pace with a group of 6-8 horses. Jonjo started talking about Hasty as we went up the hill and explaining the training regime but I could see that all the time he was trying to catch the head lads' eye. It took me a while to realise that with all the new horses arriving he simply did not know which horse was Hasty! We soon put him out of his misery and after Hasty's first run he became one of the main horses in the yard, never to be forgotten again!

Although we did not place another horse with Jonjo following Hasty Prince and Manoubi, who at 52,000 guineas was an expensive failure for us, we have remained on the best of terms with him and he recently allowed us to do a pre Cheltenham feature film from his yard.

Venetia Williams

We placed two horses bought at the Horses In Training Sale with Venetia Williams at her Herefordshire stables, Johnny Oscar and Prince Holing. Both were very useful on the flat but failed to deliver a win for us over jumps.

Venetia was very helpful to us from a client point of view and we had a marvellous and very well attended stable tour at her yard in 2003. However syndicate ownership demands quick results and we moved Prince Holing to Martin Todhunter. Unfortunately Johnny Oscar was killed at Cartmel on his third run when looking set for victory.

John Best

John Best is what I would describe as a modern trainer. He communicated very well with us in the short time he trained for us. Unfortunately the horse we had with him was killed in a training accident and accordingly we concentrated on other trainers thereafter.

Martin Todhunter

Martin Todhunter was Centaur's main trainer between 2003 and 2007 from Park Stables in Orton in Cumbria. He had a fantastic start with us winning

10 races Crathorne 3 and Ostfanni (5 in total) and two out of two with Alfy Rich.

Unfortunately his stable got a bad virus infection in 2006-7, which meant his horses underperformed for probably a year. A year in syndicate ownership is a long time and clients were starting to default on training fees with horses like Rightful Ruler and Overstrand so we began to place new horses elsewhere. Martin eventually turned things round and it was great to send Quetzal to him in 2011. He repaid our faith immediately with three wins with a horse, which had never won previously.

I have known Martin for some 35 years, from the days when he was a leading amateur rider for the powerful Gordon Richards 'Greystoke yard in Cumbria and then Head Lad for the famous trainer who was a real martinet. At the time my first wife and I used to own a Post Office and General Dealers and I can remember Martin calling in on his way back from the races every Saturday evening to buy a bottle of gin. He needed it, as life at Greystoke was not easy!

Martin is the best trainer I have used for getting a novice to jump well and he worked the oracle several times with horses we transferred to him from other yards. He would and should have been a leading trainer in my view but for two main reasons.

Despite being a very imposing man he was and is very shy. I can remember when we had a stable tour with some 30 clients at his beautiful Lakeland stable he disappeared for most of the time until I found him hidden behind the house puffing away heavily on a cigarette. The second reason was a reluctance to run horses in the south, Steve my number three used to say Martin got a nosebleed when he travelled south of Wetherby!

Dermot Weld

Centaur was privileged to have horses trained by Dermot Weld and Francois Doumen two of the greatest trainers in the world.

I rang Dermot more in hope than expectation to tell him that I was hoping to buy a horse called Mesmeric at the October 2003 Newmarket Sales and was wondering if he would like to train it. The horse had a flat rating of 101 and I was delighted when Dermot agreed to take the horse even though he normally did not take on older horses. To have a horse trained by the only European to win the Melbourne Cup was evidence of the fact that Centaur's reputation was building.

I was expecting to pay over 40,000 guineas for Mesmeric but there was a strong rumour that the horse had problems. I rang Dermot and said that the horse may have issues and he said do not go over 25,000 but he was a vet and was confident that he could cure most things if given time.

We bought Mesmeric for 18,500 guineas and I can remember his trainer Ed Dunlop coming up to me and saying the best of luck as he did not think we could get the horse back on the track.

Dermot certainly had his work cut out with Mesmeric but the horse was back on the track in April 2004 in a novice hurdle at Navan. He ran a very promising 4th in a big field.

Prior to this in March 2004 came one of my most enjoyable days at the helm of Centaur. We arranged a stable visit to Dermot's yard at the Curragh. The visit was fully attended despite the fact that we had to travel to Ireland and back. As Dermot has over 100 horses in training, I expected that the tour would be carried out by one of his assistants, however Dermot not only welcomed us personally but spent the whole morning with us and gave us a personal tour around all of his horses. Awesome!

Mesmeric ended up winning one race for Dermot and finished a close second twice. He then asked if we would transfer the horse at the end of his year as he was taking on board additional two year olds.

Having that year with Dermot was for me a case of " Living the dream" something I will never forget.

Francois Doumen

There was only one thing that I could have wished for more than to have the opportunity to spend hours with Dermot Weld and that was to have a horse trained by Francois Doumen.

Francois' had taken the racing world by storm with his amazing multi group 1 winning horse on the flat Jim and Tonic and was a regular group 1 contender in UK national hunt races winning both the King George and Cheltenham Gold Cup with The Fellow.

Andrew and I had been talking about having a horse trained in France because the prize money was massively better than in the UK, the only drawback was that betting opportunities were virtually non-existent. We spent a week touring several French trainer's yards before the 2003 Arc de Triomphe but had not come to a decision before we went to the first day of the two day Arc meeting at Longchamp.

We were sitting chilling in the leafy paddock before the first race with a bottle of champagne, when who should be walking up towards us but Monsieur Doumen. I plucked up the courage to approach him and the rest was easy as his English was a lot better than mine. ! Francois had never trained a horse for a syndicate before and most of his owners came from the social elite of Europe, however I think the prospect appealed to his egalatarian instincts. More persuasively his son Thierry was about to start training too and he asked if he did well for us would we place a horse with Thierry in the future. We agreed to do so and we were off.

The only thing Francois insisted on was that he would have to select the horse for us. He was keen on buying a non-thoroughbred like The Fellow, as there were subsidy incentives for this type of horse.

Three months later Centaur owned Monzon, a 4-year old non-thoroughbred purchased for 35,000 guineas.

We managed to syndicate the horse on Francois' reputation although most of the owners were concerned about the lack of betting opportunities. I said that our aim should be to try to cover costs which was a realistic possibility given the prize money in France.

The Monzon partnership got off to a wonderful start. In the early spring, Francois invited us to his stable in the heart of Normandy to see the horse work. I pointed out that this would necessitate an overnight stay due to ferry times but he said that was no problem as he had a house near the gallops, which he used for owners to stay.

Six of us made the journey in my estate car and we arrived at the house at about nine am. Francois was there to meet us and we all enjoyed a wonderful, continental, breakfast. Then it was off to the lovely wooded gallops to see Francois's string work including Monzon. The horse worked well and I thought that that would be the end of the day.

Mais non!

What followed was undoubtedly my best day ever at Centaur. Francois told us that he would like us to return to his home for lunch. This seemed to be way beyond the call of duty but we were delighted to accept. He suggested that my son Chris travel with him to give us more room in my car and that we should follow him home, about 15 kilometres.

I will never forget that journey. I am not known for being a slow driver but in the next six to seven minutes along winding French country roads I don't think my speedometer dropped below 70mph. The ordeal did not last long however and I was rather pleased with myself that I had managed to keep Francois'car in view. Chris, who was ashen faced when we met up, and I often talk about that journey still today.

We were met by Francois' lovely wife Elizabeth.She quickly made us feel at home . Lunch was brought out about 1.30pm and the ensemble soon struck up a real rapport. It transpired that Francois and his son were very keen rugby fans and the imminent World Cup led to some spirited discussions. One of the Centaur owners Gerry Stevens was still playing rugby himself and at one time during the afternoon he took Francois's son out for some coaching.

I have never known time pass as quickly as it did that afternoon/evening. Towards the end of daylight Francois took us for a walk around the paddocks surrounding his home and there was the recently retired Jim and Tonic with some of his other famous horses. When we got back dinner was laid out! It was well after midnight that we finally left. I regret that I never had the opportunity to return Francois' wonderful hospitality.

Unfortunately Monzon did not live up to the expectations created by our amazing first visit to France. He proved to be extremely temperamental, refusing to start on two occasions when poor Andrew had taken syndicate members a long way to see him. Francois managed to win a bumper with him and place once over hurdles and fences at Auteuil but suggested we took him over to England to see if his temperament could be improved.

The horse had spells with Brendan Powell and Martin Todhunter but would not adapt to a training regime so we gave him to one of our long time owners, Tony O Gorman. Tony asked Chris Gordon, a new trainer, to see if he could get Monzon to race and thanks to his skill and perseverance he achieved a mInor miracle, getting the horse to run regularly between 2007 and 2009 and win twice.

Amazingly as I was typing this chapter on the 29th September 2012, there was Francois again on TV winning a fillies group 1 at Newmarket with Siyouma. He truly is a timeless and brilliant trainer.

Brendan Powell

I met Brendan Powell for the first time at Sedgefield in the summer of 2004. I was impressed that he had travelled up himself from his south coast base to meet the owner of a pretty moderate horse, which is the kind of customer- based ethic which we looked for in our trainers.

I introduced myself to Brendan and we placed three horses with him eventually. Mesmeric who joined him from Dermot Weld, Monzon from Francois Doumen and a promising three -year old, Obay, who I bought out of Ed Dunlop's stable at the October 2004 Newmarket Sales.

Things got off to a great start with Brendan. Mesmeric placed and won in his first two races and Obay made a fantastic debut in a juvenile hurdle at Fontwell in December 2004 running the useful and experienced Verasi to a photo finish after looking the likely winner. After this race he was in the forefront of betting for the 2005 Triumph Hurdle.

However after this I am afraid things went downhill fast. Mesmeric got a leg injury and lost his form, eventually being retired the following year. He is still enjoying his retirement in the Devon countryside at the home of Peter Tosh a long- term Centaur client.

Obay ran really badly in his next race over hurdles at Sandown running with his head on one side, which is indicative of pain/injury. It transpired he had major wind problems. Despite two operations he never recovered his form and ended up tailing off in a selling hurdle at Hexham in 2006. We sold Obay cheaply shortly afterwards to race in Dubai and one year later to our amazement he finished third in a group 1 race on the all weather surface at Djebel Ali where he was able to run on lasix and bute, which counteracts bleeding.

Bursting blood vessels is one of the most common risks to racehorse welfare in the UK and, unlike some other countries, owners are not allowed to run horses on tranquilising drugs. The most common reaction is to try and run horses with a tongue- tie if the wind problem is minor or to have an operation to repair the tear in the horses' windpipe, if more serious. Centaur had to have these operations done on several occasions. They never worked and it would be interesting to see some statistics on the various operations and their success rate.

Brendan's stable suffered a dip in form in 2006 and we did not replace our retiring horses with him. I must say however that Brendan was an excellent communicator who kept us well informed of the horses welfare and who gave our owners some excellent betting information on other horses during the last winless year.

Noel Wilson

Noel Wilson is a hard working smaller dual- purpose trainer based near Malton in Yorkshire. We got together with Noel in 2008 when I heard that he was looking to sell one of his horses, Arctic Ghost.

Arctic Ghost was a massive grey horse, who had won Centaur clients money when winning a bumper and then two novice chases. He had run very consistently until he did not take to the right-handed Carlisle track on his final outing for his former owner Paul Dixon. He was a horse I liked a lot and I thought he could be a grand staying chaser and a possible Scottish National type.

I went to see the horse do a strong gallop at Noel's before I made up my mind about trying him to buy him and he put in a sensational piece of work. This persuaded me to buy him for £20,000. Even though he was 8 years old there was little mileage on the clock.

Eighteen months later, the Centaur clients suggested that the horse should be renamed " Keith's Folly!" Arctic Ghost never recovered his form, he dropped steadily down the handicap and unfortunately we went over the cliff a few times on the betting front before we sold the horse for £2,000 in 2009.

We even tried transferring him to Ferdy Murphy to see if he could work a miracle but even a great horseman like Ferdy could not work the oracle.

Arctic Ghost was one of my, thankfully infrequent, purchasing mistakes.

Noel did win two races for us with Rightful Ruler and was a short head away from a third on the flat at

Wolverhampton with Johnmanderville. He is an excellent trainer given the right ammunition.

Micky Hammond

Another horse that turned out to be a big disappointment for us was Arctic Cove who I bought at the October 2005 Newmarket Sales and sent to be trained near Richmond by Micky Hammond.

Although he was a cheap buy we had high hopes for this horse as he was schooling brilliantly over hurdles and had us reminiscing of Hasty Prince's fast daisy cutting hurdling style.

After an introductory run we decided to go for a punt on Arctic Cove in what turned out to be quite a good novice hurdle at Newcastle in February 2006. The owners backed the horse each way at 33/1 and he was backed down to 14/1. He was travelling smoothly and jumping immaculately when he slightly over-jumped the 4th hurdle, took a couple of strides and did the splits!

There was no betting recovery with Arctic Cove. He was found to have a severe wind problem after his third run and ended his career with no wins from 20 runs over hurdles. Micky, who is a fantastic bloke, did his best for us and like Brendan tipped us some winners for the owners but we did not renew our relationship following Arctic Cove.

It was great to see him doing so well in 2015/16.

Allison Thorpe

Allison Thorpe trained 4 horses for us from her stable near Fishguard in South Wales between 2008 and 2011. Allison's yard was one of the best managed I have seen. She used every yard of space to best effect and her work ethic was second to none among those who trained for Centaur. I have covered her magnificent achievements with Treaty Flyer earlier in the book and cannot say how stunning that performance was winning 8 races in a year and taking an 8 year old mare's official rating from 95 to 137.

We rewarded Allison by buying four more horses for a total of £70,000 and placing them with her. Allison did win a race with Murcar, an expensive purchase, and with Crathorne on his return from injury however three of the horses with her sustained serious leg injuries and we sold Treaty.

Unfortunately Allison gave up training in 2012, a real loss for horseracing.

Wilf Storey

Wilf Storey is a veteran northern trainer who combines training with sheep farming. We placed two cheaply bought horses with Wilf in 2005/6, but neither of them showed any real promise. It was worth having the horses trained by Wilf though, his wife Brenda made the best Victoria Sponge I have ever tasted!

Tony Carroll

I met Tony Carroll for the first time at the October 2009 Newmarket Sales. I was keen to place a horse with Tony who I regarded as one of the best trainers in the UK for adding value to a horse's performance. Unfortunately I could not acquire the right horse at those sales with the budget I had available but I assured Tony that he would have the next horse we bought.

As things turned out, we were able to place three horses with Tony before the next October. During this time my original high opinion of Tony was confirmed. He did a fantastic job with Maze who we transferred to him from David Nicholls and also with Bengal Tiger who came to him unraced from Charlie Mann. He managed to get the horse back on the track and win a race with him after a two- year absence.

I would describe Tony as " The thinking man's trainer". He leaves no stone unturned in trying to find the key to a horse and, ably assisted by his assistant trainer James, he provides the best value in racing in my opinion. His supreme achievement was to win a listed race in France with the first two- year old he trained, a filly, who cost only 2000 guineas.

The Naughty Corner

You can see from this chapter so far that Centaur's policy of spreading our assets and a willingness to move horses to seek improvements in performance led us to use a lot of trainers.

Let me say now that I would not hesitate to send a horse to any of the above 15 trainers should I re-enter bloodstock management.

There are 4 trainers who we used who I would not employ again.

Charlie Mann

We spent over £200,000 placing horses with Charlie Mann between 2004 and 2009. This was influenced by the fact that Charlie was prepared to go 50/50, using my judgement on some purchases. This was good for Centaur as it increased the number of horses I could buy.

We enjoyed some success with him, notably with Bagan but not in comparison per pound spent with other trainers.

At the time we were with him, Charlie had a magnificent establishment in the Lambourn Valley. Some of my most enjoyable days were spent going to watch our horses work with Charlies' on the rolling Lambourn hills.

However, Charlie was perhaps the best example I can use of a trainer who thought the horses belonged to him rather than the owner and practised "mushroom" management as far as Centaur were concerned.

The best example of this was with a horse we paid 38,000 guineas for at the November 2009 sales, Bengal Tiger. I enquired after the horse two or three times in the 2009 winter and was told that he would be running early in 2010 but on an unannounced visit to the stable when Charlie was away racing we saw the horse tethered in his box. He apparently had had a tendon operation and had not been in any kind of work!

This followed another incident, which demonstrated Charlie's refusal to communicate. We had two useful novice hurdlers in 2006, which we owned 50/50 with Charlie, Song of Vala a former miler on the flat and Mt Desert a winning stayer on the flat. Charlie told me that he had entered both horses on the 30th April at Wetherby and Ludlow and that both were working really well and that we should have a good bet. At the time I had an owner who was prepared to invest a lot of money with Centaur if we could deliver him a winning gamble.

I was flying back from Tenerife on the 30th and went straight to Wetherby and did not read the Racing Post as normal. I bought a paper on arrival and gasped when I looked at the two races our horses had been entered in. Song of Vala barely stayed 2miles but had been entered in a 2mile 5 furlong novice hurdle at Wetherby and Mt Desert who would stay all day had been entered in a 2 mile Novice Hurdle at Ludlow one of the sharpest jumping courses!

It did not take a genius to detect what happened. Song of Vala, who had been backed from 9/4 to 11/8 , travelled like the winner all the way but failed to stay on after the last and Mt Desert was taken off his feet but stayed on really well to finish a close third. As our big, shortly to be ex, client wasted no time in telling me if both horses had been entered in the opposite race they would have both won!

The final chapter in our story with Charlie came with the campaigning of Bagan. I deal with this in the jockey chapter below.

David Nicholls

David Nicholls is without doubt the finest trainer of sprinters in Europe .His CV is remarkable with multiple wins in the Ayr Gold Cup and top sprint races at Ascot and Goodwood as well as numerous group races.

However, using David as a trainer proved to be a disaster for Centaur from a client relationship perspective. The reason for this was that he considered that the horses you had in training with him were his to run and bet on as he liked,. You were privileged to have him as your trainer.

David did a great job in training Border Artist for Centaur between 2002 and the end of 2004 winning 5 races and raising the horse's official rating from 52 to 69. However in terms of providing betting advice for our clients, we were able to contact David only once on a race day! The horse was heavily backed on several occasions when he won. This made things difficult as you can imagine with his owners, who we were only able to inform using our own views not the trainers'.

The best example of how David felt about syndicate owners came when I rang him in spring 2003 and asked him to run Border Artist down south a few times as most of the owners in his syndicate were based in the South. His response was " Are you telling me how to train the horse" to which I replied" No, but I am the owner and I would like you to run the horse occasionally at southern racecourses".

The next thing to happen was that Border was entered up in 3 races between the 7th and 10th July at Windsor, Kempton and Epsom. I tried to contact David several times before the 7th to see what his plans were but he was not answering his phone and the stable secretary could not give us an answer. Border was entered to run first at Windsor so we assumed he would run and several of the syndicate turned up. We managed to get hold of David's son Adrian who was down to ride the horse and he said that the horse had an each way chance. He did not know if he would be running on the Tuesday or

Thursday. You can imagine how that made us look in front of our owners and their mood was not improved when the horse finished 12th of 17 without ever threatening to win.

Andrew and I assumed that would be it and the horse would return north, but no, when we opened the Racing Post the next day he was entered up in a women jockeys race at Kempton that evening and had a top female jockey on board. Border was priced up as third favourite and liked running 7 furlong on a right- handed track like Kempton. He was prominent in the betting, but again David was not contactable so all we could do was advise a small each way bet.

Shortly before the race, there was a jockey change on Border. The talented and, experienced rider, who was due to ride,,was replaced by an inexperienced rider. Border finished a running on third beaten only 2.5 lengths, so at least our owners made a small profit however he might conceivably have won the race had the original jockey been on board. Again there was no sign of David in the paddock only an inexperienced stable girl who had difficulty saddling the horse and had to have some help from another stable. Our owners were not best pleased.

The final insult came two days later when Border appeared in a class 4 race at Epsom over 6 furlongs. This represented a raise in class from his two previous races and the horse had previously been campaigned on flat tracks. No contact from David again and his third race in 4 days on what appeared to be an unsuitable track. We advised no bet to his owners other than a fun £10 each way. That morning the horse was smashed in the betting from 20/1 to 6/1 and he came with a withering late run to win the race. We had been made to look complete fools.

David had a reputation as a prickly customer and he was not used to being tackled in the flesh by angry owners. However I think I earned brownie points when I turned up at his stables the next morning and walked straight in on him. We had a full and frank discussion and after that things improved he even hosted a stable day for the Border Artist syndicate.

All in all we had 3 horses with David but I ended the relationship when he pulled another stunt with a horse called Maze who finished last when we were told to have a good bet on him but won next time after being heavily backed after we were told not to bet.

The lesson we learned from having syndicate horses with David was that winning was not everything.

Two other trainers who we had brief associations with which I definitely would not renew were Brian Ellison and Gordon Elliott. Both are extremely successful but both were found to be billing us for horses in training when in fact they were confined to box rest with injuries.

Hopefully the last two paragraphs have given the reader a balanced view of Centaur's ownership history. Fantastic success on a number of occasions and great betting wins but a few occasions where we had to experience the other side of the coin.

CENTAUR JOCKEYS

The Difference Between Winning and Losing

Most of Centaur Bloodstock winners came in National Hunt races and that is reflected in this chapter, which recalls some of the incidents that occurred when we had top jockeys on board our horses.

Before I go on to describe them I should say what I am looking for when I make a jockey booking. Three things;

- ❖ Firstly a horseman. In that I mean a jockey that can consistently present a horse correctly at an obstacle. I prefer this to a jockey who employs strength in the saddle as his main attribute. For example I would prefer a Timmy Murphy ride to a Tony McCoy ride. I believe that jockeys like Timmy and Paul Carberry prolong a horses' career as they hit fewer obstacles.
- ❖ Secondly, good feedback on the horses performance after a race. Too many jockeys tell the owner what they think they want to here or are simply unable to think objectively in the heat of battle. Getting the right feedback can help in planning a horses' future campaign.
- ❖ Thirdly, to obey riding instructions. In my experience many top jockeys think they know best and are reluctant to take instructions on how to ride a horse. Graham Lee is a notable

exception .I have to say that if given a free hand I would most often use an up and coming apprentice who tend to make up for their lack of experience by riding to instructions and by taking fewer chances.

Which jockeys did I use who consistently met these criteria?

Ruby Walsh, but he only had one ride for us due to external commitments. That was Overstrand's victory in the William Hill hurdle at Sandown.

 Nina Carberry was similarly brilliant when we brought her over from Ireland especially to ride Rightful Ruler in a lady riders race at Musselburgh in January 2008 .The horse won easily and never knew he had been in a race, landing some massive bets for us on the day.

Otherwise, outstandingly Graham Lee, whose post race feedback led to many, future wins for us. Graham also endeared himself to the Centaur owners by saving Rightful Ruler's life after he had won for us at Cartmel.

Although Rightful won easily that day, he returned to the winning enclosure with a nasty gash close to his tendon. It was the last race and we were worried that the veterinary surgeon may have left but Graham walked the horse to the stables and sent me in search of the vet. Fortunately I found her before she left the course and she administered some creams and healing antibiotics. Graham raced back and made the weigh in so all went well. It is great to see Graham make such a successful transition back to flat racing.

I rate Paul Carberry as one of the best national hunt jockeys ever to have ridden. Watching him is like watching poetry in motion as horse and jockey become one. Unfortunately the Irish public have been treated to the best of Paul. However, even the best make mistakes and Paul was guilty of ignoring Dermot Weld's instructions, on a day that cost Centaur's owners and clients dearly.

The horse in question was Mesmeric, the venue Leopardstown on the 29th February 2004. Mesmeric had made a very satisfactory debut over hurdles and Dermot told me he was confident of a win on his second outing even though it looked a warm novice hurdle. Most of the syndicate travelled over and we advised a heavy bet to the owners and later to Centaur clients. Mesmeric was backed in from 9/2 to 9/4.

We were all gathered round Dermot when Paul Carberry came up for his riding instructions. Dermot told him to give the horse an exaggerated waiting ride and under no circumstances to hit the front till after the last hurdle. These tactics were perfect for Paul who was a jockey who exuded confidence and there was an air of supreme confidence among our owners.

Off they went and for the first six hurdles Mesmeric sat out the back, last of the 14 runners, at least 10 lengths off the pace. Then as the horses were approaching the bend into the straight Paul moved him out and gave him a squeeze. The response was electric, Mesmeric cruised past the whole field and went 5 lengths clear approaching the last hurdle. There was much jumping up and down and hugging going on! However this turned out to be premature. Mesmeric did not take the last too well and after looking like a 10 length winner he tired dramatically on the run in. He was caught on the line and beaten a head by Point Barrow, a useful novice trained by Dessie Hughes who went on to win a Group 1 novice hurdle.

Paul was ashen faced when he rode the horse into the winning enclosure. I think Dermot told him that we had backed Mesmeric to win over £1 million. He apologised to each one of the owners present saying that he could not believe how well the horse was travelling and did not want to disappoint him.

Even the best get it wrong some times!

I have commented about the Tony Dobbin jinx earlier in the book and I should now set the record straight. Tony was on board Crocadee when it ran out costing Andrew and I the Scoop 6 and he was on board Hasty Prince when he was almost killed and on board Prince Holing when he lost his life at Sedgefield. However, Tony was also responsible for the best ever ride given to a Centaur horse when Crathorne won a class 2 Handicap hurdle at Wetherby on the 12th October 2005.

Crathorne ran and jumped his heart out in this race, ably assisted by Tony who got every ounce of effort out of the horse. He was joined by the favourite, Mexican Pete before the second last and the two horses went at it hammer and tongs until Crathorne edged in front near the line, winning us a nice prize of £9,000.

I will close this chapter by describing the behaviour of a jockey who proved my biggest disappointment and led to the break up of a 4- year relationship with his trainer.

Before I describe these events I need to let the reader know that it is an unfortunate truth that in every racing partnership you form there will be some owners who do not trust you and who think you are trying to put them away. I will never forget the day at Market Rasen when Crathorne ran his only poor race for us. This followed 7 wins and some successful bets. One of his owners, a loud mouthed Yorkshire businessman, came up to me and told me we had been put away by the trainer and we should move the horse!

Multiply that frame of mind across two thousand tipping clients and you can see the pressures that bloodstock ownership brought with it.

Bagan was a high profile horse for Centaur and was capable of contending top handicap chases in 2007/8. He had won a novice handicap chase at Newbury in December 2007 in devastating style for his third win over fences. Bagan was ridden in all his races by Noel Fehily, who had been Charlie Mann's stable jockey for a number of years and is a highly talented jockey, one of the best jockeys riding in presenting a horse at a fence.

It was crunch time for Bagan in early 2008. He was entered in the £60,000 Skybet Handicap Chase at Doncaster and got in with the eye- catching weight of 10 stone 3 pounds after a hugely impressive win at Newbury. Everything seemed fine as he had his favoured good ground. I was not the only person to fancy him strongly and he was widely tipped in the racing press.

What happened next was nothing short of a complete disaster. There were 20 runners in the race and for some reason Noel held up the horse last of 20. I watched in dis-belief, as he did not try to improve his position until after a mile. He then met with repeated interference over the next two miles and ended up a strong finishing 8th behind an extremely well ridden winner.

I let my disappointment show after the race when I went to the unsaddling area to see the horse, Charlie and Noel. I had already had many texts from clients telling me how much money they had lost and that they had never had a run for their money. I asked Noel why he had ridden the horse in last place and I got a pretty flippant answer back. I should point out here that I suppose I was talking out of a pocket, not mine but that of hundreds of Centaur clients who were definitely short- changed by what had happened.

I rang Charlie the following week and asked for an assurance that Bagan would be ridden more prominently in future. After a discussion in which he said that he should decide on the tactics, as he was the trainer, I insisted that the horse should run at Warwick in early February in a class 2 handicap chase and that he be ridden prominently. The horse ran, he took up the running 5 fences out and won by 12 lengths!

I thought that the matter was sorted now. How wrong could I be! Bagan's next race was the Racing Post Chase at Kempton at the end of February, one of the biggest handicap chases of the year. He was strongly fancied following his Warwick performance. Again hopes were high and he had come out of his Warwick run very well. He was well backed.

The owners congregated in the paddock before the race in front of a very big Kempton crowd. Bagan was toward the front of the betting. Noel was standing with Charlie and I asked him how he was going to ride the horse. He gave me a wide grin and said he was going to drop him right out! I thought he was winding me up. However when the race started, there he was in last place. I was just turning angrily to Charlie who had agreed to him being ridden in the first four like Warwick, when the second last horse fell. It brought Bagan down, something that clearly would not have happened had he been ridden prominently.

This farce brought about the end of our association with Charlie Mann and worse the horse injured himself in the fall and never fully recovered his form. I remain convinced that, good horse that he was, we never saw the very best of Bagan.

Centaur's bloodstock operation came to an end at the end of 2011 just prior to the company going into liquidation. We had owned some 30 horses, won over 60 races and over £500,000 in prize money. Writing this chapter has brought it all back, the highs and the lows. Still it was a much better way to spend 10 years than signing off the external audit of London Boroughs!

CENTAUR GREYHOUNDS

A Success From Trap To Line

I like to think that the considerable success, which Centaur achieved in selecting and managing racehorses, was down to the skill and professionalism that Andrew and Steve and I applied to the task.

However I have to admit that the even more stunning success, which we achieved with Centaur Greyhounds was down initially to luck.

Centaur greyhounds came about due to an after dinner conversation with my wife Hazel in 2002. Hazel has been a dog lover all her life and we had kept cocker spaniels in the first 15 years we were married. This became impractical after Centaur took off and we were living in four different homes, including one in Tenerife. Hazel said that she was missing having a dog and that I should buy some racing greyhounds so she could get involved with them when we were in the UK.

I gave this some thought and the more I thought about it the more I liked it. I thought that Centaur could buy three or four greyhounds and place them with trainers in different parts of the country .We could leave our owners passes for clients to use and go and see the dogs as a social benefit of being a Centaur client. Also if we named the dogs with a

Centaur prefix it would be free advertising and PR for the business.

It should be easy to buy 4 dogs or so I thought. After three months of approaching trainers and owners I was being quoted some silly prices and getting nowhere. Pretty much the same happens if you try to buy racehorses outside the sales. Then I bumped into Gary Wiltshire at Ludlow races. Gary was a big racecourse bookmaker, both horseracing and greyhounds, where he was the principal layer at Oxford and Milton Keynes tracks. He also put money on for Andrew and I on the course.

I met Gary in late summer 2002 and mentioned that I was trying to buy some greyhounds but was not having much success. Gary said that he could get some decent pups for me from Ireland and asked how much I would like to spend. We agreed on him getting me four dogs for £20,000.

Four weeks later I received a call from Gary to say that he had a breeder in Ireland called Baby Doyle who could sell me two dogs and a bitch who all had decent form at Limerick. We agreed on £17,000 as a price and Gary arranged transport to the trainers I had selected.

My plans had been to locate one greyhound at Hove to be trained by Brian Clemenson, one at Belle Vue in Manchester with Andy Heyes and one at Sunderland with Harry Williams. I travelled to meet the trainers and introduce myself. Things went okay with Brian and Andy, however Harry told me that he was about to retire and was not taking any more dogs. This turned out to be one of his worst ever decisions and a great stroke of luck for Brian.

Because we did not have much time I rang Brian and asked him if he could take two dogs not one and he agreed. I planned to move one of the dogs later to Newcastle but at the time they did not have any proven open race trainers.

Andrew and I travelled down to see Centour Flyer (The BGRB made a mistake registering the dogs due to my handwriting which has been likened to a spider crawling across a page.) trial at Wimbledon We carried on to see Centour Galloper and Centour Corker at Brian Clemenson's kennels near Worthing. Brian was delighted with Centour Galloper who was a magnificent looking ermine dog and said that the other dog Centour Corker should be okay.

Centour Corker

Travelling down to Brian's and back was a 1000- mile journey for me from our Seahouses house and the Centaur office. I was working in the office a week later when I got a telephone call from Brian Clemenson. Brian said that if I could travel down to see the dogs trial I would see something remarkable, I told him that I was new to greyhound ownership and explained how far I had to travel for in essence a trial and he said that in all the years he had been training greyhounds he had not seen anything like the trial one of our dogs had done.

He would not be drawn further so I told him I would travel down the next day and he said he would set the trial up for two days hence. I arrived late morning for the trial and Brian led out our dog It was not the ermine dog, who he said was pretty good and should win open races but the brindle who we had called Centaur (Centour) Corker.

Brian put three dogs in the 695 metre traps. The first he explained, was a top staying bitch who had won the St Leger and the other dog was his big hope for staying races next year, Corker was the third dog.

Around came the hare and they were off. Nothing out of the ordinary for the first 400 metres, Corker was marginally behind the bitch and about a length in front of the other dog. Then something remarkable happened he went past the leader and rocketed away as if a turbo had been fitted. At the winning line he was about 8 lengths in front and was not stopping!

Brian had a broad smile on his face as he led Corker back to me .He had given the dog a four bend trial with two open race dogs the previous week and had seen him make up an unbelievable amount of ground after a slow start. We went out for lunch to discuss a programme for the dog, which he said was quite simply "a freak". This coming from the leading trainer of staying greyhounds in the UK was some complement.

Brian said that the dilemma I faced was whether to target the dog at the 2003 Greyhound Derby, as he was no slouch over four bends, or to earmark him for a career as a stayer. Brian said that if we went for the second option he thought we had a real chance of breaking Ballyregan Bob's all time record of 32 consecutive wins. I was new to greyhound racing and left it to Brian who said we would target him initially at the Golden Jacket, the premier staying competition, which was to be run at Crayford in February.

In the interim Corker ran four times at the standard 515 distance in top grade at Hove. He won three of these races including beating the previous year's Greyhound Derby winner and was a close second in the fourth after being badly hampered. I was scheduled to be in Tenerife from January until April but made plans to fly home for the final of the Golden Jacket if Centaur made it there.

Brian was not a gambling trainer, he made this clear from the start of our relationship. Otherwise he would not have entered Corker in one of the Golden Jacket Trial races in early February and we would probably been able to get odds of 10/1 or better about him for the competition. However, when he spread-eagled the field in the trial race and smashed a 6 year- old track record the bookies priced him up as 4to1 favourite for the competition. Andrew and I were gutted but we still had £10,000 on to win £40,000.

Although Brian did us no betting favours by running Corker in the triaL the massive publicity he got for his run enabled me to fully syndicate him and our two other greyhounds. I will concentrate on Corker for the rest of this section of the book but both Centaur Galloper and Centaur Flyer turned out to be good dogs in their own rights and both won open races.

Galloper won two open races and 18 out of 72 races. He improved with age and won 10 from his last 34 races when we transferred him to Paul Rutherford's kennels at Brough Park . This included one memorable evening when Hazel drove to Brough and back from Seahouses through driving snow to land some huge bets on the dog.

Flyer was a useful bitch and won 5 out of 16 races at Belle Vue and a further 6 races including one open race when we transferred her to Hove. She also had the distinction of bringing a Centaur Board Meeting to an end. While at Belle Vue she was trained by Andy Heyes who, unlike Brian was a trainer who liked to land a gamble or two. Andy had a system of rating his dogs' chances on a 1-10 scale. Getting a ten was extremely rare and given Andy's strike rate was equivalent to having a mortgage bet.

Andrew, Hazel and I were in the middle of a Board Meeting on the 13th December 2002 when my mobile rang. It was Andy saying the dog would definitely win that evening. It was already afternoon and it was a 4 hour drive from Seahouses to Manchester. There was only one thing to be done, I used my powers as Chairman to suspend the meeting and despatched Andrew with £3,000 to bet the dog! I would have sent more moneybut £3000 is about as much as you could get on at the track. And that takes some doing. While he was driving down I called a couple of other Centaur clients to meet Andrew to help him get the money on.

Andrew's breakneck journey was not in vain. Flyer bolted up by 4.5 lengths having been backed in from 7/2 to 6/4.

Back to Corker and the Golden Jacket. His progress was imperious, two 5 length victories in the qualifying rounds and a 2.5 length victory after coming from last to first in the semi final, something that was very difficult to do at the tight Crayford track. Hazel and I flew over for the final at Crayford on the 3rd March 2003 and met the new part owners of Corker who were elated to be there. I have to thank Ladbrokes for a wonderful evening at their Crayford Stadium. They laid on tables for dinner for all the finalists and provided 8 places for our syndicate. We had a wonderful evening.

We were seated next to Linda Jones' owners. She had two finalists including Kinda Sleepy who had also got through to the final unbeaten and was a heavily backed second favourite behind Corker.There was some good -natured banter between our owners and hers and a few side bets were placed. The final itself was over from the second the traps opened. Corker was not usually a fast breaker but he was out of the traps like lightning (All credit to Brian) and once round the first bend in front he pulled remorselessly away to win by 6 lengths smashing his own track record in the process.

Much jubilation among the Centaur Corker syndicate and the greyhound press were full of praise for the new staying star. Two more wins and we were off to Sheffield for the Queen Mother Cup over 660 yards at the end of March but not before an unwelcome occurrence.

The syndicate and I had gone to Swindon to see Corker run in a one -off 6 bend Open Race. We were sat in a private box having dinner when a sheepish looking Brian Clemenson came in and asked if he could have a few words with me. He said that his main owner, Roy Fremlingham would like to buy Corker. I told him I would ask the other owners out of courtesy but I had a controlling interest and definitely would not sell the dog.

I thought that was the end of it, I mentioned it to the owners but no one wanted to give up the excitement we were enjoying with Corker. An hour later a figure burst in to the room and without introducing himself said he would make us an offer we could not refuse for Corker. I remained polite and explained that there was not enough money in greyhound racing to lead us to sell the dog. He left saying that we were upstarts as far as greyhound racing were concerned and that a great dog like Corker should be owned by someone who had been in greyhound racing for most of their life.

I should say at this point that we had come to notice that there was a lot of jealousy in greyhound racing about the fact that Centaur had sensational success with our first greyhound to run in main competitions (More about this later). This was evident following the Golden Jacket final. I found this disappointing, it was not our fault that we had enjoyed such outstanding luck but I would say that over the next 5 years we put in some £400,000 into greyhound racing in rearing and training fees and sponsorship. And donated thousands of pounds to the welfare of retired greyhounds.

The Fremlingham episode did nothing to our relationship with Brian and Corker destroyed the opposition by 10 lengths in the semi-finals at Sheffield. Then came his last defeat in 15 open races in the Final in strange circumstances. For some reason the draw for the final was not made after the semi finals but the next day. When we saw it we could not believe that Corker was in trap 6 as he was a middle seed. This was the only time in his racing career that he ran from trap 6. What made the matter more unsatisfactory was that the remaining 5 local dogs ended up in exactly the traps they would have opted for.

The Yorkshire owners got the result they had hoped for. Corker, not used to being on the outside of the field broke slowly and was virtually knocked over by two dogs at the third bend. What happened next was simply amazing however. Off balance and at least 10 lengths behind the leaders he righted himself then took off after them., he could not catch the winner Frisby Fassan who was a group 1 winner but he was only beaten 3 lengths at the finishing line and before he reached the pick up where the hare stops he was in front by many lengths.

Our owners were all there and were obviously gutted by the result as we had Brian's vision of beating Ballyregan Bob's record in our mind and this meant that we would have to start again. We were soon cheered up however. We were waiting by the track exit to pet Corker a after the race. All the other trainers led their dogs to the track barrier and the dogs hopped over it, Brian led Corker up to the barrier then bent down and picked him up and carried him over. We were all smiling at this when the fanfare went up for the presentation of the trophy to Frisby Fassan. As soon as Corker heard the trumpets his ears went up and he started to drag Brian toward the ceremony, he clearly thought as we did that his rightful place was to be there receiving the prize!

Corker's next race was the Trainer's Championship at Sittingbourne on the 4th May. I still have the video of this race and watch it regularly –it is simply gobsmacking.

Despite the distance being shorter, only 642 metres and a very strong field, Corker was sent off a shade of odds on. He was badly baulked at the second bend and nearly knocked over. The video then concentrates on the first two dogs who had gone lengths clear from the rest of the field. These two dogs are the only things in the picture as they race up the back straight for the second time approaching the last bend .The viewer does not see another dog but then hears this mounting crescendo of noise. This was the roar of the crowd as Corker came roaring after the leaders, hurtled past them on the final bend and won going away by 2.5 lengths. A truly awesome win.

Next on Corkers agenda was his second group 1 event, the Ladbrokes Summer Classic over 684 metres at Monmore. No problems in the first round with a clear- cut win and then a mouth-watering clash with the 2002 St Leger winner Alibulk Lad, winner of his last 7 races. Again Corker was slowly away and as they approached the last bend Alibulk Lad was a clear leader, with Corker some 4 lengths behind. We feared the worst, but he suddenly kicked in the turbo to get up and win by half a length.

We did not know then but he had probably broken Alibulk's heart, as in the final Corker massacred the field smashing the trap record and recording a time half a second faster than his semi –final win. Alibulk was tailed off and only ran one more race before retiring.

Five days after the Ladbrokes Summer Classic Final, Corals staged a televised £5,000 one off invitation 930 metre marathon at Corker's home track, Hove. The event was by invitation only and the aim was to have the top 6 marathon dogs in the country take part. Corker had never run beyond 714 metres but such was his reputation that Coral's knew it would cause massive interest in the greyhound world if he took part. Brian rang me four days before the race to say they had asked him if Corker would take part. I asked him if the dog was tired following the three round summer classic and he said Corker had not taken anything out of him-self and was as fresh as a daisy.

Nothing ventured, nothing gained and we were in. This meant another 500- mile drive for me but Hazel and I arrived at Hove Stadium in good time and we were met in the restaurant by my son Darren, a Sergeant in the Parachute Regiment stationed at nearby Portsmouth. We were just starting to have dinner when a representative from Sky TV came up and asked if I would do a 5- minute interview with hosts Gary Newbon and Jonathan Hobbs at the start of their show.

I knew Jonathan, who was the Racing Post's greyhound editor, as I had been to the Racing Post on many occasions to discuss Centaur's advertising budget but had not met his co presenter. The interview focussed on Corker's sensational start to his staying career and went fine until I was asked by Newbon if I was not being a bit greedy for running the dog only 5 days since he won a Group 1 final. Another example of how our arrival in the greyhound world was not well received by everyone. My reply was that I left everything regarding the dog's training programme to Brian Clemenson and he thought the dog would stay, I added that if that was the case he was a remarkable price at even money. Clearly my remarks must have carried some weight as the dog went off at 1to 2!

Sky viewers were treated to a virtuoso performance by Corker who led shortly after the first bend and broke the 4, 6 and 8 bend clocks on his way to a staggering 10 length win. Some of the previous season's top marathon dogs were beaten huge distances. This win more than anything convinced me that if Corker had any sort of injury free run he would break Ballyregan Bob's record.

However, two races later it was all over.

After a trial at Oxford where we were considering running him in the Caesarewitch, Corker's next run was back at Hove on the first of July to decide whether he ran in their grade 1 Olympic Stayers Competition over 695 metres or at Oxford. Brian had contacted me after the Oxford trial saying that he thought Corker had pulled up sore but that his vet could not find anything. Accordingly we gave the Caesarewitch a miss as a precaution. Before the run at Hove, Brian had the dog checked again by 2 more vets and we ended up 2to 1 in favour of running.

As always, I left things to Brian to decide. His view was that we should run in the first round of the three-round competition and if there was any sign of soreness we could withdraw him rather than carry on. As things went, Corker turned in a great performance, narrowly failing to beat the track record. After this he was 1to 5 to win his third group 1.

The semi-finals were held a week later and as usual Corker attracted a bumper crowd, he had hundreds of fans at his local track and Andrew was kept busy replying to e mails via the Hove site. I could not make it due to business meetings but Andrew was there. Everything was going well and Corker was just starting to pull away from the field on the back straight when he faltered badly and stopped. There was a gasp from the crowd.

As I mentioned I was not there but Andrew said he has never seen so many men in tears, including himself, when Brian was carrying the dog off the track. Corker had shattered his hock and was in pain and the track vet wanted to put him down as he said an operation would cost thousands and the dog would not run again. Andrew said to give him painkillers and that we would pay for the operation regardless of the cost.

That was it for Corker's racing career but the operation, which was carried out by a top vet in Ireland, was a success and he went on to have a successful stud career based at Jimmy Fenwick's Morpeth stud farm. This was followed by a very enjoyable, five year retirement living with Hazel and I and Hazel's sister Ann in Seahouses until he died in July 2012 at the age of 12. The dog became a well known personality in the town as Hazel gave him his daily walk in his Ladbroke's Golden Jacket winner's jacket.

A sad epitaph to his racing career came when he failed to win the Stayer Of The Year award at the annual greyhound awards dinner, due to his career finishing early in the year. However if you look at Appendix 2 which follows the book you will see a fitting tribute to Corker written by Richard Birch of the Racing Post some 9 years after the end of his brilliant career.

Centour Para

Folllowing Centour Corker's premature retirement, Andrew and I thought it only right to ask Brian Clemenson to try to buy us another good greyhound. We did not expect to follow the dog of a lifetime with another group 1 winner but that is what happened.

Brian took his time in buying a new dog for Centaur. His philosophy was not to buy pups from Ireland but to try and look for value in more experienced dogs. He contacted us in September 2003 to say that he liked an Irish dog that was two and a quarter years old and was out of a slightly unfashionable sire, Judicial Pride. The dog had excellent form however and we eventually concluded a deal at a very reasonable £7,000.

Centour Para turned out to be another fantastic dog. He won the Grade 1 Champion Stakes at Romford in July 2004 and was second in a Grade 2 final and almost made the Greyhound Derby semi-finals, losing in the quarter- finals after landing some heavy bets for his owners when winning his third round heat.

Para only won 12 races in his career but was an extremely reliable greyhound when the money was down. We landed one of the biggest- ever betting wins in greyhound racing when he won the Champion Stakes final at Romford. On the morning of the race he was the 12/1 outsider of the field in the final, however I thought the make up of the field was perfect for him, as all of the early paced dogs had been knocked out except him. I rang Brian and he agreed saying that he thought he could be 2-3 lengths clear after the first bend and then would be difficult to catch on a tight track like Romford.

Para went off at 5/1 and we never had a moments worry. He led round the first bend by 3 lengths then used his superb middle pace to go 6 lengths clear of the field before hanging on to win from the staying on field by almost 2 lengths. A great night then ensued. The owners were invited to walk around the circuit wth the trophy and Para and did so to tumultuous applause. We then had a great party in the superb facility that Coral's had provided for the finalists.

Para's career ended in early 2006 and since then has lived with Hazel's nephew Darren and his wife Vicki.

The Centaur Greyhound Partnership

Until the end of 2004, I sourced greyhounds and syndicated them on an ad hoc basis. There was never any shortage of demand from Centaur's client base given the success of Corker and Para. We would probably have carried on in this manner but for an unfortunate event at the end of 2004.

Unbeknown to Andrew and I, a couple of our main owners Gerry Stevens and John Shaw, a lecturer at Manchester University, were plotting a coup. They had been sowing dissent amongst the owners about the way the syndicates were being run and called a special meeting at the Novum Hotel in Stevenage. By this time Corker had started serving bitches and Para looked sure to win another Grade 1 competition.

When I found out what was happening I rang Jimmy Fenwick, the UK'S top breeder who was rearing Corkers litters. Jimmy was not best pleased about the lack of loyalty being shown and said that if the meeting went against Andrew and I he would want the pups picked up immediately and reared elsewhere.

The meeting started with 8 owners present. Gerry announced that there was only one item on the agenda, a vote of no confidence in Andrew and I in running the syndicates. He told the meeting that we were too busy running Centaur and that John and he would do a much better job in managing the syndicates. He then said that he had proxy votes from the two absentees in favour of himself and John.

I responded by saying that I was disappointed that no one had voiced any concerns to me and given me a chance to put any concerns right and that I thought that the meeting should hear from Jimmy Fenwick who was rearing some 20 pups born to four of the 5 brood bitches we had purchased with Corkers ' profits. I asked for a non- binding vote before this telephone call-it was 6-4 in Gerrys favour, so much for loyalty!

I then rang Jimmy on the telephone and put him on speaker -phone. He told Gerry and the mutineers that if the vote went against me that they had better turn up and collect the pups from Morpeth tomorrow morning and find someone else to rear them. He also told Gerry and John what he thought of them.

I asked for a vote straight after the call and it was 6-4 in my favour. Gerry and John got up and left the meeting. They started another syndicate and paid

£30,000 for a top Irish Dog, which dropped down dead on its first run in England and they achieved very little success thereafter.

I was extremely disappointed with what had happened and decided that I did not want multiple owners any more. I then bought out the remaining owners using a valuation by the editor of the Greyhound Star.

Shortly afterwards I was approached by a Centaur client, Scott Fraser, who had heard what had happened and said that he would be interested in forming a new partnership with me. I met Scott originally at The Alternative Investment Exhibition at Docklands in Spring 2004. He was a managing partner in a Property Company in Edinburgh who had a passionate interest in greyhound racing. At the time we met I did not have any shares available in greyhounds so Scott bought some shares in our racehorses, notably Crathorne.

Scott and I had a couple of planning meetings in early 2005 and he was very much in favour of setting up a major breeding programme using the Centaur brood bitches. We needed around £100,000 to deliver the programme we had agreed and were going to put in £50,000 each but when I said that I thought I could attract 2 more partners who would invest £25,000 each Scott was delighted. He undertook to manage the partnership and to maintain all records which was fine by Andrew and I as Andrew was under pressure keeping Centaur bloodstock records and acting as Finance Director.

The partnership got underway in March 2005. Scott and I were joined as partners by Ian Craig ,who was a long term Centaur Client and was IT Director for Bank of America and Michael Gill who had shares in several Centaur racehorses and owned a chain of estate agencies in London.

The partnership lasted until the end of 2007 by which time it had won two grade 1 competitions and narrowly lost a third, three grade two competitions and a number of open races on Sky TV. It broke up due to increasing business commitments for Scott and Michael.

Centaur Striker

Centaur Striker was the first star to emerge from the Centaur breeding programme. The partnership had employed Jimmy Fenwick as breeding manager and when the pups were coming up to racing age, Jimmy asked if he could train them until we assessed whether they were of sufficient ability to transfer to our preferred leading trainers Mark Wallis, Brian Clemenson and Charlie Lister.

Striker was an August 2004 pup whelped by Murlens Chance, one of our own brood bitches. He showed precocious early speed at Brough Park and won 8 from his first 13 races in top grades even though the standard distance at Brough Park was too far for him at 480 metres.

Charlie Lister took over the dog from October 2006 and he wasted no time in dropping him down to sprint distances. In no time at all he had won the grade2 Betfred Sprint at Sheffield and the category 1 British Sprint Championship at Nottingham in December 2006.

We were really excited about Striker as Charlie planned a 2007 campaign to take in the category 1 Coral Sprint at Romford and then the Greyhound Derby as we knew he stayed 4 bends. Then disaster struck, he was due to run at Coventry in January 2007 when he escaped from the back of Charlies' van and ran straight into a concrete post.

It took 5 months for Striker to get back on the track and he never quite recovered his former brilliance although he was runner up in the 2007 British Sprint Final.

Centaur Decree

While the Centaur Greyhound Partnerships' puppies were developing, we bought a few dogs to maintain interest. Undoubtedly the best of these was Centaur Decree. He won the partners their initial stake and training fees back over 2 years.

Leading trainer Mark Wallis contacted Scott in early October 2006 saying that he had seen a pup he really liked in Ireland. The sire was a new American stud dog Kiowa Sweet Trey. We conferred with Jimmy, who liked the breeding and bought the pup for £10,000.

Decree did not look top class in his early runs winning only 3 out of 10 races and failing to make the final of two puppy competitions at Monmore and Hall Green. He was approaching his second birthday in April 2007 when Mark entered him in the Ocean Trailers Puppy Stakes at his home track, a grade 2 competition covered by Sky Television.

Decree was un-fancied by the bookmakers pricing up the event as Mark had the two ante post favourites and Decree was priced at 33/1! Not for long, Mark rang Scott to say that the dog had really taken off at home and was showing brilliant early. When the event started Decree was only 3/1 and after a wide margin trap to line win in his semi-final he went into the final a 11/10 favourite which gives you some idea of how heavily his owners had backed him.

The final was interesting as, although nearly all of Decree's owners and friends turned up for the private facility that Walthamstow laid on for us, there was one notable exception. Ian Craig was in New York attending a Bank of America Board Meeting, he was gutted he could not be there but asked me to ring him and give him a live commentary.

The commentary went;

"They are going in the traps"

" The hare is running"

" The traps have opened"

" He has gone round the first bend 5 lengths in front- its all over"

Much jigging about on both sides of the Atlantic after a simply devastating performance by Decree, who won by 9 lengths,, equalling the five- year old track record in the process.

After this performance, Decree was prominent in the Greyhound Derby betting. However, he did not take to Wimbledon, going out in the first round despite being sent off 6to4 favourite in his heat. Decree did not show his real form throughout the remainder of 2007 although he did finish a creditable third in the Category 1 Eclipse Stakes at Nottingham in November

Walthamstow's main competition each year was The Arc, probably ranked second to the Greyhound Derby in status. The 2008 event was scheduled for February. One would have thought the main bookmakers would have learnt their lesson after the massive gamble on Decree the previous year, not so, Paddy Power priced him at 50/1 in their ante-post market and all of the other bookmakers went 33/1.

All we needed was the green light from Mark and when he said he was having a few quid on himself, déjà vu! Decree was not as impressive as in the

Ocean Spray in fact in qualifying for the final he did not win any of his three races against top class opposition..The final was different, however he showed the same electric pace to the first bend as in the Ocean Spray and romped to a 5- length victory.

Following the race the owners were at the Sky presentation and were obviously elated. I liked to keep a low profile at these things and kept in the background however the sky interviewer had done his homework and found me with the mike and asked for my comments. I thanked Sky for covering the event which enabled thousands of people to enjoy top class greyhound racing and thanked the sponsors Ladbrokes for their valuable contribution but most of all I thanked Paddy Power for going 50/1 in the ante post market!

Decree finished his racing career in late 2009 and was looked after by one of his loyal owners John Porter until he died in mid 2012.

Centaur Trooper

Centaur Trooper was another product of the Centaur Greyhound Partnership breeding programme. She started her career as a pup at Brough Park and showed a lot of promise. A friend of mine Trevor Alderson, who was a successful racehorse owner, was keen to get into greyhound ownership and bought a half share in Trooper on condition we sent her to be trained by Terry Dartnall a leading southern trainer based at Reading.

Trooper soon showed she was a top class stayer. All in all she won 7 of her 13 six- bend races including two category 2 competitions and a £500 Sky Open. Her trademark was her blistering early pace and at sharp 6 bend tracks like Crayford, Monmore and Peterborough she was virtually unbeatable.

Her main target was the 640 metre William Hill Stayers at Sunderland, which carried with it a massive £20,000 in prize money. The track seemed perfect for Trooper and she was a hot ante post favourite for the competition after she beat the sprint clock in a pre first round trial. However our best-laid plans came to naught when she injured herself badly in the first round and never raced again.

I carried on owning a few greyhounds after we sold off the assets of the Centaur Greyhound Partnership, until the liquidation in 2012 but on a much reduced scale. I did not have any further big race success, although Centaur Marine, trained for me by Chris Allsopp at Monmore finished third in the Steels City Cup at Sheffield and the Laurels at Belle Vue.

That concludes my account of the ten years which I spent managing bloodstock. I was often asked by the media and by clients whether I preferred owning horses or greyhounds. A difficult question to respond to as both gave me moments of sheer unadulterated joy. The one thing I would say is that in the five seconds or so waiting for the greyhound traps to fly open in major finals in which I had a runner my stomach was a tight knot, a feeling that I have never experienced elsewhere in life.

Sky filmed two twenty minute specials on Centaur greyhounds, these can be viewed on U Tube.

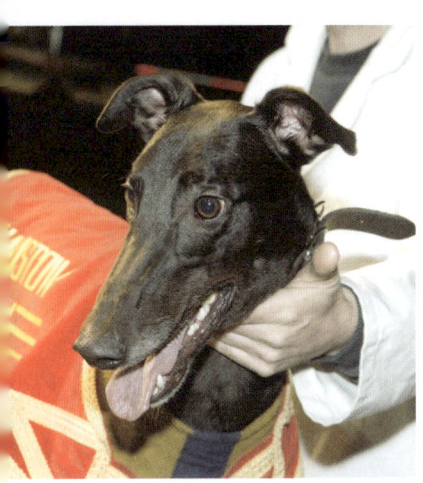

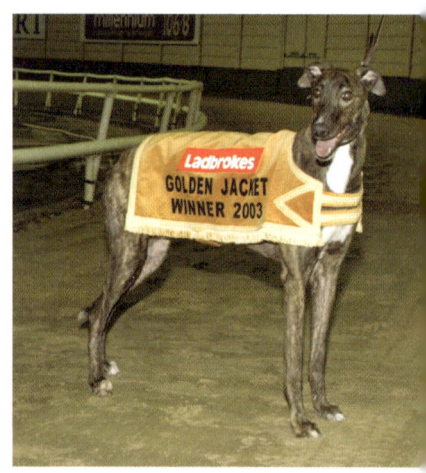

TROUBLE AND STRIFE

Until we appointed Andy Mcinally in mid 2004, Andrew, Hazel and I had run things at Centaur and with the exception of the Alan Bentley episode, everything had run smoothly and staff relations had been extremely good. However little did we know that we were in for eight years of unremitting trouble and strife which made me regularly question whether I should have packed Centaur up and gone back to betting professionally.

Things started in 2004 with the discovery that Mel Turner, who was our head of sales had got himself into gambling difficulties with two of the bookmakers who took the money from our managed accounts, Gary Wiltshire and David Lawson. Not only that, he had persuaded them to set him up as a tipster in return for giving them a stolen copy of our database. This was particularly painful for me as I had counted Gary and David as friends and when I appointed Mel I had got a solemn promise from him in front of his wife, who we employed too, that he would give up gambling. I dismissed Mel following the discovery and he went on to lose his house some time later over his gambling habit.

Next came the end of Andy' Mcinally's period as managing director. Andy's main tasks were to market our new product Bismark in the investor market, to develop and market a franchising scheme for Centaur products I had developed with one of my long term clients Jane Boast and to work with Alan Moore to halt the decline in income from the punter market relating to our horseracing products. During his period at the helm, Andy increased staff numbers by almost fifty per cent at a time when income was falling rapidly and while he spent a lot of time playing the Managing Director of Centaur role at client meetings and racecourses He failed significantly to address his key goals. Two things that really upset me were, that he stopped the monthly colour magazine, which Andrew and I had written and sent out every month to all Centaur clients since Centaur began and at the same time he awarded his wife's company our mail distribution contract without telling me.

When I sat down with him to discuss his performance against his targets in February 2005 things were not good. Andy had stopped marketing the Bismark as it had had a losing run. He had earlier changed the selection policy from that operated in the first two successful years. The franchising scheme also failed to meet its objectives due to a change in legislation affecting tele marketing. Accordingly, income had decreased significantly over the last 6 months. Andy and Alan Moore had had a major falling out and I had not renewed Alan Moore's contract at Andy's request. Worryingly the business cash account, which had a balance of around £900,000 when we appointed Andy, had reduced to £250,000.

Andy was confident that he would turn things round but when I invited him to put in £50,000 of equity in return for stock he declined. Things came to a head three months later and I arranged a meeting at Newcastle Airport. The cash account was down to less than £100,000 and there were no upward trends from Andy's marketing efforts.

I told Andy that I was going to have to let him go and offered him a payoff of £50,000 to go quietly, which I thought was a generous offer. To my surprise he said that there was no way he would accept this offer as he had a three- year fixed term contract, which had over two years to run. I thought he was having me on as we had had his contract drawn up by legal experts and it should have included a six- month notice clause. However to my dismay it turned out that owing to a drafting error by Hay and Kilner, Andy was right.

This disastrous news in effect meant the probable end of the Centaur Group of companies as we faced a potential employee tribunal payout of £250,000 to Andy. He had also mishandled correspondence with a Bismark client, which also could cost us a significant pay out. Rodney Jones, a partner at Hay and Kilner responsible for the contract drafting and our retained lawyer told us that he would submit our case to the firm's insurers but any chance of a payout was likely to take up to two years. Rodney also said that due to the potential of a claim by ourselves, Hay and Kilner could not represent us in the Mcinally case.

It was at this time that our retained accountants and lawyers really proved worth their while. After weeks of meetings and exploring different options we decided to "Run Off" the Centaur Companies into a new company Maxnet Media Limited, who would buy the remaining assets at an independent expert valuation. These funds would be left in Centaur Group Holdings to fund the legal costs of the hearing and meet any settlement.

As things turned out Andy Mcinally was awarded £250, 000 as, surprise surprise, he had not found other employment in the year after he left Centaur but there were no funds left in Centaur Companies to meet this payment. He was the only creditor. Andy turned up at the hearing and told me me he was going to slag me and Centaur off throughout what his lawyer had told him would be a three- day hearing and he had alerted the press to be there. However our barrister pleaded guilty straight away and this prevented any evidential proceedings. I can remember winking at Andy, as he turned purple, he had brought the case using his legal insurance and they would not fund any more action.

That was pretty much the end of the Mcinally saga. He tried to blacken our name several times via the Internet and the press without success. He was however responsible for bringing down the initial group of Centaur companies and for losing me close to £1million. Despite this I felt no bitterness toward him as his failure was pretty much down to incompetence rather than malice or theft and I was responsible for his appointment. I felt no regret for our actions towards him as I had offered him a pay off of £50,000, which was pretty much all the funds we had left.

There was an interesting postscript to the affair two years later when Andrew and I went to a meeting in London with the managing director of Telephone Express Limited who had taken over our telephone business from Greenland. At that meeting he asked if Andy Mcinally still worked for us, when we told him what had happened, he said that he was not surprised as Andy was on gardening leave for non - performance when we offered him our job! Another example of my woeful recruitment skills!

At the same time that we were going through the dismissal of Andy Mcinally we had another staff issue, which was not as costly but was deeply upsetting for Andrew and I as we had always prided ourselves on the way in which we treat our key staff.

Craig Forsyth joined Centaur in 2002 as office manager including responsibility for information technology. I met Craig by chance at Berwick –Upon-Tweed railway station in May 2002. He was going to York races for the Dante Meeting and I was going to London for some buiness meetings. We both were carrying Racing Posts, which gave away our interest in horse racing.

The two hours to York passed very quickly as we discussed many aspects of horseracing. Craig was extremely knowledgable and knew about Centaur and the impression we were making on racing. He told me that he worked in the information and technology department at Berwick –Upon- Tweed Borough Council and clearly had excellent IT skills which was a key area for Centaur and one in which we currently bought in networking and programming skills. Craig was also a director of Berwick Rangers Football Club. At the end of the journey I asked him if he would be interested in coming in for an interview for the Office Manager post at Centaur and he said he was really interested.

Craig started with Centaur in mid 1992 and over the next three years he was very much part of the inner circle. He was instrumental in developing our Betting Exchange Seminars with Steve Taylor who was a friend of his who came to work for Centaur shortly afterwards and his presence increased the reliability of our IT systems considerably. The three years from 1992 onward were probably my most enjoyable at Centaur, the office had a real buzz about it and we regularly took afternoons off in recognition for the success we were achieving and played golf or went racing.

Things changed for Craig in 1994 when out of the blue he found out that his 22 year- old sister, who lived at home with him, had contracted Mad Cow Disease. This was a massive blow and led to her dying slowly and painfully at home over the next year. Andrew and I did everything we could to help. We gave Craig unlimited time off and when he had his pockets picked on a management outing to Cheltenham to watch Hasty Prince run in the Champion Hurdle at Cheltenham we gave him the £1,000 back out of our own pockets.

Disaster struck for our relationship at Christmas 2004. Craig was not best pleased about our appointment of Andy Mcinally as Managing Director even though I spoke to him at length before hand explaining that I thought that he needed another three to five years of experience in handling corporate issues before he could discharge the responsibilities of managing director successfully. Obviously the uncertainty over his sister also needed to be considered.

Between September when Andy took over and Christmas, Craig took a fair bit of time off and he was on a week's leave leading up to the Christmas leave period when the board met in late December to discuss the significant trading losses in the last two quarters. At that meeting we reluctantly decided to reduce staffing costs making two of the nine staff redundant and making a 25% salary reduction for the remaining staff. I told Andy that I would go out to see Craig and let him know the news face to face, however, without my knowledge, he sent out a letter to all staff including Craig informing them of our decision.

Craig took this very badly and when Andrew and I went to see him thinking we were going to let him know the news and explain the reasons, he was extremely hostile and made a number of threats. Our previous actions and relationship seemed to have gone out of the window. This was confirmed a few days later with headlines in the Daily Record " North East Racing Firm behave badly to family of Mad Cow Disease Victim. ".

Craig's next action was to go on extended sick leave and to threaten us with more disclosures if we did not agree to make him a financial settlement. Much against my better judgement, Andy persuaded me to agree to this and we did not see Craig again. It was no surprise however when Craig renegued on this agreement and gave a statement to Andy Mcinally in support of his employment tribunal claim against Centaur. Craig was an individual who thought the world revolved around him. I understand he now acts as a radio tipster for William Hill and operates a small tipping service. I have to say this is extremely surprising given his appalling record as a tipster when he was with Centaur.

Following this cluster of betrayals things were pretty quiet until 2008. In the intervening three years our managed horse racing business built up and the managed football product Maxnet exceeded our wildest expectations raising client funds of approaching £7 million. This made it extremely important that we developed robust procedures for investing monies in the horseracing and football markets. We made some early mistakes and were let down badly by prominent bookmakers Gary Wiltshire and Alan Ballard and a northern bookmaker John Hutchinson. However when a major new betbroker arrived on the scene, Betbrokers PLC, it looked as if our security issues had been answered.

In 2006 Betbrokers signed a Trust agreement with Centaur that stated that the betting funds we deposited with Betbrokers would be held in Trust and not used for any other purposes than for betting as directed by Centaur. Our relationship with Betbrokers worked well for two years and we gradually increased the amounts we bet with them on horseracing and football. Our main betting market for football was Betfair where we regularly bet or laid £500,000 on individual games but the attractions of getting a fixed price from Betbrokers meant that we could bet on occasions up to £100,000 with them.

In 2008 there were a number of articles in the press, which hinted that Betbrokers PLC might be in trouble however their Chief Executive Wayne Lochner continually assured us that our deposits were safe and covered by the Trust Agreement.

In August 2008 I decided to test things and asked for the £220,000 we had on deposit to cover two large football bets to be refunded. After a series of excuses we managed to get £50,000 recovered and then Betbrokers went into administration and subsequently liquidation. After two years, despite evidence of false accounting and in our case breach of trust, the liquidators Vantis whom Lochner had used previously had not recovered a penny for creditors. I withdrew Centaur from the process and we were taking separate action for recovery using our solicitors SNG of Manchester until this foundered due to Centaur's liquidation. To this day I find it incredible given the role of the FSA that the clear breach of trust that occurred was not subject to criminal action.

Unfortunately we were not finished with losses from betbrokers, in 2008, i was approached by a bookmaker who was based in Northern Ireland . Sean Murphy was one of the leading poker players in Europe at the time and operated a retail and credit betting business from Belfast. We started off by having a tipping competition for £10,000, which ended up in a draw and then met socially on a number of occasions including at the House of Lords, where Sean invited us to meet one of his backers. Sean appeared to have sound credentials and when he offered to take up to £50,000 of our football liability on a weekly basis we agreed after obtaining a written agreement that the funds we transferred to him would be used solely for betting purposes.

No problems at first as we embarked on a rare losing run of football trades which necessitated us topping up our £50,000 imprest with Sean a couple of times. Then normal service kicked in and we had a run of winning trades. We asked for repayment at £70,000 and, after various promises and a bounced cheque we ceased business with Murphy owing us £120,000.

We pursued Murphy over the next year and eventually succeeded in having him arrested by Cumbria Police only for him to skip bail to Northern Ireland. Due to the ineffectiveness of reciprocal arrangements between the two police forces he was able to avoid prosecution. I did achieve a small amount of revenge by getting an article published in the Belfast Telegraph telling about Murphy's arrest and penchant for dodgy dealings. This caused him some embarrassment but as for hard cash-nothing.

Things could have been much worse with Murphy who was obviously an accomplished fraudster. We almost entered into a property deal with him to buy two properties in Belfast only for our solicitor to point out to us there were some inadequacies in the security aspects of the transaction. The last I heard of Murphy was when I met Charlie Mann, one of our racehorse trainers, at the Doncaster sales. Charlie told me he had been the subject of an audacious fraud and had lost £50,000, The name of the fraudster was Sean Murphy.

The last incidence of financial loss from betbroking and betrayal came in mid 2011. I had just appointed Neil Daldy as Commercial Director with the prime task of closing the deals on the sale of our Education products to the major bookmakers. Daldy's CV seemed ideal for this purpose as his previous job was as Acting Vice President with VCBET and I knew from previous meetings with him that he was well connected within the bookmaking industry. What I was not aware of however was that he was an alcoholic whose behaviour caused a number of scenes in the short time he remained with Centaur.

Having been responsible for handling big betting clients with VCBET, Daldy identified that one of our critical tasks was getting the money on our horseracing investments. He introduced us to a private layer, Stuart Jones, a big equity trader in the City. Jones was an owner with Brian Meehan, passed financial scrutiny and said he could take bets with a liability of up to £200,000. We started cautiously and as with Murphy we had a poor run. There was no problem with us receiving payment under our agreement for some small wins. Then in Autumn 2011 he agreed to take a bet of £20,000 win on Tell Dad at 8/1 at Newmarket. The horse won easily and then the fun and games started.

Jones told us he had placed part of the bet with an independent bookmaker who said he would not pay him till the end of the month and the balance with another bookmaker who was also experiencing financial difficulties. He said that we would get our money back and urged us to keep on trading. He did not know we had been through all of this before and we referred matters to SNG immediately. They had recovered £53,000 of the debt and were set to recover the balance when Centaur went into liquidation. Jones clearly had run up big gambling debts himself and was using Centaur's money to stave off the inevitable.

So Daldy did not make the best of starts with us, come to think of it he achieved nothing in the six months he was with us other than alienate most of the other directors and staff with his behaviour. He was aptly described as a popinjay by one of his former associates on Google. His tenure came to an end when I found out he was plotting with one of our major shareholders to open up a rival academy in the city. Another of my great recruitment decisions!

If I aggregate all of the losses the Centaur Client Account sustained as a result of betbrokers defaulting since management accounts began it comes to £630,000. Most of you are probably sitting there thinking what crass stupidity it was to pursue this avenue continuously. However, by using Betbrokers rather than placing all monies on the betting exchanges, our clients still achieved a net benefit due to consistently achieving better prices than the betting exchanges.

As is often the case in life all is not as it seems although I have to say that, had I not come up with " The Big Idea", we would probably have abandoned the managed accounts and gone back to telephone tipping.

THE BIG IDEA

The Andy McInally/Craig Forsyth saga left me drained and, apart from my personal betting accounts, pretty much penniless. Once again betting came to my rescue and, after a very successful period, the new Centaur was adequately funded to carry on trading, but the question was did I want to?

I felt indebted to the 5 remaining staff in the Centaur office but they had all been well rewarded over the previous 5 years as we always paid more than local rates of pay and offered a number of other benefits.

I decided to go to Ireland for three months with Hazel and think things through. We rented a cottage in Cleggan a small village on the Connemara coast. In that time I became something of a legend as I cleaned out the Paddy Power shop in Clifton, the nearest town of any size on numerous occasions. It got so that if I walked into the shop people would start to appear out of the woodwork waiting to see what I was going to back.

Spending quality time with Hazel always does the trick for me and after three months away I came back refreshed for the battle. I had decided that the way forward for the new Centaur was to launch a new football product into the investor market as I had seen at the investor exhibition that investors were turned off by horseracing. The problem for me was that I had tried previously to appoint a good football selector without success.

There was nothing for it, I would have to become that person. I spent most of the three months in Ireland doing football research and by the end of this period I felt confident that I could operate a profitable football laying service (I have never been lacking in self confidence). The next task was to plan and launch a marketing campaign to launch the product into the investor market. I turned to Alan Moore again and we came up with the brand name Maxnet and, with the help of a design firm Paradigm from Bristol, we came up with a product- brochure.

Maxnet's launch went like a dream .The product brochure really struck a chord with investors around the proposition that clients would have two of the three possible outcomes in a football match in their favour and that when a football match kicked off they were already winning. Within 6 months we took over £500,000 in fees. Fortunately the results did not let the hype down. In the first three years, Maxnet delivered annual tax- free returns of 46%, 36% and 77% for its clients with a consistent strike rate of around 80 per cent correct. By Spring 2008 we were holding almost £7million in client deposits for Maxnet.

Things turned for Maxnet in summer 2008 when I decided that I would invest client funds in the World Cup. Commercially that seemed a sound decision as it meant that clients would not withdraw their funds following the end of the UK soccer season. Sometimes clients who had won over the winter did not reinvest the following autumn after taking their funds out having found something else to spend them on.

Things started well in the World Cup. Steve and I had done a lot of research and we both liked Australia, managed by Gus Hiddink and rank outsiders to come through their group. We invested around 500k in them not to lose against the USA in their opening match and did not have too many worries as they ended up winning. Even better was to come when we took them not to lose against Croatia who were around two to one on. Australia came through with flying colours and we had increased clients balances by well over £1 million at that stage,.

Next came the big test of our convictions, the remaining game in their group was against Italy, one of the favourites for the competition. Italy,needed to win to go through to the next round while Australia needed only to draw.

I was in Tenerife with Hazel during the World Cup in the villa we rented each year. Everyone in the pub I used to go to, Strikers Bar, which showed the horseracing as well as the football, was following the Centaur bets. Those of you who know me know that I am superstitious and I made sure that the landlord Chris kept my usual chair free for me to watch the match. Steve and I had decided to go for it on the basis that the Australians were playing really well and seemed to have an excellent defence and also we felt that Italy often did not play well when they were strong favourites, in this case almost one to three. We staked £1 million to win £2.5million.

At that time, football was considerably more important to Centaur than horse-racing as in 2007 I had my first, and only, losing year for horseracing clients. This was due in part to the fact that I had several skin cancer operations that year which made it difficult for me to follow my proven routine. It was really important to the business that we continued our success on Maxnet and I made sure that I followed the exact routine that had been successful in the first two matches, arriving at Strikers some 15 minutes before kick off.

For 90 minutes I was in Nirvana, Italy never had a shot on target and had a player sent off just after half time. Australia did not go all out to win against the ten men knowing that a draw was good enough for them to win the group. The officials held up the board with three minutes extra time but I was relaxed. Surely Italy who had hardly mustered a serious attack in the whole game could not score.

Then it happened, Hazel who had never watched any of the games to date walked into the bar and headed toward me. I don't know why but I had this dreadful premonition and asked her if she wouldn't mind popping out for five minutes. To those of you who know my darling wife you will not be surprised by the response she gave me and she sat herself firmly down. At that moment in time the ball was in the Italian goalkeepers hands. He launched a kick out to the left hand side of the pitch and there seemed no danger as the winger collecting the ball was being marshalled by the Australian fullback. For the first time in the match the Italian got past his marker and sped to the by line. There still seemed little danger as the Australian centre half came across to tackle, as there were no Italiian forwards in the box. For some reason the defender slid into the tackle and although there was no way it should have been, the referee awarded a penalty from which Italy duly scored.

There will never be a better example to justify that football is a cruel game. From looking certain to win the group, Australia went out of the competition and that last minute goal made a £2.5 million difference to the Maxnet client account. I was so gutted I told Hazel that I needed to go for a walk as I literally could not speak knowing the commercial impact of what had just happened. Worse was to follow I lost a further 15% on client accounts over the remainder of the competition which wiped out the profit brought forward from the second half of the UK football season.

My poor form carried on when the UK season commenced in August and at the end of 2008 Maxnet clients suffered their first losing year with a deficit of around 15% on their investment bank. Shortly afterwards the Credit Crunch hit the UK and the Maxnet funds we held on deposit suffered a massive hit. Unlike most hedge funds, we did not impose redemption penalties. By the end of 2009 client funds in Maxnet deposit accounts totalled less than £2 million. Maxnet, or Socrates as it became from 2010, never recovered the glories of 2006/8 and despite my trying new well qualified analysts, such as Tony Cascarino, client funds gradually withered and we had less than £0.5 million on deposit when Centaur went into liquidation in January 2012.

Maxnet was certainly a good idea and was extremely well promoted. However, it was not the Big Idea. This came about by chance in 2006.

Professor Leon Goldman was a long -term friend and client of Centaur. I met Leon originally when I was a Senior Manager with the Audit Commission. He came to see me alleging a fraud by a Consultant at the North Middlesex Hospital. I arranged for his allegations to be investigated and brought to a successful conclusion. Leon contacted me again in 2001 and was interested in joining the horse racing service.

Over the next five years, Leon did extremely well betting on Centaur tips, to the point that he would suspend his lectures for 5 minutes while he got his bets on the numerous bookmaker accounts he maintained! He did less well on his ventures into bloodstock with us seemingly having the knack of choosing the few horses that were unsuccessful.

Andrew and I often used to meet up with Leon when I was down in London, our chosen venue being The Captain Kidd in Wapping, which maintained an excellent restaurant overlooking the river Thames. We were sitting chatting at one such meeting about racing and Leon said that he found it very stimulating not to mention profitable. He said that he wished that the subjects he taught at college were as interesting.

Wham! Those words certainly struck a chord with me. For the remainder of the meeting, I could bearly concentrate upon the topics of conversation, all I could think about was the concept of developing a gambling degree, after all we had already written and developed a number of one and two day courses. I went back to Seahouses and did some research on gambling education in the next week or two.

What seemed to be the case was that although gambling/gaming was one of the biggest industries in the world with a turnover of over £400 billion there was nothing in the way of structured education provision. Salford University in the UK had carried out sociological research on behalf of several governments in to gambling for several years and offered a limited degree course, which was not too successful. A University in Arizona offered a degree in casino management and that was about it. All of the big bookmaking firms in the UK and Betfair ran internal management development programmes with occasional input from universities.

After discussing my findings with Andrew we arranged another meeting with Leon to discuss the feasibility of developing the first Professional Gambling Degree in the world. Leon was extremely excited and enthusiastic when I spoke to him on the telephone and by the time we met up to discuss the project in Autumn 2006 he had assimilated a lot of relevant information. Over the next three months Leon and Andrew met weekly and developed a business plan for the project, which I edited when we had a sign off meeting. The project seemed feasible and we estimated that it would take about eighteen months to have the degree ready and we felt that £1 million working capital would be sufficient if we could rent/lease suitable property in London.

Over the next six months I had my first experience of the City as we tried to raise the working capital to progress the project. We had no success, even when we offered full security in property charges to our own bankers Barclays. Andrew and I went out to Cyprus to discuss the project with Demitris and his advisors too but he felt that we would struggle to get parents to fund their children's education in something like gambling even though he agreed there was considerable scope within the industry for well-trained employees.

Undeterred, we decided to write the degree, which Leon strongly felt should in fact be an MBA as he saw the subject appealing to more mature post graduate students. After 18 months hard work, we felt the product was ready and in early 2008 I tried again to raise the capital.

We were initially steered toward an IPO by Wayne Lochner, the CEO of Betbrokers, with almost disastrous consequences. Over a period of several months, Lochner, who we employed as a consultant for a while, introduced us to a number of people who had invested previously in his businesses. It did not take us long to realise that these meetings were going to continue to be unproductive as both of Lochner's businesses had failed and he was not regarded warmly in city circles.

The IPO, which Lochner steered us toward was administered by Rivington Street Capital who assured us that raising £1 million in capital on the Plus Market was achievable and that total fees would be in the region of £150,000. The IPO began in April 2009 and after three months Andrew and I were exhausted by the documentation requirements and had been told that the amount to be raised was now likely to be less than £500,000. Fees had already reached £190,000 and I eventually blew my top when the legal firm involved sent 5 staff up to the Seahouses Office for one day of due diligence. They were not expecting me to be there and certainly did not appreciate my asking them how many solicitors it took to change a light bulb in their office.

I terminated the IPO and Lochner's contract. However, all was not lost as a former associate of Lochner, Tony Woodhams approached me saying that he had heard about our proposal and as long as Lochner was not involved he felt confident that he could get us the money we were looking for. I had heard this several times before but in this case, Tony was as good as his word. A former futures trader in the City he had maintained close contact with several of the major traders based in Gibraltar.

One of that circle, Adam Nash, who founded and managed a major trading group, showed a considerable interest in Centaur as both a trading and a potential major education business. Adam's passion was cricket and he understood sports betting well, being a regular user of Betfair. Adam and his IFA spent some time carrying out due diligence on Centaur and then asked me to go over to Gibraltar for a meeting to discuss the business plan.

The meeting in Gibraltar took place in July 2009 and Adam and I struck up an immediate rapport. We were both used to managing high levels of risk and taking decisions associated with that. Adam was fascinated by the fact that I did not use computerised algorythms to arrive at my selections as his decisions were based on the use of complex software and charts as befitted someone with a double first in maths.

Tony and he were convinced that we could develop a Trading Fund based upon sportstrading and we all felt that moving to the City would benefit Centaur's traditional trade to expiry funds. He was unsure about the success of the Gambling Degree but said that he would get to grips with the issues involved over the next few months and was happy to provide initial funding. Before I left the meeting Adam handed me a cheque for £500,000 to meet our initial working capital requirements and another for £300,000 as an investment in Centaur's sports funds.

When I look back now I sometimes wonder, given subsequent events, if we would have been better off not raising the investment capital for the degree. However if that had been the case I would have gone to my grave saying that I had an idea for a global business that never got the chance to bear fruit. I hope that after reading this book you agree that I did everything I could to make it a success.

CENTAUR MOVE TO THE CITY

Over the next few days in London, Tony and I set about acquiring some premises for Centaur. We got on well together. He had an engaging personality and a strong work ethic having run his own entertainments business previously only for it to fall victim to cutbacks in the City following the dreaded credit crunch. One night at dinner Tony asked me if I would give him a shot at being Managing Director of Centaur Group Holdings. He knew my health was not brilliant and that I would have to travel back and forward from Seahouses to the City each week and would probably not be able to spend the winter months in Tenerife as I was used to.

I agreed to think it over and to give him my answer in a week's time. In the meantime he came up to the Seahouses office and met our staff there. Tony stayed at our house for a few days and after he left I discussed his proposal with Hazel. She is far more cautious than me and felt that we should wait six months so we could assess Tony more closely. However a couple of things happened which forced the issue. Firstly we had the chance of taking over the rental of a fantastic suite of offices in the heart of the City close to the Guildhall and then Tony came up with the idea of creating a Sports Trading Academy in those offices.

The offices were some 4500 square feet and contained a ready made lecturing theatre. Also, on the ground floor of City Tower, where they were located, there was an empty basement with a further 13,500 square feet available if we needed to expand. The full rent of this accommodation was over £20,000 per month however we were able to negotiate an escalator starting at only £8,000 per month in year 1 and rising to £11,000 by year three. With service charges and business rates we were still looking at outgoings of over £20,000 per month, quite a shock after Seahouses!, However the offices were spectacular and were a perfect launchpad for the Academy and College and an impressive base for marketing Centaur Funds and Galileo, a new fund concept that Tony brought to the table.

The idea of a Sports Trading Academy came as a result of a chance meeting with a friend of Tony's, Steve Ward, who was a principal lecturer at the well-established Schneider School for Financial Traders. Over dinner we discussed our ideas for education with Steve, he was a well respected sports psychologist in his spare time and lived for sport being a keen triathlete.. Steve and Tony felt that there could not be a better time to launch a Sports Trading Academy as hundreds of financial traders were being made redundant in the City and theoretically would be interested in making the switch to trading sport, given proper training.

If we took this course of action it would mean postponing the launch of the degree for a while and giving priority to the setting up of the Academy. However Steve told us he had a data- base with 8000 traders'names who had either received or applied to receive training. That swung things for me as I thought that even a 5per cent take up would generate income of over £500,000. Adam knew of Steve and after visiting a couple of trading establishments to discuss the feasibility of our Academy we decided to go ahead. Steve was offered the post of Education Director.

It was no use renting City Tower without getting cracking and the two main tasks were to fit out the academy and to start marketing. Over the next month we appointed another acquaintance of Tony's, Paul Hole, who was a co director of his in a property letting business as IT and Facilities Management director. Paul did an excellent job in fitting out the Academy on a limited budget and the finished refurbishment was truly awesome to the beholder.

When it came to marketing we explored a few options and interviewed several companies. We eventually settled for a firm called Meanstreak headed by Richard Evans- Thomas who had an impressive CV Richard's brief was to change Centaur's image and make us City facing rather than being investor and punter friendly which is how I would describe the existing website, which I had designed with my long standing website designer Jason Thompson of Sound Ideas.

After three months of " Blue Sky Thinking " days involving all of the staff, we ended up, having spent around six figures, with a new website and brochures based upon the concept of " Sports Intelligence" as our trademark. All of our sports funds were renamed after philosophers, for example our horseracing fund became Newton and Maxnet became Socrates.

As the person responsible for all of our previous advertising and websites, I found this process extremely difficult but I managed to bite my tongue and stay silent as my work was dismantled piece by piece. Richard worked very hard and clearly believed in what he came up with but what we ended up with was three "wallpaper" sites for the Centaur Funds, Centaur Academy and Galileo, the new Sports Trading Hedge Fund which Tony was pursuing hard.

I was coming round to the idea of vacating the MD role and moving up to Chairman and decided to coopt some wise heads onto the Board of Centaur Group Holdings to provide support and mentoring for Tony if I moved upstairs. One of these Frank Roseman, who I had met at a Centaur Fund marketing event and who ran his own gold fund, gave us his views of Richard's efforts at the next Board meeting.

Most of that meeting was given over to Richard's presentation of the new Centaur image. Following Richard's eloquent presentation Frank congratulated him on a very good presentation of a very "clever" concept. He then went on to draw Maslow's hierarchy of needs pyramid on the flipchart and said in his opinion the new site was so clever it would miss out all of the tiers except the pinnacle!

Having run some 60 businesses in the city, Frank was not someone whose opinion should have been taken lightly and following a long discussion the board, particularly myself, agreed with his viewpoint. We decided to keep the " Sports Intelligence"theme but scrap the remainder of Richard's work and let him go. So, we had pretty much wasted £100,000 contemplating our navel and were consigned to developing a new fund and Academy site. This process took well over a year and cost another £60,000.

Tony could not be blamed for this disaster and when it came to November I decided to let him take over as Managing Director till the following July. He was to give me a weekly report and discuss anything major with me by telephone before taking definitive action. I would attend the monthly Board meetings.

This arrangement turned out to be an unmitigated disaster. I was not aware but Tony was in dire financial straits following the collapse of his business and one of his first actions, as MD, was to try to get the trusty Andrew, our Finance Director to pay him a £4,000 cash advance. Big mistake. He was also trapped in a very unhappy marriage, which was creating a lot of stress for him.

This situation led to him behaving inappropriately with one of our junior female employees, which led to my having to fly back for a while to sort matters out. Tony became fixated upon his project Galileo, the Sports Hedge Fund and completely ignored the Centaur Sports Funds to such an extent that they collected no new income over the 7 months he was CE0. This led to a major decrease in CGH's turnover.

I had an inkling from my visits to board meetings that all was not well and was aware that Tony had had to get Adam to invest a further £200k to keep the ship afloat. He and I had raised a further £500,000 in share capital but this appeared to be getting eaten into at an alarming rate of knots. There was nothing for it but for me to come back and assume the CEO role, which I did at the end of May 2010.

Over the next month I carried out a process audit on the Academy, Galileo and Centaur Funds. This confirmed my worst fears. There were no proper processes for reconciling Academy income to courses held or for the authorisation of expenditure. Worse, less than £50,000 income had been raised by the Academy, despite it having spent more than that sum in marketing to attract delegates. My instructions to develop distance-learning material and to develop webinars had been ignored. The business aims for the Academy to achieve cross over from financial traders and income from people in the south-east seeking a new career had failed. There was no sign of any income from the database that Steve told us he was bringing to the table.

On the face of it, this may well have been compensated for by the launch of our new Sports Trading Fund, Galileo. Tony had spent most of his time developing this and had succeded in getting it approved as an Experienced Investor Fund registered in Gibraltar as part of the Quay Financials.Umbrella Fund. The Fund had attracted massive publicity and the concept of a Hedge Fund based upon trading sport was attracting international interest at a time that conventional financial markets had suffered a loss of confidence.

Our retained PR firm Templars had facilitated major articles in the money sections of The Sunday Times, Independent, Observer, San Francisco Times, New Times and leading broadsheets in Scandinavia. On the back of this Tony had been invited to take part in two half hour TV debates on CNN and Bloomberg and the latter did a major feature on Galileo.

We had hoped to launch Galileo in the second quarter of 2010 with a view to raising some much-needed income. However Tony made a gaffe in one of the tv programmes which led to Galileo's security provider Credit Suisse withdrawing. It took us a further three months to replace them with The Bank of Scotland.

There was enormous interest from investment funds in Galileo. However the 68 funds that registered a formal interest, without exception, such as AXA who pledged a miimum of £20million, said that investment would follow only if we delivered a successful trading performance over the first two quarters. Fingers had been burnt in the hedge fund sector over the last two years and no one was going to go into this new sector until we proved our trading viability.

We had been aware that this was the likely response from investment funds and for the past two months Tony had been speaking to leading sports traders with a view to recruiting them to trade Galileo. Having skilled in –running traders was a must for Galileo, which was not allowed to practise fixed odds trading. This was proving extremely difficult as the leading traders were independent and were making upwards of half a million per annum tax free from their own trading on the betting exchanges. We had tried two or three other individuals using £20,000 banks provided by Andrew and I but this had proved unsuccessful.

At the end of my stocktaking audit, I concluded that the Academy had been a major failure and had lost well over half a million pounds in nine months, this had jeopardised the success of our main objective which was to launch the Gambling Degree . The future of the Centaur Funds had also been jeopardised by Tony's complete preoccupation with

Galileo, which, while it had considerable potential, lacked the working capital to establish a proven trading team that would attract investors. Quite simply if we collected £5 million in founder investment for Galileo we would only accrue £75,000 in fees from the deal Tony had concluded with Quay and annual expenditure would likely exceed £500,000. A trading profit of over 40 per cent would be needed to break even. Tony had done nothing to boost income to the traditional trade to expiry funds despite another year of excellent trading results.

The position I faced in July 2010 was that we had less than £100,000 in working capital remaining and the Academy/College budget was losing around £1 million per annum. I was on the verge of ceasing trading and going back to Seahouses and restarting a private tipping service. This meant that I would have to make some 15 people redundant, shareholders would lose their investment and we would have to default on the 2 years remaining on our office lease. Tony Woodhams and Steve Ward clearly had to go which would save around £200,000 per annum. Both left amicably and had engineered other opportunities to go to. Tony earned himself some much-needed cash by selling most of his Centaur shares with my consent. Steve had just finished a book and went back to consultancy and promoting that.

Four things happened in the next two months, which led me to change my mind and take the biggest decision I ever took in my life.

The first thing to happen was that Tony Woodhams contacted me to say that he was doing some consultancy for Betfair and he had been approached by senior management to ask if Centaur would be interested in a trial period of running sports trading courses for their VIP customers. Betfair had hired Centaur Academy for the Cheltenham festival in March and had asked us to put on entertainment for some 50 guests. Several directors had attended and they were impressed by our facilities and the knowledge of our presenters.

Over the next three months we managed to overcome the concerns of Betfair middle management who felt somewhat threatened by this potential outsourcing development and convinced senior management that Centaur could manage a major annual education programme for them. A key factor in this result was my appointment of Tony Hargreaves as replacement Education Director.

This came about by chance, I received an email from Tony in June saying that he had read about Steve Ward's departure and was interested in applying if there was a vacancy. He explained that he lived on a remote island off the west coast of Scotland from where he ran a sports trading and education business, Badger. His wife ran a sports trading software firm.

I was aware, from the now regular meetings with Betfair about implementing an education programme, that I needed a principal lecturer who really knew their stuff. Steve Taylor was my best in house resource and I arranged for him to hold a preliminary interview with Tony at the Seahouses office. Steve rang me that night and told me that we needed to recruit Tony as soon as possible he said that he had the best technical knowledge of sports trading he had ever seen and that he had tested him on presentation and he was dynamic.

I invited Tony down to London and he was blown away by the Academy's state of art facilities. As a typical Australian Tony was extremely forthright and after a very complex set of negotiations we agreed that he would take up the post of Education Director and work three days per week in the London office and further time as required each week from home. He would roll his education business into Centaur in return for a small shareholding and Centaur would rent his wife's trading software for a period of two years. Tony's starting salary would be £60,000 per annum plus an annual bonus based upon the financial performance of the Academy.

Tony was convinced that if we revamped the Centaur Academy website,using a designer he had used, that Academy would start to perform better financially. This was music to my ears as I was desperately unhappy with the site that Richard had left us with and Paul Hole had taken 5 months and not come up with a suitable replacement. Tony worked with Steve to produce the initial courses for Betfair and they worked bigtime. Betfair got great feedback from delegates so much so that they were willing to commit themselves to a formal, rolling, six month contract and to allow Centaur to publish the fact that we were Betfair's approved Education Contractor.

The second major thing to happen was that Leon had completed the Professional Gambling Degree working with Andrew and had received informal feedback from a major accreditation body that we could have it accredited by Christmas if we acquired suitable premises. Leon had told me he was willing to give up his current job as Professor/Bursar at a college in London to work full time on the project and could bring two colleagues with him to manage the necessary administration, marketing and information technology requirements.

At a specially convened board meeting, we approved a budget for the development of Centaur College, which estimated a conservative income of £3million in tuition fees in 2011 based on two intakes in May and October with a net surplus of over £1 million per annum.

I was still worried about our cash position, which was dire, but a chance meeting with Simon Nimmo of Charles Cameron Estate Agents went some way to resolving these concerns. Simon was a well-known estate agent and investment broker in the City. He had been helping Tony to get investment interest in Galileo since early spring but had lost interest due to the lack of scope in the commission framework. He had asked if he could use the Centaur Academy for a business meeting and I ascertained from our telephone conversation that he knew nothing about Centaur's traditional trade to expiry funds. I asked if I could give a presentation on these funds to him before or after his meeting and he agreed.

Simon was completely wowed by the performance of Centaur's traditional funds and could not believe that Tony had not been promoting them. He agreed to promote them and to try to attract investment capital for Centaur on a commission/equity basis subject to carrying out his own due diligence on us and visiting our Seahouses office. He did this quickly and within two months he had introduced over £1million in investor funds to our racing and football products.

The building blocks were falling into place and while Adam had vetoed any further personal investment into Centaur he helped us to get £400,000 capital for Galileo to start up trading. I was loath to do this, as we clearly could not yet afford to employ traders with the necessary CV to make consistent profits. However Tony Hargreaves and Steve Taylor persuaded me to let them have a trial trading the World Cup. I approached ten clients including Adam and they were happy with this and each deposited £10,000 for a two- week trial. This worked out extremely well and the clients made a 13per cent profit in the two -week period. Steve and Tony worked as a team with Andrew Cork acting as Risk Manager. The one area of concern that I should have paid more attention to was that Andrew had to intervene on two occasions to prevent Tony trading outside his authorised limits.

These developments were all positive but the major event that led me to carry on was that I was approached by two major investors in September who both expressed a keen interest in a deferred purchase model for Centaur Group Holdings.

Giovanni Pannetta was CEO of Goldwinds Hedge Fund, an award winning boutique hedge fund, which was significantly funded by American investors including a lot of major sportsmen. Giovanni approached me in late August and asked if he could discuss Centaur's business model. He had been approached earlier by Simon Nimmo and his partner Tony Tadros , They had done business with Giovanni previously. He had read the publicity surrounding our sports fund and was very interested in the Education aspects of our business. Giovanni was accompanied to the meeting by his lawyers,who were heavily involved in education businesses in Italy.

After a series of meetings we agreed a deal which would result in Goldwinds purchasing a 20 per cent interst in Centaur for £2million with an option to purchase all shares at the end of 2012 at market value. Goldwinds were primarily interested in marketing the Gambling Degree and Academy world wide using their extensive education contacts. They were less interested in the Fund side of the business although Giovanni was a keen sports trader himself.

At the same time as the interest from Goldwinds, we were approached by several City venture capitalists including Peter Webb Capital, who were interested in purchasing our fund business and progressing it to develop an FSA Regulated Fund. These interests were serious and, on two occasions, both parties pursued due diligence through solicitors with a view to completing a deal/sale.

While all of these favourable developments stacked up and the cash position had stabilised due to the efforts of Simon Nimmo in marketing the funds, the expenditure profile had increased significantly too with Leon needing funds to complete the degree accreditation and Tony needing support analysts to help with Galileo Trading. I hoped to offset the latter costs and to boost the Academy by launching a daily Sports Trading Email Magazine and after three months lead in we launched The Daily Trader.

In late September 2010 I received the management accounts for the business and these showed that we had no cash resources left and were facing some significant expenditure over the next three months. I tried approaching everyone who had shown interest in investing previously to see if I could raise a further £250,000 pending completion of the Goldwinds deal. Andrew and I had already contributed nearly

£150,000 of our own money and could not provide further funds

These efforts proved unsuccessful, due primarily to the poor trading year when Tony Woodhams was at the helm. After much deliberation I took a fateful decision, I decided to borrow £250,000 from our Clients Account which held deposits for the Centaur Funds. I did this because it appeared an odds- on shot in betting parlance that we would complete a sale for the business and /or extend the profitability of Centaur Academy. Centaur Funds and Galileo. We would be able to repay the "loan" promptly. I should point out here that I made this decision alone and no one knew about it until Andrew Cork became aware when Barclays decided to close our bank accounts in mid 2011.

2011 AN ANNUS HORRIBILIS

Going into 2011 I had risked everything on the fact that one of my five "horses" would come in i.e Goldwinds, Betfair, Centaur Funds, Galileo, The Gambling Degree. During the year I was to see all of them fall at the last fence!

The year started well when Leon succeeded in obtaining the accreditation for our Gambling Post Graduate Degree and we obtained a lot of positive publicity. We were set on obtaining MBA approval but that was likely to take a further year. This meant that we were able to market the degree throughout Europe but not outside it where most of Leon's contacts were based. Still there was an air of optimism in the Academy/College as we commenced our marketing campaign.

This did not last long. In mid January I attended Goldwinds headquarters for the meeting at which the sale agreement was to be signed by Giovanni and his Chairman, as the due diligence had been completed satisfactorily. I had a premonition that all was not well when Giovanni was accompanied by a Board Director, who was not the required signatory. He went on to say that Goldwinds would not be able to complete the deal due to the fact that they had a very poor fourth quarter's trading, particularly in the investment sector in Bahrain. He said that they would review the situation later in 2011.

This was a hammer blow as I had already had to borrow over two hundred thousand and marketing the degree was likely to increase the monthly deficits on our management accounts. Simon and I redoubled our efforts to secure investment but despite many many promising meetings by the end of May, no further investment had been obtained.

Worse still, our marketing campaign in the UK and Europe for the PGD in Gambling had failed to attract the numbers of individual students we required .In fact only 7 students were willing to start the syllabus in May 2011.This was insufficient for us to commit the necessary expenditure on lecturing costs. The only bright side from our marketing had been expressions of interest from leading bookmaking firms in Britain and Europe to commit to a range of short courses aimed at developing middle management and trading staff.

I had employed Mark Davies, the former Managing Director of Betfair to use his PR company Camberton as a vehicle to bring senior management of the Bookmaking Industry to the table The two conferences we held at City Tower for the Betting Industry were both well attended and there appeared to be a commitment to send staff to a series of Centaur courses. However, as seemed to be the norm, our timing was wrong, as most of the bookmkers had committed to moving offshore and this became an overwhelming priority for them for the remainder of 2011.

These events meant that we were more dependant than ever on the success of our trading funds, Centaur and Galileo. At the end of 2011, through Simon Nimmo's auspices we had signed a contract with an investment marketing company Stratus for them to market the traditional trade to expiry funds. All of the funds were restructured at Stratus request to operate on a pay as you win basis. Ths meant that after paying Stratus commission Centaur only earned 4% up front and then 21 per cent of any profits delivered.

Things started well and Stratus soon filled up our horseracing fund Newton to the capacity we imposed of £1 million and the fund was profitable in Q4 of 2011. We then expected Stratus to fill up Socrates Fund, which had £20 million of spare capacity.

However they told us that their clients were excited by the 200 per cent profit per annum that the racing fund was delivering and were unwilling to commit to the football funds, which had failed to deiver significant profits for the last three years. In order to raise much needed income I agreed to start a second racing pool, Newton B and this filled up in less than 1 month. This sounded great but in income terms only brought in £40,000 compared to the £300,000 we would have collected on our former upfront free basis.

In Q2 performance on Newton A dipped significantly and Stratus continued to be unwilling to deliver clients to our other funds. Things came to a halt and our hopes for Centaur Funds bankrolling the business from their profits with it.

Things were even worse with Galileo. There is a well - known saying by George Bernard Shaw " Those that can, do, those that cannot, teach". This summed up Tony Hargreaves perfectly. He was undoubtedly a first rate Sports Trading Lecturer however when it came to putting theory into practice he was sadly lacking. It did not take me long to realise this as I have met a lot of compulsive gamblers in my time and Tony fit the mold exactly. He was emotionally unstable, celebrating his wins frenetically and chasing his losses dramatically. His co trader Steve Taylor shared the 4 bedroomed flat in the Barbican with Tony and I. Steve is an extremely cautious gambler but was being brow beaten by Tony into approving desperate recovery trades, as Tony was his boss.

After a promising start with a profit of around 3% at the end of Q1,Galileo slumped to a deficit of some minus 8 per cent at the end of Q2 and minus 12 per cent by the end of Q3. Most of this was due to Tony ignoring pre set limits and chasing his losses. Any chance we had of marketing the product to major investors had gone and at Quay Financials request we returned the balance of their funds to the initial investors. A final irony with regard to Galileo came at the end of 2011 when a well -known and successful City trading fund IG Index closed its' sports trading function. One of its traders Andy Harriott came to work at Centaur in our trading/media department. I interviewed Andy and was immediately impressed he had the trading outlook and discipline I had been looking for all along. I gave him £20,000 of my personal funds and he returned a surplus of 40 per cent in three months trading cricket.

Andy and two of his former colleagues could have been the focus of a relaunched Galileo but it was not to be, Centaur went under before we could attract the necessary backing.

The walls were crumbling around me by June 2011. To make matters worse I had a telephone call from Barclays Corporate telling me that the bank had decided not to retain the accounts of businesses' that were linked to gambling. This followed some well-publicised business collapses in the Sector. The fact that Andrew and I had personal accounts with them for over twenty years and business accounts for over ten years meant nothing. At one stage they were giving us less than two weeks to transfer our accounts and were going to freeze our assets if we did not comply. However I managed to get our local MP to intercede. Andrew worked his magic over the next month and we ended up being a new customer with Lloyds.

Someone should do some research about how the banks have assassinated small companies over the last five years and publish it. Had Barclays helped Centaur to obtain adequate working capital in 2009, partly covered by directors property as security, instead of taking part in the widespread abuses that came to light with the credit crunch, we could have survived and gone on to enjoy the rewards I describe in the final chapter. No shareholder or client funds would have been lost.

By the end of July 2011 I had only two throws of the dice left. We had to secure some business from the betting industry for Centaur College and monetise the Betfair contract. We had a solid foothold in both these areas but we lacked the necessary internal sales/marketing skills to capitalise. Both Leon and Tony Hargreaves were technically sound but totally ineffective in senior management client meetings. On the face of it all was well with Centaur we held regular functions in the Academy such as our pre Cheltenham buffet evenings,which were extremely well attended. In order to try to achieve the first of these objectives I made my last and probably my most disastrous director appointment, I recruited Neil Daldy from VCBET as Commercial Director.

I had met Neil a couple of times at Centaur functions which he attended in his role of acting Vice President at VC BET, responsible for corporate entertainment and their financial markets clients. Neil seemed extremely well connected within the betting industry and introduced a few of his clients to Centaur's fixed odds funds. I asked him in May to meet me one to one and at that meeting i asked him whether he could succeed in selling our education programmes into the major bookmakers using his contacts. Neil had in fact attended one of the Centaur College open days that was attended by most of the great and good within the betting industry. I told him about my vision for Centaur on the worldwide gambling stage and he said that he was interested and we arranged to meet at Chester races in a couple of weeks to hopefully firm things up.

Neil met Hazel and I at Chester Races and he let me know that there was an internal reshuffle taking place at VCBET and he had been told he would not be getting the job he had been promised. We discussed terms and although I could not meet his current package I told him that there was considerable scope to do so if he could get the main bookmaking firms to follow up on their verbal commitments re management development and trading courses for their staff. Neil made the commitment and took up his post as Commercial Director at the end of June.

Over the next six months, Neil caused considerable internal strife at Centaur with his arrogant behaviour and continuous attacks on other directors. I realised by the end of August that I had made a big mistake as he was failing completely to achieve his primary task and was trying to put up a smokescreen to avoid my taking him to task. I commented earlier on the fact that he introduced a betbroker to Centaur who in his words was " A successful raceowner and pillar of the City", who then proceded to welch on bet -placement liabilities of £160,000. Most worryingly I discovered, following an increasing number of unexplained daytime absences that Daldy was an alcholic, something that was clearly known within senior management in the betting and investment industries so that using him in those circles was having a negative rather than a positive effect.

Neil did however come up with one good idea, which if it had been given a chance to develop, could have been Centaur's saviour. He had many contacts within the City and was convinced from talking to them that if we set up a Graduate Academy for Sports Trading that it could be a commercial success. His concept involved recruiting MBA calibre students in possession of relevant degrees and allowing them to trade sport for four weeks using the Academy's systems and software then either recruiting them out into the Betting Industry or finding backers to enable them to trade in the Academy on a profit share basis going forward.

Neil convinced me to try placing advertisements in E Financials to see if there was any interest and we were both staggered when over 200 expressions of interest from relevantly qualified individuals were received. Neil then persuaded me, against my instincts, that he should recruit his own staff to manage the first course. Four weeks later, I discovered that he had gone against my specific instructions and failed to get the first tranche of students to pay for the course and had failed to supervise the trading environment so that £13,000 had disappeared out of the trading account. He had also failed to firm up on verbal agreements with VC bet to place four students at £15,000 per placement.

Worse still I discovered that Neil had been spreading rumours that Centaur were about to go out of businesss throughout the City and had been in touch with Adam Nash, who disappointingly had agreed to fund the setting up of a competitor graduate academy in the City managed by Neil. What Neil did not realise but I did was that his model was flawed in that the concept of allowing the delegates to trade on the betting exchanges unsupervised would never work and that trading using virtual markets and funds was an insufficient test of true trading ability.

I terminated Neil and his staff's contracts in November and had set up a proper training course involving twelve graduates paying £1500 per head to commence in January 2012, when Centaur folded. Following his departure we discovered information that he had defrauded two city companies he had previously been CEO of in the past. Yet another great recruitment decision!

BETFAIR TO THE RESCUE?

Centaur's relationship with Betfair should have matured into a long lasting worldwide education partnership of massive benefit to both parties or to a buyout by the betting exchange provider. The reasons that it did not were;

- Bad timing
- Betfair's flotation
- Betfair culture
- Tony Hargreaves

Betfair senior management had been convinced from our initial presentations and from the early courses and events we put on that Centaur could provide an effective solution to their continuing need to provide trading and betting education to their client base. This is estimated at between one and three million client accounts, depending upon which publications you read. Centaur were recognised internationally as expert sports traders and education providers so that our endorsement of Betfair platforms as a third party would carry more weight than self -endorsement. This was a factor in the run up to Betfair flotation that was taking place in 2010/11.

While this support existed at the top of Betfair's structure it certainly did not extend to the sticky swamp that was Betfair middle management. Having been told about this from other parties that had business dealings with Betfair I still could not believe the reluctance that we faced to implement board instructions and had to vent my frustration at many of the meetings we had with Lee Childs and his support team who seemed to spend 110 per cent of their time in meetings and took longer than Nero to implement simple tasks. It came as no surprise that when Betfair employed management consultants to review the establishment post- flotation that the whole of this so- called team disappeared.

Despite this, we managed to get the first rolling contract with Betfair in place and underway in August 2010 (Some three months late) and much to Mr Child's frustration scored consistently excellent feedback from the 400 or so Betfair clients who attended our first schedule of courses which took place mainly in London but also in Manchester and Dublin.

Although the courses were successful, they were not the solution to Centaur's financial problems bringing in only around £250 per client. I had allowed Tony Hargreaves to build up his establishment to 5 staff to provide the courses, to support Galileo trading and more importantly to build up a library of course and distance learning material covering a range of sports such as horse racing, football, tennis, cricket, golf and NFL. However my regular progress checks showed little progress and there appeared to be ample evidence that what we had created was a "talking shop".

Things came to a head in Spring 2011 when I had succeded in getting the second Betfair Contract to include provision for weekly sports trading "webinars" . These would be live broadcasts immediately prior to the midweek Sky TV programmes. Centaur experts would analyse the scheduled football matches pre kick off and give advice on trading and exit strategies. They would continue to provide advice at 15- minute intervals during the matches with a summing up after the final whistle.

The idea was that Betfair clients could access their accounts pre kick off and get continuous trading advice throughout the course of a programme of matches. Betfair and we were confident that this would boost football trading turnover and were prepared to set up two focus groups of 2500 clients to track the experiment and to pay Centaur £2.50 per client.

This income would hopefully grow considerably after the trial period and would have meant that the Betfair contract should have delivered Centaur well over £1,million per annum. However, in order for it to be successful, it required an effective team effort from Centaur and support from Betfair middle management, in particular their team leader Neil Brown. To my intense frustration, Hargreaves and Brown proved incapable of getting the project off the ground. Hargreaves was so out of touch with reality that he continuously argued for Centaur Academy to offer its courses at cut-price rates and even allowed Betfair to force the price down for Trading Courses in Contract 2. By July I had enough of him and his continual behaviour that the Academy was his personal fiefdom and not a part of Corporate Centaur.

Matters came to a head when he tried to get his girlfriend in London a job in his team(He was married at the time) even though there was not a relevant post to match her skills. When I refused to endorse his promise of a job he resigned saying that Centaur could not survive without him.

Hargreaves' ego was so large he could not believe it when I accepted his resignation on the spot and he got the same answer when he came back shortly afterwards pleading to be reinstated.

Despite these setbacks, there appeared to be an excellent chance of a business sale to Betfair for at or around £10,million. Their Finance Director and Acting Chief Executive, Stephen Morana, asked me to present to him in late August on Centaur's business model and a new product that I had developed LEARNTOBET.COM,

This was a one stop betting website that contained details of every betting activity and game in the world together with brief but informative descriptions of how to bet/play. The site was to work as a recruitment aid for the betting/exchange industry aimed at evolving worldwide betting markets such as the USA and eventually China. This presentation was scheduled for 30 minutes but went on for almost 2 hours. Stephen was enthusiastic about what we had to offer in the worldwide market. The fact that California had announced in April 2011 that they were going to deregulate internet betting and New Jersey were set to follow meant that my vision of a Centaur/Betfair Sports Trading Academy in each deregulated state with parallel development for LEARNTOBET.COM. appeared to be a reality.

At the end of the presentation, Stephen said that he would take the sale to the main board and arranged for us to have a series of meetings with Betfair's Head of Mergers and Acquisitions. These meetings took place and in the meantime Betfair achieved a better than anticipated price on their flotation. Everything seemed set fair, then our 2011 luck struck again. California issued a press release saying that Internet betting deregulation would be delayed for at least 12 months due to a number of objections having been received that would have to be considered by the legislature. One month later, I was told by the Head of M and A at Betfair that they would not be purchasing at this point in time. They would monitor developments in the USA and would keep the matter under review. They did not realise, and I could not tell them without undermining our relationship, that we were on the point of going under.

THE END

Stewards Enquiry

Betfair's decision meant that the end was nigh. I had used up the money in the clients account by August 2011. I had kept the business going by covering excess expenditure over income by betting with my own money on behalf of the clients. Between August and December 2011 I won some £150,000 which I ploughed straight back into the business account. This also helped to pay back clients who wished to close their managed accounts.

Normally this would have involved only small sums however Neil Daldy had stirred up a lot of discontent and in December we had a call of some £700,000 to repay which we could not meet. There was no alternative but to cease trading and put the business in the hands of a liquidator. I paid the staff their December salaries out of Hazel and my bank account and then gave them their notice.

Centaur was officially placed in liquidation on the 9th January 2012 with Liquidators from Begbies Traynor (Central) LLP. I left a detailed statement to be read out to the Meeting of Creditors accepting full and sole responsibility for unmet liabilities. Whether it was the pressure of these events or the normal effect of the British winter (I normally wintered in Tenerife for health reasons) I contracted an extremely bad chest virus that left me bed ridden for nearly three months.

As soon as I was feeling better I arranged a meeting with the liquidators and over a period of three months and with Andrew's assistance we came to a settlement acceptable to them. The agreement that we concluded prevents me from disclosing the details of the settlement.

So, Centaur had fallen from its mighty perch within the betting industry. Why did we fail?

Was it due to poor leadership? It is difficult for me to answer that question.

The fact that I created Centaur Academy and Centaur College and that they did not stand the test of time does not mean that these were bad decisions. The fact that in March 2013 that both New Jersey and China have announced that they are deregulating internet betting in the future would have increased Centaur's worth hugely had we raised enough founder capital to stay in the game.

At a personal level I could not have put in more effort to deliver my vision for Centaur shareholders, any of the staff would testify that I was always first in and last out of the Centaur offices and worked a 7 day week when in the UK. Andrew, Hazel and I drew nil salary from March 2011 and were owed over £300,000 in expenses at the date of liquidation.

Other than getting the timing of our Education launch wrong, our marketing strategy placed too much emphasis on the UK and not enough on emerging markets and distance learning.

The other main reason was a consistent failure to recruit the necessary calibre of staff at director level to take the business forward. I have spoken many times to the CEO of successful and unsuccessful small to medium businesses, most said that the most difficult task they faced was to grow the organisation from its initial core staff.

Well, that is my take on things, let me conclude again by thanking the many Centaur clients who have supported me and my new businesses KSTIPS.COM and LEARNTOBET..COM since 2012.

THE PHOENIX RISES

In early 2012, I was at an all time low.

Centaur had gone under and I had to surrender our three homes in the UK as part of the liquidation process.

My health was never good during the UK winter and I developed chronic bronchitis in the first quarter of 2012 after we moved to the Republic of Ireland. It takes a lot for Hazel not to be her normal indefatigable self but she too was depressed and contracted shingles, the only time in the 26 years I have known her, that she had to receive treatment from a doctor

The weather matched my state of health. We only had two days of sunshine in our first 180 days in Ireland living near the beautiful coastal town of Clonakilty in County Cork.

However, when the sunshine eventually came, things began to pick up. I travelled back to England for a series of meetings with the Liquidator and thrashed out a settlement.

More importantly, I had a number of letters from long- term Centaur clients asking after my health and telling me they would be willing to pay a significant annual fee if I started a private tipping service.

After notifying the Liquidator that I intended to start a new sole trader business, I launched KSTIPS.COM, a private tipping service in mid 2012. I am pleased to say that this has been a huge success as you can see by visiting the website. I have repaid the faith that people had in me with mega profits in every year since 2012. Some of my main supporters have won over £500,000 in this period.

KSTIPS branched out into football and tennis tipping over the following 4 years and these too have been successful, especially tennis.

In 2013, I was feeling much healthier and the fact that I had no business worries was making my betting for clients a huge success. It helped that I was able to move back to the UK after taking possession again of my homes in the Lake District and Seahouses albeit with significant mortgages.

I have always been a frustrated writer and have created all of my websites myself. I embarked on two major projects in 2013. I wrote an autobiography " Stick Or Twist" which I am delighted to say you are reading now and completed my debut novel " Migrants" in mid 2016. I am pleased to say that this was accepted very quickly for publication and should be on the shelves before the end of 2017.

Also, I was totally convinced that the world was ready for a major Betting Education business, Given the fact that the USA and China appeared to be set to deregulate Internet betting. I set myself the task of writing a comprehensive, one stop, betting website covering every sport in the world that you could bet on.

This took me almost a whole year and I paid my long-term friend and website developer of 14 years, Jason Thompson to make it come to life. As usual, I was delighted with Jason's work and LEARNTOBET.COM went live in late 2014.

The next task was to get investment funding to finance advertising of the website and the development of a parallel site for the USA. I soon found out that it was pointless going to the City and other traditional sources of investment due to the events at Centaur. I was not surprised by this, as I had found in the past that the City was pretty much incapable of original thought and usually wanted to latch onto something that was already a proven success.

Again, former Centaur clients came to the rescue. I sent a circular letter around the KSTIPS database and was delighted when 5 clients invested sufficient funds to achieve my initial aims and provide sufficient capital to commence advertising in the USA.

LEARNTOBETUSA.COM went live on the 10th February 2016 and if you check out google we are already on the home page for most education enquiries. We commenced a digital marketing and Media advertising campaign on the 1st of July 2016.

If you like what you see on www.kstips.com and the learntobet sites, don't hesitate to get in touch. I am always happy to take on more clients and am looking for funding to finance a major advertising/media campaign in the USA and Asia.

The Lord loves a trier

This week: Centour Corker

BALLYREGAN BOB had just been retired when I first became interested in greyhound racing. I missed out on the Scurlogue Champ/Ballyregan Bob/White City era.

If you asked 1,000 people in the sport to name the top three greyhounds and trainers of all-time, the names Ballyregan Bob and his trainer George Curtis would feature in 99 per cent of both lists. I've never had the honour of meeting George, but a cherished telephone conversation with him some years ago confirmed what everybody had told me – when Curtis speaks it makes sense to listen.

In 2003 he said to Brian Clemenson: "That dog's the best I've seen since Ballyregan Bob". That dog was Centour Corker.

Greyhound racing's own fabulous freak

WATCHING the fabulous freak that is Frankel strut his sensational stuff on the Sussex Downs on Wednesday somehow rekindled magnificent memories of a greyhound who was trained just several miles north-east of Goodwood at Billingshurst.

Frankel is relentless. You get the impression that once Tom Queally asks him to lengthen, he will continue lengthening for another circuit if necessary. I used to get that same impression about Centour Corker.

The brindle son of prolific Aussie sire Smooth Rumble burst on to the British scene in February 2003. For five months he had the greyhound world at his feet. We were all mesmerised by his talents. Yet by July he was gone, having cruelly suffered a career-ending injury after landing his opening round of the Regency.

Centour Corker fizzed through the Ladbrokes Golden Jacket in the manner of a superstar. A track record of 45.02sec for Crayford's 714 metres in a trial stake heralded the arrival of something special, and he duly went undefeated through the three-round competition without breaking sweat, his aggregate margin of success a cool 14 lengths.

In the final he didn't trap particularly fast from box four, but held a conspicuously straight line to the bend before unleashing superior speed and cutting across to lead. By the second bend he was comfortably clear.

Even round the ridiculously tight, cramped confines of Crayford, a track which provides no assistance to the true greats, you could only gape in astonishment at the majesty of Centour Corker.

He possessed a beautiful, long, raking stride. His action was exquisite. He was wonderful to watch. A six-and-a-quarter-length destruction of

Centour Corker: a class apart over staying trips

'You could only gape in astonishment at the majesty of Centour Corker'

Slaheny Sally in a fastest-ever 44.74sec clinched the Golden Jacket, and a new star had definitely been born.

Centour Corker went on to win opens at Hove, Sheffield and Sittingbourne as his reputation soared. He set new figures at his home track of 40.74sec for 695 metres, slamming Honors Best by nearly ten lengths as 1-5 favourite. He had the natural ability to slice significant time off clocks at will.

More track records were to come. Despite being knocked sideways at the second bend in the Ladbrokes Stayers Supreme Classic final at Monmore, Centour Corker proved an entirely appropriate winner of the race, powering up the home straight to melt Iceman Yank's hopes of victory and score by five lengths. His winning time of 40.60sec was the fastest ever over the Wolverhampton track's 684 metres.

Less than a week later he stepped up to eight bends at Hove. There had never been any doubts he would get the trip. Indeed, he absolutely relished it, turning the 930-metre event into a procession, and destroying Missed The Putt by ten and a quarter lengths in a record 56.29sec.

Clemenson had a kennel of blue-bloods at the time and Hove boasted a strong strength of top six-benders, but there was never any doubt that Centour Corker was in a totally different league to the rest.

At that time he was pretty well unbeatable over six and eight bends, and it is highly likely that would have proved to be the case for a very long time but for the most savage of misfortune to intervene.

Why does it always seem to happen to the very best? That question has been asked so many times over the years when a true great breaks down that the replies would fill the Encyclopaedia Britannica.

Prior to the Regency the off-course bookmakers made the decision not to quote ante-post prices because Centour Corker was so much better than the rest. When you recall the opposition included some startlingly fast performers such as Micks Best Hero and Soviet Gypsy that's a perfect reflection of how good this dog really was.

Centour Corker duly hosed up in round one, scoring by five and three-quarter lengths. However, he suffered a injury during that contest, and we never saw him again.

It was very hard to accept at the time. I'd only seen him once in the flesh – that never-to-be-forgotten night when he made his eight-bend debut at Hove – and drove back up the M23 with the feeling he could have achieved anything he wanted to. Just like Frankel.

Read Richard Birch's Get It Ready! every Tuesday in the racing & football **outlook**

KSTIPS RACING LEVEL STAKES 2017

DATE	HORSE	PRICE	STAKE	WIN/EW	RESULT	POINTS	FORM>30	GOING>30	DIST>20	KSTIPS TRACK>20	SELECTION CLASS>30	SYSTEM FITNESS>30	CANDD10	TRAINER>20	JOCKEY>20	NOTE>50	TOTAL	RISK HCAP	FACTORS RUNNERS	ADJ TOTAL	PTS STAKED	REMARKS
1st Jan	A GOOD SKIP	12TO1	1PT	EW	LOST	-2	12	20	20	16	18	20		18	18	20	172	172	-20	132	1EW	IN HANDICAPPERS GRIP
	MARQUIS OI	3TO1	1PT	WIN	LOST	-1	15	20	10	10	20	30		10	12	10	139	139	0	139	1PT WIN	
2ND JAN	TURTLE CASK	7TO1	1PT	WIN	LOST	-1	10	20	16	15	15	25		3	12	30	156	156	-10	126	1PT EW	
	LOCHNELL	4TO1	1PT	WIN	LOST	-1	25	20	20	20	20	30	10	12	20	20	197	197	0	177	1PT WIN	LIMITED TO 1 PT AS I LIKED 2 HORSES IN RACE
3RD JAN	GWORN	9TO1	0.5PT	EW	LOST	-2	5	15	3	10	20	30	0	2	5	20	110	110	0	110	0.5PT EW	RAN WELL CAUGHT A TARTAR
	TWO SWALL(	7TO2	1PT	WIN	LOST	-1	25	20	15	10	15	20	0	10	15	10	140	140	0	140	1PT WIN	
6TH JAN	FLASHJACK	5TO1	1PT	WIN	LOST	-1	15	25	5	20	20	10	0	18	17	20	150	150	-20	130	1PT WIN	JUMPED APPALLINGLY
	DOUBLE		0.5PT	WIN	LOST	-1																
7TH JAN	MOORES RO	4TO1	1PT	EW	WON	4.8	30	30	15	20	20	30	0	3	15	30	193	193	0	173	1PT EW	LIMITED STAKE AS LIKED 2 IN RACE
10TH JAN	STEELCITY	11TO2	0.5PT	EW	WON	-2	10	25	15	15	20	30	0	5	3	30	153	153	-20	113	0.5PTEW	
12TH JAN	POLITICAL Q	15TO2	1PT	EW	WON	9	12	25	10	5	25	20	0	3	20	40	162	162	-20	122	1PT EW	
	BALLYBEN	6TO1	0.5PT	WIN.	LOST	-1	20	20	15	10	10	30	0	20	20	10	155	155	-20	115	0.5PT WIN	ABYSMAL RUN
	STRAIDNAH	8TO1	0.5PT	WIN.	WON	8	10	30	15	15	20	30	0	17	18	10	160	160	-20	120	0.5PT WIN	
	SMART CATC	33TO1	0.5PT	WIN.	LOST	-1	5	20	10	15	10	20	0	7	5	10	112	112	0	112	0.5 PT WIN	
	SCALES	16TO1	0.5PT	WIN.	LOST	-1	5	25	10	10	10	20	0	18	3	10	111	111	0	111	0.5PT WIN	
14th JAN	MODUS	11TO1	1PT	EW	WON	12.5	15	25	10	15	25	20	0	18	16	30	174	174	-20	134	1PTEW	FACILE WINNER CORAL HURDLE NEXT?
	GREY GOLD	4TO1	1PT	WIN	LOST	-1	10	5	20	20	30	20	0	18	20	5	148	148	-20	128	1PT WIN	ADVERSE GROUND CHANGE
15TH JAN	GRAND VISIC	7TO2	1PT	WIN	WON	-1	10	25	15	12	25	5	0	8	7	25	125	125	0	125	1PT WIN	NEEDED RUN
17TH JAN	BINDON MIL	7TO1	1PT	EW	WON	8.4	12	20	5	15	15	25	0	5	10	20	137	137	0	137	1PT EW	FACILE WINNER CAN FOLLOW UP
	SIDEWAYS	14TO1	0.5PT	EW	ECOND	2.5	12	20	10	7	15	15	0	10	20	10	119	119	0	119	0.5PT EW	
21ST JAN	ZERO WOLF	9YO4	1PT	WIN	WON	2.25	25	25	20	20	10	30	0	17	20	30	187	187	0	187	1PT WIN	LIMITED STAKE AS LIKED 2 IN RACE
	VINTAGE CL(	10TO1	0.5PT	EW	LOST	-2	16	20	15	15	10	20	0	16	18	20	170	170	-20	130	0.5PT EW	JUMPING ERRORS COSTLY
23RD JAN	BIGRONONI	11TO4	1PT	WIN	NR	0																
24TH JAN	CAPT REDBE	11to2	1PT	WIN	WON	5.5	18	25	15	15	20	30	0	10	7	20	160	160	-20	140	1PT WIN	DECISIVE WINNER
ante post	APPLES JACK	25TO1	1st	EW																		
26TH JAN	DINO VELVE	11TO4	0.5PT	WIN.	LOST	-1	15	20	20	5	25	30	0	15	12	20	172	172	0	172	1PT WIN	FAV A BIG DANGER
27TH JAN	MAN LOOK	16TO1	1PT	EW	WON	-2	5	15	5	10	10	15	0	15	12	20	107	107	0	107	0.5PT EW	
28THJAN	THEATREBA4	5TO1	1.5PT	WIN	LOST	-1	25	10	20	20	10	30	0	5	2	50	167	167	-20	137	1.5PT WIN	RAN WELL DID NOT COPE WITH HEAVY GROUND
29TH JAN	ASH PARK	9TO4	1PT	WIN	LOST	-1	15	20	20	12	25	20	0	10	7	20	149	149	0	129	1PT WIN	LOOKS TO HAVE WIND PROBLEM
	SPECIAL CAT	11TO4 -14.5	1PT	WIN.	WON	2.25	12	25	25	25	25	30	0	20	20	20	182	182	0	162	1PT WIN	LIMITED STAKE AS LIKED 2 IN RACE
	DOUBLE		1PT	EW	WON																		
1st FEB	BLOOD CRA2	11TO1	0.5PT	EW	LOST	-2	25	25	10	20	15	30	0	20	20	30	195	195	0	195	0.5PT EW	LIMITED STAKE-TRAV WELL IN LEAD WHEN FELL
	ALLEE BLEU	7TO1	0.5PT	WIN	WON	7	30	30	20	20	20	30	0	10	15	30	205	205	-20	165	0.5PT WIN	LIMITED STAKE
2ND FEB	NOT NEVER	4TO1	0.5PT	EW	LOST	-2	17	20	7	7	10	15	0	10	15	10	119	119	0	119	0.5PT WIN	A NON TRIER- WATCH FOR HCAP DEBUT
4TH FEB	VALHALLA	20TO1	0.5PT	EW	LOST	-2	18	25	25	12	20	30	0	18	5	10	155	155	-20	115	0.5PT EW	LOOKS TO HAVE WIND PROBLEM
	PROJECT BIL	7TO4	1PT	WIN	LOST	-1	30	25	25	20	20	30	0	15	5	20	215	215	0	215	1PT WIN	LIMITED STAKE
	PINA DORAC	50TO1	0.5PT	EW	LOST	-2	10	20	20	15	10	15	0	0	3	10	104	104	0	104	0.5PT EW	
	WESTENDOR	5TO1	0.5PT	EW	LOST	-2	18	20	10	15	15	30	0	10	15	20	153	153	0	153	0.5PT EW	LIKED 2 IN RACE-WIND PROBLEM
6TH FEB	OAK VINTAG	14TO1	0.5PT	EW	LOST	-2	6	8	5	7	15	30	0	15	15	20	101	101	0	101	0.5PT EW	NO ABILITY
	JOSEPH MEF	13/2-20P	0.5PT	WIN.	WON	5.25	22	18	8	15	12	25	0	5	2	30	156	156	-20	116	0.5 PT WIN	LIMITED STAKE AS LIKED 2 IN RACE
	WOLF SWOR	3TO1	1PT	WIN.	LOST	-1	22	25	20	20	15	30	0	2	17	18	192	192	0	172	1PT WIN	
ANTE POST	CLOUDY DRE	16TO1	0.5PT	EW																		
ANTE POST	THE YOUNG	33TO1	0.5PT	EW																		
9TH FEB	ALLEE BLEU	7TO2	1PT	WIN	LOST		30	30	20	15	20	30	0	10	15	30	205	205	-20	165	1PT WIN	LIMITED STAKE -CAUGHT A TARTAR
	GLOBAL THR	10TO1	0.5PT	EW	THIRD	1	8	12	20	15	15	20	0	3	5	20	128	128	-20	108	0.5PT EW	LOOKED SURE TO WIN- FOUND LITTLE
10TH FEB	BALLYANDY	5TO1	0.5PT	WIN.	WON	5	18	15	15	12	15	15	0	15	20	20	155	155	-20	115	0.5PT WIN	CAN FOLLOW UP
	WAIT FOR M	16TO1	0.5PT	WIN	LOST	-1	16	20	20	20	20	30	0	0	20	15	160	160	0	120	0.5PT WIN	IN GRIP OF HANDICAPPER
ANTE POST	NATIVE RIVE	9TO2	1PT	EW																		
	CUE CARD	8TO1	0.5PT	EW																		

STICK OR TWIST INCENTIVE SCHEME

Thank you for reading my autobiography. I hope that you found it entertaining.

You can also make it a profitable experience.

If you have never been a member of KSTIPS you can e-mail me on enquiries @kstips.co.uk and I will be delighted to give you a one month membership of any KSTIPS service worth a minimum £69 for FREE. To obtain this –please quote the first word on page 83 then be prepared to answer a question about the book. Nominate the service you would like to trial.

Check out our results on www.kstips.com before making your choice.

The full monthly cost of our services are;

RACING £330

MULTIPLIER £83

SPORTS BETTING £83

If you want to improve your betting performance. Visit LEARNTOBET.COM and buy the videos that meet your needs. Contact us at enquiries@learntobet.co.uk and we will be delighted to offer you a discount of 50 per cent.

Good Luck

Keith Sobey